SELECTED WRITINGS

SELECTED WRITINGS

DOVER THRIFT EDITIONS

Alexander Hamilton

Edited by John Grafton

DOVER PUBLICATIONS
GARDEN CITY, NEW YORK

DOVER THRIFT EDITIONS

GENERAL EDITOR: SUSAN L. RATTINER
EDITOR OF THIS VOLUME: MICHAEL CROLAND

Bibliographical Note

This Dover edition, first published in 2021, is a new selection of documents written by Alexander Hamilton between 1780 and 1796, reprinted from standard texts. Misspellings, minor inconsistencies, and other style vagaries derive from the original texts and have been retained for the sake of authenticity. A new Introduction and Editor's Notes have been specially prepared for this edition.

Library of Congress Cataloging-in-Publication Data

Names: Hamilton, Alexander, 1757–1804, author. | Grafton, John, editor.
Title: Selected writings, Alexander Hamilton / edited by John Grafton.
Description: Garden City, New York : Dover Publications, 2021. | Series: Dover thrift editions | Summary: "This collection of the Founding Father's public and private writing provides an introduction to his life, personality, political career, and influence on the early history of the United States. Contents include Hamilton's political essays, selections from The Federalist Papers, Report on Public Credit, and personal correspondence"—Provided by publisher.
Identifiers: LCCN 2021033071 | ISBN 9780486815565 (trade paperback)
Subjects: LCSH: Hamilton, Alexander, 1757–1804. | Hamilton, Alexander, 1757–1804—Correspondence. | Hamilton, Alexander, 1757–1804—Political and social views. | United States—History—1783–1815. | United States—Politics and government—1801–1809. | United States—Politics and government—1783–1789. | Founding Fathers of the United States. | BISAC: HISTORY / United States / Revolutionary Period (1775–1800)
Classification: LCC E302.6.H2 A4 2021 | DDC 973.4092—dc23
LC record available at https://lccn.loc.gov/2021033071

Manufactured in the United States of America
81556001   2021
www.doverpublications.com

Contents

Introduction

IT IS EASY to see why interest in Alexander Hamilton has grown exponentially in the twenty-first century. The 2004 Hamilton biography by Pulitzer Prize–winning historian Ron Chernow ignited many readers' curiosity about this always intriguing Founding Father. Chernow's tour de force inspired a once-in-a-lifetime cultural event, the hip-hop musical *Hamilton*. Created by the multitalented Lin-Manuel Miranda, the show opened in New York in 2015 and brought a huge new audience into the orbit of Hamilton's fascinating life and era.

Because he was a unique and multifaceted genius, Hamilton was a great subject for a theatrical wizard such as Miranda. Hamilton came from total obscurity, overcame many roadblocks, and still, before he was thirty, stood out in the turbulent times he lived in and played a leading role in many historical events. It is crucial to his legacy that Hamilton had a unique vision of the future of America. It is equally crucial that he was able to persuade others regarding the meaning of his vision and the importance of his ideas. The force of his personality played a large role, but Hamilton, even though he was often at the center of the action, could only reach a limited number of people personally and directly in eighteenth-century America. The key factor, without which his place in history would be nothing like it is today, was his ability to put across his thoughts on paper.

Hamilton expressed his ideas and opinions, conveyed them to his contemporaries, and saved them for posterity through letters, newspaper columns, political pamphlets, and the official government reports that he created as the first secretary of the Treasury. The purpose of this book is to provide accurate texts of some of these basic writings and supply some information about the historical context in which they were created.

Early Years

Alexander Hamilton was born on the island of Nevis in the British West Indies on January 11 in either 1755 or 1757. The date has never been established with certainty, but theories abound in both directions, with the most recent research pointing more toward 1755. His father was James Hamilton, a Scottish trader, and his mother was Rachel Fawcett Lavien of British and French Huguenot descent. At the time of Alexander's birth, Rachel was married to John Lavien, an older trader. It was an unhappy marriage, which she had been unable to dissolve. Ultimately, James Hamilton abandoned Rachel and their sons—Alexander had a younger brother, James Hamilton Jr., who died at the age of thirty-three in 1786—when Alexander was a boy.

Hamilton grew up in poverty with little formal education, but he was a great reader with a sharp mind. He went to work in a business office on St. Croix at a very young age. This was his introduction to commerce and finance and how they worked in the real world, and he made the most of his experience. Within a few years, a group of local businessmen saw Hamilton's intelligence and talents at work and put together the funds needed to send him to New York for some genuine education. He arrived there in 1773, at the age of eighteen at the most. After a brief time in a preparatory academy, he enrolled at King's College, which later became Columbia University. The following year, with the conflict between England and her American colonies on the horizon, Hamilton published his first political article about America's fight against British taxes and related issues. This early 1774 effort, *A Full Vindication of the Measures of the Congress*, not excerpted here, is somewhat meandering. It lacks the logical heft of his mature political writings, such as *The Federalist Papers*, where he never drones on beyond the needs of his argument and always comes up with the perfect word when it matters most. Nevertheless, he was on his way in the worlds of politics and political controversy.

The American Revolution and the
Articles of Confederation

The battles at Lexington and Concord in April 1775 meant that the colonies were at war with England, and Hamilton left King's College to join the American side. In 1776, he was with the New York Provincial Company of Artillery in battles on Long Island and at White Plains and Trenton. In 1777, following battles at Brandywine Creek, Germantown, and Princeton, he became a lieutenant colonel in the Continental Army and an aide to General George Washington, for whom his primary duties often involved drafting important letters and other reports. In 1780, before the war was over, Hamilton married Elizabeth (Eliza) Schuyler, a daughter of General Philip Schuyler.

After the Revolution, Hamilton, although largely self-taught in this area, established a law practice in New York. He expanded his activities in the politics of New York State and the new republic, serving in the Continental Congress for several years in the 1780s. A rule exempting veterans from the usual three-year clerkship before practicing law on their own helped Hamilton get started quickly. The failures of the Articles of Confederation to provide a viable framework for an effective national government became more evident during the 1780s, and Hamilton was active in the group of national political leaders who brought about the Philadelphia Convention of 1787. Their original purpose was to discuss ways of revising and improving the government created by the Articles, but the convention soon became the vehicle for drafting a Constitution for a new government.

Even before the end of the Revolution, Hamilton shared the belief of many that the Articles of Confederation, which had been ratified by the states in 1781, did not establish a strong enough central government for the new nation to function or defend itself effectively. The problems with the Articles were many. No independent judiciary was provided for, there was no office in charge of foreign affairs, and the tools available to the government for dealing with internal and external threats were sketchy at best. The central government under the Articles had no way to raise funds, regulate trade, or do much of anything. Having funds for any purpose depended on the goodwill of the individual states, which were often protective of their power as independent entities. There were also substantial numbers of patriotic citizens who, with memories of the long conflict with England fresh in their minds, feared creating a powerful central government to rule over them. This divide informed the battle over the Constitution and the politics of the first decades in the life of the new republic.

The Constitution

In 1786, Hamilton met with a group that included Virginia's James Madison. They called for a convention of representatives from all the states to meet in Annapolis, Maryland, in September to discuss revising the Articles. When the time came, only twelve delegates from five states were able to get to Annapolis, and they decided to take up their issues in Philadelphia on the second Sunday of May of the following year. The Constitution was created at the Philadelphia Convention during the long, hot summer of 1787. The summer was made hotter for the delegates because of the decision to keep the windows in Convention Hall shut so that no details of their deliberations would leak to the press or anyone else until they were ready for their work to be made public. While some of the delegates who arrived in May had plans for limited revisions to the Articles, Hamilton and others were thinking of a new structure for the government.

Hamilton did not take a major role in putting ideas before the delegates at the Philadelphia Convention. Each state delegation only had one vote on any issue that came up for a decision, and Hamilton was one of three members of the New York delegation. His two colleagues did not share his views on what the new Constitution should look like, which left him powerless and in the minority as far as New York's votes were concerned. Hamilton participated early on with committees that planned the work of the convention, but otherwise his attendance was sporadic. He did have an opportunity to speak, and on June 16 he took his turn without a prepared text—just some not very detailed notes—for six hours. He spoke about the deficiencies of the Articles and the need for a new Constitution. It was a temporary misstep that some of his proposals, involving the possibility of life terms for some offices, were widely seen as not sufficiently democratic, thus giving opponents an opening to attack. He corrected this course in the battle over ratification. Reprinted in full in this volume is the transcript of a speech Hamilton gave at the special New York State convention that was held on ratification of the Constitution in Poughkeepsie in 1788. As many as two-thirds of the delegates to that convention were opposed to the Constitution at the start of the discussion. The efforts of Hamilton and others gradually turned the tide, and ultimately the New York State convention voted for ratification by a narrow majority.

Battle for Ratification

Hamilton's major efforts on behalf of the Constitution mostly took a different form than giving speeches. In making these efforts, he left us a significant part of his written and published legacy,

The Federalist Papers. During the months following the end of the Philadelphia Convention in September 1787—while politicians in the individual states were debating ratification—Hamilton joined with Madison and John Jay to write the eighty-five essays now collectively known as *The Federalist Papers*. The essays supported the plans for the Constitution, which the Philadelphia Convention had drafted. Hamilton wrote fifty-one of the essays. Jay wrote five, his efforts being curtailed by ill health, and Madison wrote the remaining twenty-nine. The papers discussed at length many of the topics that the delegates had debated in Philadelphia, the nature of the two houses of Congress, details concerning the new office of president and how the president would be elected, aspects of the new nation's judiciary, and many other issues. They are still read today by students, scholars, politicians, and even Supreme Court justices, who often refer to precedent-setting points made by Hamilton, Madison, and Jay over two hundred years ago. Hamilton's authorship of many of *The Federalist Papers* was not made public until after his death in 1804. A substantial selection of Hamilton's *Federalist* essays appears in the pages that follow.

The new Constitution, which the Philadelphia Convention had drafted and Hamilton had argued for in *The Federalist Papers*, took effect on June 21, 1788, when New Hampshire became the ninth of the original thirteen states to ratify it. New York did not ratify the Constitution until a few days after New Hampshire, late to the party largely because of an ongoing debate over the Bill of Rights, which was not a part of the original Constitution but which was ratified soon after the Constitution took effect. It was decided that the new government would begin work on March 4, 1789. The first elected president, George Washington, was inaugurated in New York City on April 30. The following year, the government moved to Philadelphia.

Secretary of the Treasury

Washington appointed Hamilton to be the first secretary of the Treasury, and he took office in September 1789. At the top of his agenda, following a request by Congress to prepare a report on the issue, was working out a plan to deal with the debts that had been incurred by the American government and the individual states during the Revolution. The amount owed by the nation was about $54 million. Hamilton wanted to put the new government on a

sound fiscal basis. He believed this could not be done without a plan
to deal with the money the country owed, to show financiers—
American and others—and governments in Europe that the new
country would pay its bills and could be trusted. Hamilton developed
a plan to issue bonds and raise funds via taxes and tariffs to fund
them. His plan also called for the government to assume the states'
war debts of about $25 million and deal with them the same way.
"The debt of the United States . . . was the price of liberty,"
he said.

His plan immediately became a major issue between the northern
Federalist Party, which Hamilton represented, who were in favor,
and the southern, agrarian states, represented by Jefferson and
Madison's Democratic Republicans. The latter did not trust the
North's financial and business interests and feared giving away
too much power to the national government. On June 20, 1790,
following negotiations that led to the "dinner table agreement,"
Madison and Jefferson agreed to back Hamilton's plan for dealing
with the debts and establishing a federal system for tax collection.
In return, Hamilton agreed that the new city of Washington, the
permanent site of the new federal government, would be on the
Potomac River, where it is today. Establishing the permanent center
of the government in the South made the arrangement much more
palatable to the political leaders of Virginia and other southern states.
It should be noted that George Washington was philosophically a
Federalist, but he never joined the party, no doubt for very sound
political reasons.

Hamilton's next major accomplishment followed in short order:
the establishment of the First Bank of the United States, which was
designed to be the financial agent of the Treasury Department.
During the debate over this plan, Hamilton prepared a report
for Washington, giving his thoughts on why he believed the law
establishing the National Bank would be constitutional even though
no such project is mentioned in the Constitution. The United States
Mint was also established at this time. In the political wrangling to
bring it about, the Mint ended up under the control of Jefferson's
State Department and only became part of the Treasury in 1873.
Hamilton's reports on the constitutionality of the National Bank
and a final one on how he saw the future of manufacturing in the
United States—along with his First Report on the Public Credit,
written during the debate on the war debts issue—are vital parts
of his written legacy.

Washington's Farewell and Last Years

Hamilton resigned from the Treasury in 1795, before the end of Washington's second term. His salary as secretary of the Treasury was $3,500 per year, and he had a large family—ultimately including eight children—to support. He retreated to his New York law practice. He continued to advise his successor, Oliver Wolcott, and, of course, Washington, as seen in his vital role in drafting the president's historic Farewell Address.

Hamilton remained busy with his law practice, unofficially advised members of the government he was friendly with, and wrote many newspaper articles on issues of the day, including columns on America's foreign policy. His actual influence was never the same after Washington left office. He often advised members of the cabinet of Washington's successor, John Adams—many were holdovers from Washington's administration—but Hamilton's relationship with Adams had never been warm. Hamilton's communication with members of his government greatly displeased Adams, who took steps to counter Hamilton's influence.

One high spot of these years was Hamilton's argument before the Supreme Court in the case *Hylton v. United States*. He defended the constitutionality of a federal tax—of $16 per year—on the ownership of carriages by individuals or businesses. This was the first Supreme Court case on the constitutionality of an act of Congress. The court upheld the tax.

In 1791, while secretary of the Treasury, Hamilton was involved in an adulterous affair with a woman named Maria Reynolds. He paid blackmail to her husband so that he would keep quiet about it. The affair was likely always an extortion scheme by the couple. Gossip about it reached some influential people, but nothing came of it while Hamilton was at the Treasury Department.

Several years later, the scandal flared up. A Philadelphia journalist accused Hamilton of somehow combining the affair with Mrs. Reynolds with illegal activities involving Hamilton, Reynolds's husband, and speculation in public funds. Hamilton issued a famous pamphlet in his defense, known as the Reynolds pamphlet, entitled *Observations on Certain Documents in Which the Charge of Speculation Against Alexander Hamilton, Late Secretary of the Treasury, Is Fully Refuted*. Hamilton admitted, in print, his embarrassment over the affair but denied any misuse of public funds. By this time he was out of office, and the scandal more or less died down. Although the case has been made, it seems like a stretch to say that this affair prevented Hamilton from ever becoming president. He had many enemies by the late 1790s, including Adams, a member of his own Federalist Party. Could this fractured Federalist Party with Hamilton and Adams at odds with each other have taken a presidential election from the Virginia aristocracy? The fact that Adams's single term was followed by three two-term presidents from Virginia—Jefferson, Madison, and James Monroe—suggests the answer. The complete, lengthy text of the Reynolds pamphlet may be found on the Founders Online website.

Alexander Hamilton died on July 12, 1804, after being shot in a duel with one of his longtime political enemies, Aaron Burr. Duels had played a role in Hamilton's life for a long time. In 1778, during the Revolutionary War, Hamilton was a second for his friend John Laurens in a duel between Laurens and the irascible and controversial General Charles Lee, in which Lee was wounded. In 1801, three years before Hamilton's duel with Burr, Hamilton's oldest son, Philip, died in a duel with a political ally of Burr, who had insulted the Hamilton family in a speech at Columbia University.

Although they had a long relationship and occasionally worked together, Hamilton had often been disparaging about Burr, calling him "the most unfit and dangerous man of the community." When Hamilton would not retract the comment, Burr challenged him to a duel. On July 11, 1804, they faced each other with loaded pistols at a site often used for dueling in Weehawken, New Jersey—across the Hudson River from New York—where Philip Hamilton had also been killed. Hamilton fired and missed, perhaps on purpose; no one really knows. Burr fired and gravely wounded Hamilton, who was taken back to New York, where he died the following day. His grave is in the cemetery at New York's Trinity Church at Broadway and Wall Street.

SELECTED WRITINGS

1

Letter to James Duane, September 3, 1780

James Duane (1733–97) was a close friend of Alexander Hamilton
during the Revolution and the subsequent battles over the drafting
and ratification of the Constitution. Duane had been a delegate to the
Continental Congress and a signer of the Articles of Confederation.
He was a member of the New York Senate from 1783 to 1790 and
the mayor of New York from 1784 to 1789. He was a judge for the
United States District Court for New York from 1789 to 1794. He
died in 1797.

Hamilton sent this letter to Duane on September 3, 1780, fourteen months before the Battle of Yorktown brought an end to the
Revolutionary War and while Hamilton was still on active duty
with the Army. It indicates that things were looking good enough
to Hamilton—and no doubt to others in George Washington's inner
circle—that Hamilton could contemplate what the new nation would
look like after the war and the direction that its political organization
should take. As a private letter to a friend, it presents a more personal
view of Hamilton's thinking than some more "historic" documents.
It clearly sets out his views on many of the issues that would occupy
him and his coauthors of *The Federalist Papers* several years later,
including the need for a more effective central government than was
provided for by the Articles of Confederation.

From March 1777 to April 1781, Hamilton was an aide-de-camp
to Washington, drafting much of his urgent correspondence to
major political and military figures. Hamilton's position while still
a very young officer in Washington's command was crucial to the
development of his later outlook. His war service enabled him to be

involved in the whole American war effort, not just the battles of any particular state. His experience gave him insight into how the war effort had been hampered by the jealousies and conflicts between and among the individual states and how badly a more effective central authority was needed.

One idea Hamilton suggests to Duane is "calling immediately a convention of all the states with full authority to conclude finally upon a general confederation, stating to them beforehand explicit[l]y the evils arising from a want of power in Congress." Hamilton discusses several other ideas that were later at the forefront during the campaign for ratification of the Constitution and in his work as secretary of the Treasury, including the establishment of a national bank.

Hamilton addresses this letter as being sent from "Liberty Pole." The name commemorates a famous Liberty Pole—a tall, wooden pole—erected in the Englewood/Teaneck, New Jersey, area in 1766 to celebrate the repeal of the Stamp Act. Washington's headquarters was near there. The pole has been replaced several times, but there is still a Liberty Pole at that location, along with other historical markers.

[Liberty Pole, New Jersey, September 3, 1780]

Dr. Sir

Agreeably to your request and my promise I sit down to give you my ideas of the defects of our present system, and the changes necessary to save us from ruin. They may perhaps be the reveries of a projector rather than the sober views of a politician. You will judge of them, and make what use you please of them.

The fundamental defect is a want of power in Congress. It is hardly worth while to show in what this consists, as it seems to be universally acknowleged, or to point out how it has happened, as the only question is how to remedy it. It may however be said that it has originated from three causes—an excess of the spirit of liberty which has made the particular states show a jealousy of all power not in their own hands; and this jealousy has led them to exercise a right of judging in the last resort of the measures recommended by Congress, and of acting according to their own opinions of their propriety or necessity, a diffidence in Congress of their own powers, by which they have been timid and indecisive in their resolutions, constantly making concessions to the states, till they have scarcely left themselves the shadow of power; a want of sufficient means at their disposal to answer the public exigencies and of vigor to draw forth those means; which have occasioned them to depend on the states individually to fulfil their engagements with the army, and the consequence of which has been to ruin their influence and credit with the army, to establish its dependence on each state separately rather than *on them*, that is rather than on the whole collectively.

It may be pleaded, that Congress had never any definitive powers granted them and of course could exercise none—could do nothing more than recommend. The manner in which Congress was appointed would warrant, and the public good required, that they should have considered themselves as vested with full power *to preserve the republic from harm*. They have done many of the highest acts of sovereignty, which were always chearfully submitted to—the declaration of independence, the declaration of war, the levying an army, creating a navy, emitting money, making alliances with foreign powers, appointing a dictator &c. &c.—all these implications of a complete sovereignty were never disputed, and ought to have been a standard for the whole conduct of Administration. Undefined powers are discretionary powers, limited only by the object for which they were given—in the present case, the independence and freedom of America. The confederation made no difference; for as it has not been generally adopted, it had no operation. But from what I recollect of it, Congress have even descended from the authority which the spirit of that act gives them, while the particular states have no further attended to it than as it suited their pretensions and convenience. It would take too much time to enter into particular instances, each of which separately might appear inconsiderable; but united are of serious import. I only mean to remark, not to censure.

But the confederation itself is defective and requires to be altered; it is neither fit for war, nor peace. The idea of an uncontrolable sovereignty in each state, over its internal police, will defeat the other powers given to Congress, and make our union feeble and precarious. There are instances without number, where acts necessary for the general good, and which rise out of the powers given to Congress must interfere with the internal police of the states, and there are as many instances in which the particular states by arrangements of internal police can effectually though indirectly counteract the arrangements of Congress. You have already had examples of this for which I refer you to your own memory.

The confederation gives the states individually too much influence in the affairs of the army; they should have nothing to do with it. The entire formation and disposal of our military forces ought to belong to Congress. It is an essential cement of the union; and it ought to be the policy of Congress to des(troy) all ideas of state attachments in the army and make it look up wholly to them. For this purpose all appointments promotions and provisions whatsoever ought to be made by them. It may be apprehended that this may be dangerous to liberty. But nothing appears more evident to me, than that we run much greater risk of having a weak and disunited federal government, than one which will be able to usurp upon the rights of the people. Already some of the lines of the army would obey their states in opposition to Congress notwithstanding the pains we have taken to preserve the unity of the army—if any thing would hinder this it would be the personal influence of the General, a melancholy and mortifying consideration.

The forms of our state constitutions must always give them great weight in our affairs and will make it too difficult to bend them to the persuit of a common interest, too easy to oppose whatever they do not like and to form partial combinations subversive of the general one. There is a wide difference between our situation and that of an empire under one simple form of government, distributed into counties provinces or districts, which have no legisla(tures) but merely magistratical bodies to execute the laws of a common sovereign. Here the danger is that the sove[re]ign will have too much power to oppress the parts of which it is composed. In our case, that of an empire composed of confederated states each with a government completely organised within itself, having all the means to draw its subjects to a close dependence on itself—the danger is directly the reverse. It is that the common sovereign will not have power sufficient to unite the different members together, and direct the common forces to the interest and happiness of the whole.

The leagues among the old Grecian republics are a proof of this. They were continually at war with each other, and for want of union fell a prey to their neighbours. They frequently held general councils, but their resolutions were no further observed than as they suited the interests and inclinations of all the parties and at length, they sunk intirely into contempt.

The Swiss-cantons are another proof of the doctrine. They have had wars with each other which would have been fatal to them, had not the different powers in their neighbourhood been too jealous of one-another and too equally matched to suffer either to take advantage of their quarrels. That they have remained so long united at all is to be attributed to their weakness, to their poverty, and to the cause just mentioned. These ties will not exist in America; a little time hence, some of the states will be powerful empires, and we are so remote from other nations that we shall have all the leisure and opportunity we can wish to cut each others throats.

The Germanic corps might also be cited as an example in favour of the position.

The United provinces may be thought to be one against it. But the family of the stadtholders whose authority is interwoven with the whole government has been a strong link of union between them. Their physical necessities and the habits founded upon them have contributed to it. Each province is too inconsiderable by itself to undertake any thing. An analysis of their present constitutions would show that they have many ties which would not exist in ours; and that they are by no means a proper mode for us.

Our own experience should satisfy us. We have felt the difficulty of drawing out the resources of the country and inducing the states to combine in equal exertions for the common cause. The ill success of our last attempt is striking. Some have done a great deal, others little or scarcely any thing. The disputes about boundaries &c. testify how flattering a prospect we have of future tranquillity, if we do not frame in time a confederacy capable of deciding the differences and compelling the obedience of the respective members.

The confederation too gives the power of the purse too intirely to the state legislatures. It should provide perpetual funds in the disposal of Congress—by a land tax, poll tax, or the like. All imposts upon commerce ought to be laid by Congress and appropriated to their use, for without certain revenues, a government can have no power; that power, which holds the purse strings absolutely, must rule. This seems to be a medium, which without making Congress altogether independent will tend to give reality to its authority.

Another defect in our system is want of method and energy in the administration. This has partly resulted from the other defect, but in a great degree from prejudice and the want of a proper executive. Congress have kept the power too much into their own hands and have meddled too much with details of every sort. Congress is properly a deliberative corps and it forgets itself when it attempts to play the executive. It is impossible such a body, numerous as it is, constantly fluctuating, can ever act with sufficient decision, or with system. Two thirds of the members, one half the time, cannot know what has gone before them or what connection the subject in hand has to what has been transacted on former occasions. The members, who have been more permanent, will only give information, that promotes the side they espouse, in the present case, and will as often mislead as enlighten. The variety of business must distract, and the proneness of every assembly to debate must at all times delay.

Lately Congress, convinced of these inconveniences, have gone into the measure of appointing boards. But this is in my opinion a bad plan. A single man, in each department of the administration, would be greatly preferable. It would give us a chance of more knowlege, more activity, more responsibility and of course more zeal and attention. Boards partake of a part of the inconveniencies of larger assemblies. Their decisions are slower their energy less their responsibility more diffused. They will not have the same abilities and knowlege as an administration by single men. Men of the first pretensions will not so readily engage in them, because they will be less cospicuous, of less importance, have less opportunity of distinguishing themselves. The members of boards will take less pains to inform themselves and arrive to eminence, because they have fewer motives to do it. All these reasons conspire to give a preference to the plan of vesting the great executive departments of the state in the hands of individuals. As these men will be of course at all times under the direction of Congress, we shall blend the advantages of a monarchy and republic in our constitution.

A question has been made, whether single men could be found to undertake these offices. I think they could, because there would be then every thing to excite the ambition of candidates. But in order to this Congress by their manner of appointing them and the line of duty marked out must show that they are in earnest in making these offices, offices of real trust and importance.

I fear a little vanity has stood in the way of these arrangements, as though they would lessen the importance of Congress and leave them nothing to do. But they would have precisely the same rights and powers as heretofore, happily disencumbered of the detail. They would have to inspect the conduct of their ministers, deliberate upon their plans, originate others for the public good—only observing this rule that they ought to consult their ministers, and get all the information and advice they could from them, before they entered into any new measures or made changes in the old.

A third defect is the fluctuating constitution of our army. This has been a pregnant source of evil; all our military misfortunes, three fourths of our civil embarrassments are to be ascribed to it. The General has so fully enumerated the mischief of it in a late letter of the [text omitted in the original document] to Congress that I could only repeat what he has said, and will therefore refer you to that letter.

The imperfect and unequal provision made for the army is a fourth defect which you will find delineated in the same letter. Without a speedy change the army must dissolve; it is now a mob, rather than an army, without cloathing, without pay, without provision, without morals, without discipline. We begin to hate the country for its neglect of us; the country begins to hate us for our oppressions of them. Congress have long been jealous of us; we have now lost all confidence in them, and give the worst construction to all they do. Held together by the slenderest ties we are ripening for a dissolution.

The present mode of supplying the army—by state purchases—is not one of the least considerable defects of our system. It is too precarious a dependence, because the states will never be sufficiently impressed with our necessities. Each will make its own ease a primary object, the supply of the army a secondary one. The variety of channels through which the business is transacted will multiply the number of persons employed and the opportunities of embezzling public money. From the popular spirit on which most of the governments turn, the state agents, will be men of less character and ability, nor will there be so rigid a responsibility among them as there might easily be among those in the employ of the continent, of course not so much diligence care or economy. Very little of the money raised in the several states will go into the Continental treasury, on pretence, that it is all exhausted in providing the quotas of supplies, and the public will be without funds for the other demands of governments. The expence will be ultimately much greater and the advantages much smaller. We actually feel the insufficiency of this plan and have reason to dread under it a ruinous extremity of want.

These are the principal defects in the present system that now occur to me. There are many inferior ones in the organization of particular departments and many errors of administration which might be pointed out; but the task would be troublesome and tedious, and if we had once remedied those I have mentioned the others would not be attended with much difficulty.

I shall now propose the remedies, which appear to me applicable to our circumstances, and necessary to extricate our affairs from their present deplorable situation.

The first step must be to give Congress powers competent to the public exigencies. This may happen in two ways, one by resuming and exercising the discretionary powers I suppose to have been originally vested in them for the safety of the states and resting their conduct on the candor of their country men and the necessity of the conjuncture: the other by calling immediately a convention of all the states with full authority to conclude finally upon a general confederation, stating to them beforehand explicity the evils arising from a want of power in Congress, and the impossibily of supporting the contest on its present footing, that the delegates may come possessed of proper sentiments as well as proper authority to give to the meeting. Their commission should include a right of vesting Congress with the whole or a proportion of the unoccupied lands, to be employed for the purpose of raising a revenue, reserving the jurisdiction to the states by whom they are granted.

The first plan, I expect will be thought too bold an expedient by the generality of Congress; and indeed their practice hitherto has so rivetted the opinion of their want of power, that the success of this experiment may very well be doubted.

I see no objection to the other mode, that has any weight in competition with the reasons for it. The Convention should assemble the 1st of November next, the sooner, the better; our disorders are too violent to admit of a common or lingering remedy. The reasons for which I require them to be vested with plenipotentiary authority are that the business may suffer no delay in the execution, and may in reality come to effect. A convention may agree upon a confederation; the states individually hardly ever will. We must have one at all events, and a vigorous one if we mean to succeed in the contest and be happy hereafter. As I said before, to engage the states to comply with this mode, Congress ought to confess to them plainly and unanimously the impracticability of supporting our affairs on the present footing and without a solid coercive union. I ask that the Convention should have a power of vesting the whole or a part of the unoccupied land in Congress, because it is necessary that body should have some property as a fund for the arrangements of finance; and I know of no other kind that can be given them.

The confederation in my opinion should give Congress complete sovereignty; except as to that part of internal police, which relates to the rights of property and life among individuals and to raising money by internal taxes. It is necessary, that every thing, belonging to this, should be regulated by the state legislatures. Congress should have complete sovereignty in all that relates to war, peace, trade, finance, and to the management of foreign affairs, the right of declaring war of raising armies, officering, paying them, directing their motions in every respect, of equipping fleets and doing the same with them, of building fortifications arsenals magazines &c. &c., of making peace on such conditions as they think proper, of regulating trade, determining with what countries it shall be carried on, granting indulgencies laying prohibitions on all the articles of export or import, imposing duties granting bounties & premiums for raising exporting importing and applying to their own use the product of these duties, only giving credit to the states on whom they are raised in the general account of revenues and expences, instituting Admiralty courts &c., of coining money, establishing banks on such terms, and with such privileges as they think proper, appropriating funds and doing whatever else relates to the operations of finance, transacting every thing with foreign nations, making alliances offensive and defensive, treaties of commerce, &c. &c.

The confederation should provide certain perpetual revenues, productive and easy of collection, a land tax, poll tax or the like, which together with the duties on trade and the unlocated lands would give Congress a substantial existence, and a stable foundation for their schemes of finance. What more supplies were necessary should be occasionally demanded of the states, in the present mode of quotas.

The second step I would recommend is that Congress should instantly appoint the following great officers of state—A secretary for foreign affairs—a President of war—A President of Marine—A Financier—A President of trade; instead of this last a board of Trade may be preferable as the regulations of trade are slow and gradual and require prudence and experience (more than other qualities), for which boards are very well adapted.

Congress should choose for these offices, men of the first abilities, property and character in the continent—and such as have had the best opportunities of being acquainted with the several branches. General Schuyler (whom you mentioned) would make an excellent President of War, General McDougall a very good President of Marine. Mr. Robert Morris would have many things in his favour for the department of finance. He could by his own personal influence give great weight to the measures he should adopt. I dare say men equally capable may be found for the other departments.

I know not, if it would not be a good plan to let the Financier be President of the Board of trade; but he should only have a casting voice in determining questions there. There is a connection between trade and finance, which ought to make the director of one acquainted with the other; but the Financier should not direct the affairs of trade, because for the sake of acquiring reputation by increasing the revenues, he might adopt measures that would depress trade. In what relates to finance he should be alone.

These offices should have nearly the same powers and functions as those in France analogous to them, and each should be chief in his department, with subordinate boards composed of assistant clerks &c. to execute his orders.

In my opinion a plan of this kind would be of inconceivable utility to our affairs; its benefits would be very speedily felt. It would give new life and energy to the operations of government. Business would be conducted with dispatch method and system. A million of abuses now existing would be corrected, and judicious plans would be formed and executed for the public good.

Another step of immediate necessity is to recruit the army for the war, or at least for three years. This must be done by a mode similar to that which is practiced in Sweeden. There the inhabitants are thrown into classes of sixteen, and when the sovereign wants men each of these classes must furnish one. They raise a fixed sum of money, and if one of the class is willing to become a soldier, he receives the money and offers himself a volunteer; if none is found to do this, a draft is made and he on whom the lot falls receives the money and is obliged to serve. The minds of the people are prepared for a thing of this kind; the heavy bounties they have been obliged to pay for men to serve a few months must have disgusted them with this mode, and made them desirous of another, that will once for all answer the public purposes, and obviate a repetition of the demand. It ought by all means to be attempted, and Congress should frame a general plan and press the execution upon the states. When the confederation comes to be framed, it ought to provide for this by a fundamental law, and hereafter there would be no doubt of the success. But we cannot now wait for this; we want to replace the men whose times of service will expire the 1st of January, for then, without this, we shall have no army remaining and the enemy may do what they please. The General in his letter already quoted has assigned the most substantial reasons for paying immediate attention to this point.

Congress should endeavour, both upon their credit in Europe, and by every possible exertion in this country, to provide cloathing for their officers, and should abolish the whole system of state supplies. The making good the depreciation of the currency and all other compensations to the army should be immediately taken up by Congress, and not left to the states; if they would have the accounts of depreciation liquidated, and governmental certificates given for what is due in specie or an equivalent to specie, it would give satisfaction; appointing periodical settlements for future depreciation.

The placing the officers upon half pay during life would be a great stroke of policy, and would give Congress a stronger tie upon them, than any thing else they can do. No man, that reflects a moment, but will prefer a permanent provision of this kind to any temporary compensation, nor is it opposed to economy; the difference between this and between what has been already done will be insignificant. The benefit of it to the widows should be confined to those whose husbands die during the war. As to the survivors, not more than one half on the usual calculation of mens lives will exceed the seven years for which the half pay is already established. Besides this whatever may be the visionary speculations of some men at this time, we shall find it indispensable after the war to keep on foot a considerable body of troops; and all the officers retained for this purpose must be deducted out of the half pay list. If any one will take the pains to calculate the expence on these principles, I am persuaded he will find the addition of expence from the establishment proposed, by no means a national object.

The advantages of securing the attachment of the army to Congress, and binding them to the service by substantial ties are immense. We should then have discipline, an army in reality, as well as in name. Congress would then have a solid basis of authority and consequence, for to me it is an axiom that in our constitution an army is essential to the American union.

The providing of supplies is the pivot of every thing else (though a well constituted army would not in a small degree conduce to this, by giving consistency and weight to government). There are four ways all which must be united—a foreign loan, heavy pecuniary taxes, a tax in kind, a bank founded on public and private credit.

As to a foreign loan I dare say, Congress are doing every thing in their power to obtain it. The most effectual way will be to tell France that without it, we must make terms with great Britain. This must be done with plainness and firmness, but with respect and without petulance, not as a menace, but as a candid declaration of our circumstances. We need not fear to be deserted by France. Her interest and honor are too deeply involved in our fate; and she can make no possible compromise. She can assist us, if she is convinced it is absolutely necessary, either by lending us herself or by becoming our surety or by influencing Spain. It has been to me astonishing how any man could have doubted at any period of our affairs of the necessity of a foreign loan. It was self evident, that we had not a fund of wealth in this country, capable of affording revenues equal to the expences. We must then create artificial revenues, or borrow; the first was done, but it ought to have been foreseen, that the expedient could not last; and we should have provided in time for its failure.

Here was an error of Congress. I have good reason to believe, that measures were not taken in earnest early enough, to procure a loan abroad. I give you my honor that from our first outset, I thought as I do now and wished for a foreign loan not only because I foresaw it would be essential but because I considered it as a tie upon the nation from which it was derived and as a mean to prop our cause in Europe.

Concerning the necessity of heavy pecuniary taxes I need say nothing, as it is a point in which everybody is agreed; nor is there any danger, that the product of any taxes raised in this way will over burthen the people, or exceed the wants of the public. Indeed if all the paper in circulation were drawn annually into the treasury, it would neither do one, nor the other.

As to a tax in kind, the necessity of it results from this principle—that the money in circulation is not a sufficient representative of the productions of the country, and consequently no revenues raised from it as a medium can be a competent representative of that part of the products of the country, which it is bound to contribute to the support of the public. The public therefore to obtain its due or satisfy its just demands and its wants must call for a part of those products themselves. This is done in all those countries which are not commercial, in Russia, Prussia, Denmark Sweden &c. and is peculiarly necessary in our case.

Congress in calling for specific supplies seem to have had this in view; but their intention has not been answered. The states in general have undertaken to furnish the supplies by purchase, a mode as I have observed, attended with every inconvenience and subverting the principle on which the supplies were demanded—the insufficiency of our circulating medium as a representative for the labour and commodities of the Country. It is therefore necessary that Congress should be more explicit, should form the outlines of a plan for a tax in kind, and recommend it to the states, as a measure of absolute necessity.

The general idea I have of a plan, is that a respectable man should be appointed by the state in each county to collect the taxes and form magazines, that Congress should have in each state an officer to superintend the whole and that the state collectors should be subordinate and responsible to them. This Continental superintendent might be subject to the general direction of the Quarter Master General, or not, as might be deemed best; but if not subject to him, he should be obliged to make monthly returns to the President at War, who should instruct him what proportion to deliver to the Quarter Master General. It may be necessary that the superintendents should sometimes have power to dispose of the articles in their possession on public account; for it would happen that the contributions in places remote from the army could not be transported to the theatre of operations without too great expence, in which case it would be eligible to dispose of them and purchase with the money so raised in the countries near the immediate scene of war.

I know the objections which may be raised to this plan—its tendency to discourage industry and the like; but necessity calls for it; we cannot proceed without [it], and less evils must give place to greater. It is besides practiced with success in other countries, and why not in this? It may be said, the examples cited are from nations under despotic governments and that the same would not be practicable with us; but I contend where the public good is evidently the object more may be effected in governments like ours than in any other. It has been a constant remark that free countries have ever paid the heaviest taxes. The obedience of a free people to general laws however hard they bear is ever more perfect than that of slaves to the arbitrary will of a prince. To this it may be added that Sweden was always a free government, and is so now in a great degree, notwithstanding the late revolution.

How far it may be practicable to erect a bank on the joint credit of the public and of individuals can only be certainly determined by the experiment; but it is of so much importance that the experiment ought to be fully tried. When I saw the subscriptions going on to the bank established for supplying the army, I was in hopes it was only the embryo of a more permanent and extensive establishment. But I have reason to believe I shall be disappointed. It does not seem to be at all conducted on the true principles of a bank. The directors of it are purchasing with their stock instead of bank notes as I expected; in consequence of which it must turn out to be a mere subscription of a particular sum of money for a particular purpose.

Paper credit never was long supported in any country, on a national scale, where it was not founded on the joint basis of public and private credit. An attempt to establish it on public credit alone in France under the auspices of Mr. Law had nearly ruined the kingdom; we have seen the effects of it in America, and every successive experiment proves the futility of the attempt. Our new money is depreciating almost as fast as the old, though it has in some states as real funds as paper money ever had. The reason is, that the monied men have not an immediate interest to uphold its credit. They may even in many ways find it their interest to undermine it. The only certain manner to obtain a permanent paper credit is to engage the monied interest immediately in it by making them contribute the whole or part of the stock and giving them the whole or part of the profits.

The invention of banks on the modern principle originated in Venice. There the public and a company of monied men are mutually concerned. The Bank of England unites public authority and faith with private credit; and hence we see what a vast fabric of paper credit is raised on a visionary basis. Had it not been for this, England would never have found sufficient funds to carry on her wars; but with the help of this she has done, and is doing wonders. The bank of Amsterdam is on a similar foundation.

And why can we not have an American bank? Are our monied men less enlightened to their own interest or less enterprising in the persuit? I believe the fault is in our government which does not exert itself to engage them in such a scheme. It is true, the individuals in America are not very rich, but this would not prevent their instituting a bank; it would only prevent its being done with such ample funds as in other countries. Have they not sufficient confidence in the government and in the issue of the cause? Let the Government endeavour to inspire that confidence, by adopting the measures I have recommended or others equivalent to them. Let it exert itself to procure a solid confederation, to establish a good plan of executive administration, to form a permanent military force, to obtain at all events a foreign loan. If these things were in a train of vigorous execution, it would give a new spring to our affairs; government would recover its respectability and individuals would renounce their diffidence.

The object I should propose to myself in the first instance from a bank would be an auxiliary mode of supplies; for which purpose contracts should be made between Government and the bank on terms liberal and advantageous to the latter. Every thing should be done in the first instance to encourage the bank; after it gets well established it will take care of itself and government may make the best terms it can for itself.

The first step to establishing the bank will be to engage a number of monied men of influence to relish the project and make it a business. The subscribers to that lately established are the fittest persons that can be found; and their plan may be interwoven.

The outlines of my plan would be to open subscriptions in all the states for the stock, which we will suppose to be one million of pounds. Real property of every kind, as well as specie should be deemed good stock, but at least a fourth part of the subscription should be in specie or plate. There should be one great company in three divisions in Virginia, Philadelphia, and at Boston or two at Philadelphia and Boston. The bank should have a right to issue bank notes bearing two per Cent interest for the whole of their stock; but not to exceed it. These notes may be payable every three months or oftener, and the faith of government must be pledged for the support of the bank. It must therefore have a right from time to time to inspect its operations, and must appoint inspectors for the purpose.

The advantages of the bank may consist in this, in the profits of the contracts made with government, which should bear interest to be annually paid in specie, in the loan of money at interest say six per Cent, in purchasing lives by annuities as practiced in England &c. The benefit resulting to the company is evident from the consideration, that they may employ in circulation a great deal more money than they have specie in stock, on the credit of the real property which they will have in other use; this money will be employed either in fulfilling their contracts with the public by which also they will gain a profit, or in loans at an advantageous interest or in annuities.

The bank may be allowed to purchase plate and bullion and coin money allowing government a part of the profit. I make the bank notes bear interest to obtain a readie currency and to induce the holders to prefer them to specie to prevent too great a run upon the bank at any time beyond its ability to pay.

If Government can obtain a foreign loan it should lend to the bank on easy terms to extend its influence and facilitate a compliance with its engagements. If government could engage the states to raise a sum of money in specie to be deposited in bank in the same manner, it would be of the greatest consequence. If government could prevail on the enthusiasm of the people to make a contribution in plate for the same purpose it would be a master stroke. Things of this kind sometimes succeed in popular contests; and if undertaken with address; I should not despair of its success; but I should not be sanguine.

The bank may be instituted for a term of years by way of trial and the particular privilege of coining money be for a term still shorter. A temporary transfer of it to a particular company can have no inconvenience as the government are in no condition to improve this resource nor could it in our circumstances be an object to them, though with the industry of a knot of individuals it might be.

A bank of this kind even in its commencement would answer the most valuable purposes to government and to the proprietors; in its progress the advantages will exceed calculation. It will promote commerce by furnishing a more extensive medium which we greatly want in our circumstances. I mean a more extensive valuable medium. We have an enormous nominal one at this time; but it is only a name.

In the present unsettled state of things in this country, we can hardly draw inferences from what has happened in others, otherwise I should be certain of the success of this scheme; but I think it has enough in its favour to be worthy of trial.

I have only skimmed the surface of the different subjects I have introduced. Should the plans recommended come into contemplation in earnest and you desire my further thoughts, I will endeavour to give them more form and particularity. I am persuaded a solid confederation a permanent army a reasonable prospect of subsisting it would give us treble consideration in Europe and produce a peace this winter.

If a Convention is called the minds of all the states and the people ought to be prepared to receive its determinations by sensible and popular writings, which should conform to the views of Congress. There are epochs in human affairs, when *novelty* even is useful. If a general opinion prevails that the old way is bad, whether true or false, and this obstructs or relaxes the operation of the public service, a change is necessary if it be but for the sake of change. This is exactly the case now. 'Tis an universal sentiment that our present system is a bad one, and that things do not go right on this account. The measure of a Convention would revive the hopes of the people and give a new direction to their passions, which may be improved in carrying points of substantial utility. The Eastern states have already pointed out this mode to Congress; they ought to take the hint and anticipate the others.

And, in future, My Dear Sir, two things let me recommend, as fundamental rules for the conduct of Congress—to attach the army to them by every motive, to maintain an air of authority (not domineering) in all their measures with the states. The manner in which a thing is done has more influence than is commonly imagined. Men are governed by opinion; this opinion is as much influenced by appearances as by realities; if a Government appears to be confident of its own powers, it is the surest way to inspire the same confidence in others; if it is diffident, it may be certain, there will be a still greater diffidence in others, and that its authority will not only be distrusted, controverted, but contemned.

I wish too Congress would always consider that a kindness consists as much in the manner as in the thing: the best things done hesitatingly and with an ill grace lose their effect, and produce disgust rather than satisfaction or gratitude. In what Congress have at any time done for the army, they have commonly been too late: They have seemed to yield to importunity rather than to sentiments of justice or to a regard to the accomodation of their troops. An attention to this idea is of more importance than it may be thought. I who have seen all the workings and progress of the present discontents, am convinced, that a want of this has not been among the most inconsiderable causes.

You will perceive My Dear Sir this letter is hastily written and with a confidential freedom, not as to a member of Congress, whose feelings may be sore at the prevailing clamours; but as to a friend who is in a situation to remedy public disorders, who wishes for nothing so much as truth, and who is desirous of information, even from those less capable of judging than himself. I have not even time to correct and copy and only enough to add that I am very truly and affectionately D Sir   Your most Obed ser*

                                                                A. Hamilton

Liberty Pole
Sept. 3d 1780

---

*Dear Sir, Your Most Obedient Servant

2

The Continentalist Essays, 1781–82

The Articles of Confederation, the first attempt at a "national" government for the original thirteen colonies, were adopted by Congress
in 1777. However, they were not ratified by all the states until
March 1, 1781, while the war with England was still going on and
building toward the final confrontation at Yorktown the following
October. Only a few months following ratification of the Articles,
Alexander Hamilton published the first of his *Continentalist* essays
in *The New-York Packet*. This series of six relatively brief newspaper
articles outlined his perspective on the uselessness of the Articles and
the government they had created. The term "Continentalist" indicates
that his thoughts had turned toward creating a single, unified country
and what it would take, in terms of political thinking and execution,
for the nation to get there. In this way, the six *Continentalist* papers
serve as a preview of the ideas he developed, including taking a broad
view of the powers that Congress should have, during the several
years leading up to the drafting of the Constitution in 1787 and in *The
Federalist Papers* during the campaign for its ratification.

The Continentalist essays were first published in *The New-York Packet*
on the following dates:

No. I: July 12, 1781
No. II: July 19, 1781
No. III: August 9, 1781
No. IV: August 30, 1781
No. V: April 18, 1782
No. VI: July 4, 1782

NO. I

It would be the extreme of vanity in us not to be sensible that we began this revolution with very vague and confined notions of the practical business of government. To the greater part of us it was a novelty; of those who under the former constitution had had opportunities of acquiring experience, a large proportion adhered to the opposite side, and the remainder can only be supposed to have possessed ideas adapted to the narrow colonial sphere in which they had been accustomed to move, not of that enlarged kind suited to the government of an independent nation.

There were, no doubt, exceptions to these observations—men in all respects qualified for conducting the public affairs with skill and advantage. But their number was small; they were not always brought forward in our councils; and when they were, their influence was too commonly borne down by the prevailing torrent of ignorance and prejudice.

On a retrospect, however, of our transactions, under the disadvantages with which we commenced, it is perhaps more to be wondered at that we have done so well than that we have not done better. There are, indeed, some traits in our conduct as conspicuous for sound policy as others for magnanimity. But, on the other hand, it must also be confessed, there have been many false steps, many chimerical projects and Utopian speculations, in the management of our civil as well as of our military affairs. A part of these were the natural effects of the spirit of the times, dictated by our situation. An extreme jealousy of power is the attendant on all popular revolutions, and has seldom been without its evils. It is to this source we are to trace many of the fatal mistakes which have so deeply endangered the common cause; particularly that defect which will be the object of these remarks—a want of power in Congress.

The present Congress, respectable for abilities and integrity, by experience convinced of the necessity of change, are preparing several important articles, to be submitted to the respective States, for augmenting the powers of the Confederation. But though there is hardly at this time a man of information in America who will not acknowledge, as a general proposition, that in its present form it is unequal either to a vigorous prosecution of the war or to the preservation of the Union in peace; yet when the principle comes to be applied to practice, there seems not to be the same agreement in the modes of remedying the defect; and it is to be feared, from a disposition which appeared in some of the States on a late occasion, that the salutary intentions of Congress may meet with more delay and opposition than the critical posture of the States will justify.

It will be attempted to show, in a course of papers, what ought to be done, and the mischiefs of a contrary policy.

In the first stages of the controversy, it was excusable to err. Good intentions, rather than great skill, were to have been expected from us. But we have now had sufficient time for reflection, and experience as ample as unfortunate, to rectify our errors. To persist in them becomes disgraceful, and even criminal, and belies that character of good sense, and a quick discernment of our interests, which, in spite of our mistakes, we have been hitherto allowed. It will prove that our sagacity is limited to interests of inferior moment, and that we are incapable of those enlightened and liberal views necessary to make us a great and a flourishing people.

History is full of examples where, in contests for liberty, a jealousy of power has either defeated the attempts to recover or preserve it, in the first instance, or has afterward subverted it by clogging government with too great precautions for its felicity, or by leaving too wide a door for sedition and popular licentiousness. In a government framed for durable liberty, not less regard must be paid to giving the magistrate a proper degree of authority to make and execute the laws with rigor, than to guard against encroachments upon the rights of the community. As too much power leads to despotism, too little leads to anarchy, and both, eventually, to the ruin of the people. These are maxims well known, but never sufficiently attended to, in adjusting the frames of governments. Some momentary interest or passion is sure to give a wrong bias, and pervert the most favorable opportunities.

No friend to order or to rational liberty can read without pain and disgust the history of the Commonwealths of Greece. Generally speaking, they were a constant scene of the alternate tyranny of one part of the people over the other, or of a few usurping demagogues over the whole. Most of them had been originally governed by kings, whose despotism (the natural disease of monarchy) had obliged their subjects to murder, expel, depose, or reduce them to a nominal existence, and institute popular governments. In these governments, that of Sparta excepted, the jealousy of power hindered the people from trusting out of their own hands a competent authority to maintain the repose and stability of the Commonwealth; whence originated the frequent revolutions and civil broils with which they were distracted. This, and the want of a solid federal union to restrain the ambition and rivalship of the different cities, after a rapid succession of bloody wars, ended in their total loss of liberty, and subjugation to foreign powers.

In comparison of our governments with those of the ancient republics, we must, without hesitation, give the preference to our own; because every power with us is exercised by representation, not in tumultuary assemblies of the collective body of the people, where the art or impudence of the *Orator* or *Tribune,* rather than the utility or justice of the measure, could seldom fail to govern. Yet, whatever may be the advantage on our side in such a comparison, men who estimate the value of institutions, not from prejudices of the moment, but from experience and reason, must be persuaded that the same *jealousy of power* has prevented our reaping all the advantages from the examples of other nations which we ought to have done, and has rendered our constitutions in many respects feeble and imperfect.

Perhaps the evil is not very great in respect to our State constitutions; for, notwithstanding their imperfections, they may for some time be made to operate in such a manner as to answer the purposes of the common defence and the maintenance of order; and they seem to have, in themselves, and in the progress of society among us, the seeds of improvement.

But this is not the case with respect to the Federal Government; if it is too weak at first, it will continually grow weaker. The ambition and local interests of the respective members will be constantly undermining and usurping upon its prerogatives till it comes to a dissolution, if a partial combination of some of the more powerful ones does not bring it to a more *speedy* and *violent end.*

NO. II

July 19, 1781.

In a single state where the sovereign power is exercised by delegation, whether it be a limited monarchy or a republic, the danger most commonly is, that the sovereign will become too powerful for his constituents. In federal governments, where different states are represented in a general council, the danger is on the other side—that the members will be an overmatch for the common head; or, in other words, that it will not have sufficient influence and authority to secure the obedience of the several parts of the confederacy.

In a single state the sovereign has the whole legislative power as well as the command of the national forces—of course an immediate control over the persons and property of the subjects; every other power is subordinate and dependent. If he undertakes to subvert the constitution, it can only be preserved by a general insurrection of the people. The magistrates of the provinces, counties, or towns into which the State is divided, having only an executive and police jurisdiction, can take no decisive measures for counteracting the first indications of tyranny; but must content themselves with the ineffectual weapon of petition and remonstrance. They cannot raise money, levy troops, nor form alliances. The leaders of the people must wait till their discontents have ripened into a general revolt, to put them in a situation to confer the powers necessary for their defence. It will always be difficult for this to take place; because the sovereign, possessing the appearance and forms of legal authority, having the forces and revenues of the state at his command, and a large party among the people besides—which with those advantages he can hardly fail to acquire—he will too often be able to baffle the first motions of the discontented, and prevent that union and concert essential to the success of their opposition.

The security, therefore, of the public liberty must consist in such a distribution of the sovereign power, as will make it morally impossible for one part to gain an ascendency over the others, or for the whole to unite in a scheme of usurpation.

In federal governments, each member has a distinct sovereignty, makes and executes laws, imposes taxes, distributes justice, and exercises every other function of government. It has always within itself the means of revenue; and on an emergency, can levy forces.

If the common sovereign should meditate or attempt any thing unfavorable to the general liberty, each member, having all the proper organs of power, can prepare for defence with celerity and vigor. Each can immediately sound the alarm to the others, and enter into leagues for mutual protection. If the combination is general, as is to be expected, the usurpers will soon find themselves without the means of recruiting their treasury or their armies; and for want of continued supplies of men and money, must, in the end, fall a sacrifice to the attempt. If the combination is not general, it will imply that some of the members are interested in that which is the cause of dissatisfaction to others, and this cannot be an attack upon the common liberty, but upon the interests of one part in favor of another part; and it will be a war between the members of the federal union with each other, not between them and the federal government. From the plainest principles of human nature, two inferences are to be drawn; one, that each member of a political confederacy will be more disposed to advance its own authority upon the ruins of that of the confederacy, than to make any improper concession in its favor, or support it in unreasonable pretensions; the other, that the subjects of each member will be more devoted in their attachments and obedience to their own particular governments, than to that of the union.

It is the temper of societies as well as of individuals to be impatient of constraint, and to prefer partial to general interest. Many cases may occur where members of a confederacy have, or seem to have, an advantage in things contrary to the good of the whole, or a disadvantage in others conducive to that end. The selfishness of every part will dispose each to believe that the public burdens are unequally apportioned, and that itself is the victim. These and other circumstances will promote a disposition for abridging the authority of the federal government; and the ambition of men in office in each state will make them glad to encourage it. They think their own consequence connected with the power of the government of which they are a part; and will endeavor to increase the one as the means of increasing the other.

The particular governments will have more empire over the minds of their subjects than the general one, because their agency will be more direct, more uniform, and more apparent. The people will be habituated to look up to them as the arbiters and guardians of their personal concerns, by which the passions of the vulgar, if not of all men, are most strongly affected; and in every difference with the confederated body, will side with them against the common sovereign.

Experience confirms the truth of these principles. The chief cities of Greece had once their council of Amphyctions, or States-general, with authority to decide and compose the differences of the several cities, and to transact many other important matters relative to the common interest and safety. At their first institution, they had great weight and credit; but never enough to preserve effectually the balance and harmony of the confederacy; and in time their decrees only served as an additional pretext to that side whose pretensions they favored. When the cities were not engaged in foreign wars, they were at perpetual variance among themselves. Sparta and Athens contended twenty-seven years for the precedence, or rather dominion, of Greece, till the former made herself mistress of the whole; and till, in subsequent struggles, having had recourse to the pernicious expedient of calling in the aid of foreign enemies, the Macedonians first and afterward the Romans became their masters.

The German Diet had formerly more authority than it now has, though like that of Greece never enough to hinder the great potentates from disturbing the repose of the empire, and mutually wasting their own territories and people.

The Helvetic League is another example. It is true it has subsisted nearly five hundred years; but in that period the cantons have had repeated and furious wars with each other, which would have made them an easy prey to their more powerful neighbors, had not the reciprocal jealousy of these prevented either from taking advantage of their dissensions. This and their poverty have hitherto saved them from total destruction, and kept them from feeling the miseries of foreign conquest, added to those of civil war. The federal government is too weak to hinder their renewal, whenever the ambition or fanaticism of the principal cantons shall be disposed to rekindle the flame. For some time past, indeed, it has been in a great measure nominal; the Protestants and Catholics have had separate diets, to manage almost all matters of importance; so that in fact, the general diet is only kept up to regulate the affairs of the common bailliages and preserve a semblance of union; and even this, it is probable would cease, did not the extreme weakness of the cantons oblige them to a kind of coalition.

If the divisions of the United Provinces have not proceeded to equal extremities, there are peculiar causes to be assigned. The authority of the Stadtholder pervades the whole frame of the republic, and is a kind of common link by which the provinces are bound together. The jealousy of his progressive influence, in which more or less they all agree, operates as a check upon their ill-humors against one another. The inconsiderableness of each province separately, and the imminent danger to which the whole would be exposed of being overrun by their neighbors in case of disunion, is a further preservative against the phrensy of hostility; and their importance and even existence depending entirely upon frugality, industry, and commerce, peace both at home and abroad is of necessity the predominant object of their policy.

NO. III

August 9, 1781.

The situation of these States is very unlike that of the United Provinces. Remote as we are from Europe, in a little time we should fancy ourselves out of the reach of attempts from abroad, and in full liberty, at our leisure and convenience, to try our strength at home. This might not happen at once, but if the Federal Government should lose its authority it would certainly follow. Political societies in close neighborhood must either be strongly united under one government, or there will infallibly exist emulations and quarrels; this is in human nature, and we have no reason to think ourselves wiser or better than other men. Some of the larger States, a small number of years hence, will be in themselves populous, rich, and powerful in all those circumstances calculated to inspire ambition and nourish ideas of separation and independence. Though it will ever be their true interest to preserve the Union, their vanity and self-importance will be very likely to overpower that motive, and make them seek to place themselves at the head of particular confederacies independent of the general one. A schism once introduced, competitions of boundary and rivalships of commerce will easily afford pretexts for war.

European powers may have many inducements for fomenting these divisions and playing us off against each other; but without such a disposition in them, if separations once take place we shall, of course, embrace different interests and connections. The particular confederacies, leaguing themselves with rival nations, will naturally be involved in their disputes, into which they will be the more readily tempted by the hope of making acquisitions upon each other and upon the colonies of the powers with whom they are respectively at enmity.

We already see symptoms of the evils to be apprehended. In the midst of a war for our existence as a nation—in the midst of dangers too serious to be trifled with, some of the States have evaded or refused compliance with the demands of Congress in points of the greatest moment to the common safety. If they act such a part at this perilous juncture, what are we to expect in a time of peace and security? Is it not to be feared that the resolutions of Congress would soon become like the decisions of the Greek Amphyctions, or like the edicts of a German Diet?

But as these evils are at a little distance, we may perhaps be insensible and short-sighted enough to disregard them. There are others that threaten our immediate safety. Our whole system is in disorder; our currency depreciated, till in many places it will hardly obtain a circulation at all; public credit at its lowest ebb; our army deficient in numbers, and unprovided with every thing; the Government, in its present condition, unable to command the means to pay, clothe, or feed their troops; the enemy making an alarming progress in the Southern States, lately in complete possession of two of them, though now in part rescued by the genius and exertions of a general without an army; a force under Cornwallis still formidable to Virginia.

We ought to blush to acknowledge that this is a true picture of our situation, when we reflect that the enemy's whole force in the United States, including their American levies and the late reinforcements, is little more than fourteen thousand effective men; that our population, by recent examination, has been found to be greater than at the commencement of the war; that the quantity of our specie has also increased; that the country abounds with all the necessaries of life, and has a sufficiency of foreign commodities, with a considerable and progressive commerce; that we have, beyond comparison, a better stock of warlike materials than when we began the contest, and an ally as willing as able to supply our further wants; and that we have on the spot five thousand auxiliary troops, paid and subsisted by that ally, to assist in our defence.

Nothing but a general disaffection of the people or mismanagement in their rulers can account for the figure we make, and for the distresses and perplexities we experience contending against so small a force.

Our enemies themselves must now be persuaded that the first is not the cause, and we know it is not. The most decided attachment of the people could alone have made them endure, without a convulsion, the successive shocks in our currency, added to the unavoidable inconveniences of war. There is perhaps not another nation in the world that would have shown equal patience and perseverance in similar circumstances. The enemy have now tried the temper of almost every part of America, and they can hardly produce in their ranks a thousand men who, without their arts and seductions, have voluntarily joined their standard. The miseries of a rigorous captivity may perhaps have added half as many more to the number of the American levies at this time in their armies. This small accession of force is the more extraordinary, as they have at some periods been apparently in the full tide of success, while every thing wore an aspect tending to infuse despondency into the people of this country. This has been remarkably the case in the Southern States.

They for a time had almost undisturbed possession of two of them, and Cornwallis, after overrunning a great part of a third, after two victorious battles, only brought with him into Virginia about two hundred Tories; in the State where he thought himself so well established, that he presumptuously ventured to assure the minister there was not a rebel left, a small body of continental troops have been so effectually seconded by the militia of that vanquished country as to have been able to capture a number of his troops more than equal to their own, and to repossess the principal part of the State.

As in the explanation of our embarrassments nothing can be alleged to the disaffection of the people, we must have recourse to the other cause—of impolicy and mismanagement in their rulers.

Where the blame of this may lie is not so much the question as what are the proper remedies, yet it may not be amiss to remark that too large a share has fallen upon Congress. That body is no doubt chargeable with mistakes, but perhaps its greatest has been too much readiness to make concessions of the powers implied in its original trust. This is partly to be attributed to an excessive complaisance to the spirit which has evidently actuated a majority of the States, a desire of monopolizing all power in themselves. Congress has been responsible for the administration of affairs, without the means of fulfilling that responsibility.

It would be too severe a reflection upon us to suppose that a disposition to make the most of the friendship of others, and to exempt ourselves from a full share of the burthens of the war, has had any part in the backwardness which has appeared in many of the States to confer powers and adopt measures adequate to the exigency. Such a sentiment would neither be wise, just, generous, nor honorable; nor do I believe the accusation would be well founded, yet our conduct makes us liable to a suspicion of this sort. It is certain, however, that too sanguine expectations from Europe have unintentionally relaxed our efforts by diverting a sense of danger, and begetting an opinion that the inequality of the contest would make every campaign the last.

We did not consider how difficult it must be to exhaust the resources of a nation circumstanced like that of Great Britain; whose government has always been distinguished for energy, and its people for enthusiasm. Nor did we in estimating the superiority of our friends make sufficient allowance for that want of concert which will ever characterize the operations of allies, or for the immense advantage to the enemy of having their forces, though inferior, under a single direction.

Finding the rest of Europe either friendly or pacific, we never calculated the contingencies which might alter that disposition; nor reflected that the death of a single prince, the change or caprice of a single minister, was capable of giving a new face to the whole system.

We are at this time more sanguine than ever. The war with the Dutch, we believe, will give such an addition of force to our side as will make the superiority irresistible. No person can dispute this, if things remain in their present state; but the extreme disparity of the contest is the very reason why this cannot be the case. The neutral powers will either effect a particular or a general accommodation, or they will take their sides. There are three suppositions to be made: one, that there will be a compromise *between the United Provinces* and England, for which we are certain the mediation of Austria and Russia has been offered; another, a pacification between all the belligerent powers, for which we have reason to believe the same mediation has been offered; the third, a rejection of the terms of mediation and a more general war.

Either of these suppositions is a motive for exertion. The first will place things in the same, probably in a worse, situation than before the declaration of the war against Holland. The composing of present differences may be accompanied with a revival of ancient connections; and at least would be productive of greater caution and restraint in a future intercourse with us.

The second, it is much to be dreaded, would hazard a dismemberment of a part of these States; and we are bound in honor, in duty, and in interest, to employ every effort to dispossess the enemy of what they hold. A natural basis of the negotiation with respect to this continent will be, that each party shall retain what it possesses at the conclusion of the treaty, qualified perhaps by a cession of particular points for an equivalent elsewhere. It is too delicate to dwell on the motives to this apprehension; but if such a compromise sometimes terminates the disputes of nations originally independent, it will be less extraordinary where one party was originally under the dominion of the other.

NO. IV

August 30, 1781.

The preceding numbers are chiefly intended to confirm an opinion, already pretty generally received, that it is necessary to augment the powers of the Confederation. The principal difficulty yet remains to fix the public judgment definitely on the points which ought to compose that augmentation.

It may be pronounced with confidence that nothing short of the following articles can suffice.

1st.—THE POWER OF REGULATING TRADE, comprehending a right of granting bounties and premiums by way of encouragement, of imposing duties of every kind as well for revenue as regulation, of appointing all officers of the customs, and of laying embargoes in extraordinary emergencies.

2d.—A moderate-levied tax, throughout the United States, of a specific rate per pound or per acre, granted to the Federal Government in perpetuity, and, if Congress think proper, to be levied by their own collectors.

3d.—A moderate capitation-tax on every male inhabitant above fifteen years of age, exclusive of common soldiers, common seamen, day laborers, cottagers, and paupers, to be also vested in perpetuity, and with the same condition of collection.

4th.—The disposal of all unlocated land for the benefit of the United States (so far as respects the profits of the first sale and the quit-rents), the jurisdiction remaining to the respective States in whose limits they are contained.

5th.—A certain proportion of the product of all mines discovered, or to be discovered, for the same duration, and with the same right of collection as in the second and third articles.

6th.—The appointment of all land (as well as naval) officers of every rank.

The three first articles are of IMMEDIATE NECESSITY; the three last would be of great present, but of much greater future, utility; the whole combined would give solidity and permanency to the Union.

The great defect of the Confederation is, that it gives the United States no property; or, in other words, no revenue, nor the means of acquiring it, inherent in themselves and independent on the temporary pleasure of the different members. And power without revenue, in political society, is a name. While Congress continue altogether dependent on the occasional grants of the several States, for the means of defraying the expenses of the Federal Government, it can neither have dignity, vigor, nor credit. Credit supposes specific and permanent funds for the punctual payment of interest, with a moral certainty of the final redemption of the principal.

In our situation it will probably require more, on account of the general diffidence which has been excited by the past disorders in our finances. It will perhaps be necessary, in the first instance, to appropriate funds for the redemption of the principal in a determinate period, as well as for the payment of interest.

It is essential that the property in such funds should be in the contractor himself, and the appropriation dependent on his own will. If, instead of this, the possession or disposal of them is dependent on the voluntary or occasional concurrence of a number of different wills not under his absolute control, both the one and the other will be too precarious to be trusted. The most wealthy and best established nations are obliged to pledge their funds to obtain credit, and it would be the height of absurdity in us, in the midst of a revolution, to expect to have it on better terms. This credit being to be procured through Congress, the funds ought to be provided, declared, and vested in them. It is a fact that verifies the want of specific funds that the circumstance which operates powerfully against our obtaining credit abroad is, not a distrust of our becoming independent, but of our continuing united, and with our present Confederation the distrust is natural. Both foreigners and the thinking men among ourselves would have much more confidence in the duration of the Union, if they were to see it supported on the foundation here proposed.

There are some among us ignorant enough to imagine that the war may be carried on without credit, defraying the expenses of the year with what may be raised within the year. But this is for want of a knowledge of our real resources and expenses.

It may be demonstrated that the whole amount of the revenue which these States are capable of affording will be deficient annually five or six millions of dollars for the support of civil government and of the war.

This is not a conjecture hazarded at random, but the result of experiment and calculation; nor can it appear surprising, when it is considered that the revenues of the United Provinces, equal to these States in population, beyond comparison superior in industry, commerce, and riches, do not exceed twenty-five millions of guilders, or about nine millions and a half of dollars. In times of war they have raised a more considerable sum, but it has been chiefly by gratuitous combinations of rich individuals, a resource we cannot employ, because there are few men of large fortunes in this country, and these for the most part are in land. Taxes in the United Provinces are carried to an extreme which would be impracticable here. Not only the living are made to pay for every necessary of life, but even the dead are tributary to the public for the liberty of interment at particular hours. These considerations make it evident that we could not raise an equal amount of revenue in these States. Yet, in '76, when the currency was not depreciated, Congress emitted, for the expenses of the year, fourteen millions of dollars. It cannot be denied that there was a want of order and economy in the expenditure of public money, nor that we had a greater military force to maintain at that time than we now have; but, on the other hand, allowing for the necessary increase in our different civil lists, and for the advanced prices of many articles, it can hardly be supposed possible to reduce our annual expense very much below that sum. This simple idea of the subject, without entering into details, may satisfy us that the deficiency which has been stated is not to be suspected of exaggeration.

Indeed, nations the most powerful and opulent are obliged to have recourse to loans in time of war, and hence it is that most of the states of Europe are deeply immersed in debt. France is among the number, notwithstanding her immense population, wealth, and resources. England owes the enormous sum of two hundred millions sterling. The United Provinces, with all their prudence and parsimony, owe a debt of the generality of fifty millions, besides the particular debts of each province. Almost all the other powers are more or less in the same circumstances.

While this teaches us how contracted and uninformed are the views of those who expect to carry on the war without running in debt, it ought to console us with respect to the amount of that which we now owe, or may have occasion to incur in the remainder of the war. The whole, without burthening the people, may be paid off in twenty years after the conclusion of peace.

The principal part of the deficient five or six millions must be procured by loans from private persons at home and abroad. Every thing may be hoped from the generosity of France which her means will permit, but she has full employment for her revenues and credit in the prosecution of the war on her own part. If we judge of the future by the past, the pecuniary succors from her must continue to be far short of our wants, and the contingency of a war on the continent of Europe makes it possible they may diminish rather than increase.

We have in a less degree experienced the friendship of Spain in this article.

The Government of the United Provinces, if disposed to do it, can give us no assistance. The resources of the republic are chiefly mortgaged for former debts. Happily, it has extensive credit, but it will have occasion for the whole to supply its own exigencies.

Private men, either foreigners or natives, will not lend to a large amount, but on the usual security of funds properly established. This security Congress cannot give till the several States vest them with revenue, or the means of revenue, for that purpose.

Congress have wisely appointed a superintendent of their finances, a man of acknowledged abilities and integrity, as well as of great personal credit and pecuniary influence.

It was impossible that the business of finance could be ably conducted by a body of men however well composed or well intentioned. Order in the future management of our moneyed concerns, a strict regard to the performance of public engagements, and of course the restoration of public credit may be reasonably and confidently expected from Mr. Morris' administration if he is furnished with materials upon which to operate—that is, if the Federal Government can acquire funds as the basis of his arrangements. He has very judiciously proposed a National Bank, which, by uniting the influence and interest of the moneyed men with the resources of government, can alone give it that durable and extensive credit of which it stands in need. This is the best expedient he could have devised for relieving the public embarrassments, but to give success to the plan it is essential that Congress should have it in their power to support him with unexceptionable funds. Had we begun the practice of funding four years ago, we should have avoided that depreciation of the currency which has been pernicious to the morals and to the credit of the nation, and there is no other method than this to prevent a continuance and multiplication of the evils flowing from that prolific source.

NO. V

April 18, 1782.

The vesting Congress with the power of regulating trade ought to have been a principal object of the Confederation for a variety of reasons. It is as necessary for the purposes of commerce as of revenue. There are some who maintain that trade will regulate itself, and is not to be benefited by the encouragements or restraints of government. Such persons will imagine that there is no need of a common directing power. This is one of those wild speculative paradoxes, which have grown into credit among us, contrary to the uniform practice and sense of the most enlightened nations.

Contradicted by the numerous institutions and laws that exist everywhere for the benefit of trade, by the pains taken to cultivate particular branches and to discourage others, by the known advantages derived from those measures, and by the palpable evils that would attend their discontinuance, it must be rejected by every man acquainted with commercial history. Commerce, like other things, has its fixed principles, according to which it must be regulated. If these are understood and observed, it will be promoted by the attention of government; if unknown, or violated, it will be injured—but it is the same with every other part of administration.

To preserve the balance of trade in favor of a nation ought to be a leading aim of its policy. The avarice of individuals may frequently find its account in pursuing channels of traffic prejudicial to that balance, to which the government may be able to oppose effectual impediments. There may, on the other hand, be a possibility of opening new sources, which, though accompanied with great difficulties in the commencement, would in the event amply reward the trouble and expense of bringing them to perfection. The undertaking may often exceed the influence and capitals of individuals, and may require no small assistance, as well from the revenue as from the authority of the state.

The contrary opinion, which has grown into a degree of vogue among us, has originated in the injudicious attempts made at different times to effect a regulation of prices. It became a cant phrase among the opposers of these attempts, that trade must regulate itself; by which at first was only meant that it had its fundamental laws, agreeable to which its general operations must be directed, and that any violent attempts in opposition to these would commonly miscarry. In this sense the maxim was reasonable, but it has since been extended to militate against all interference by the sovereign; an extreme as little reconcilable with experience or common sense as the practice it was first framed to discredit.

The reasonings of a very ingenious and sensible writer, by being misapprehended, have contributed to this mistake. The scope of his argument is not, as by some supposed, that trade will hold a certain invariable course independent on the aid, protection, care, or concern of government; but that it will, in the main, depend upon the comparative industry, moral and physical advantages of nations; and that though, for a while, from extraordinary causes, there may be a wrong balance against one of them, this will work its own cure, and things will ultimately return to their proper level. His object was to combat that excessive jealousy on this head, which has been productive of so many unnecessary wars, and with which the British nation is particularly infected; but it was no part of his design to insinuate that the regulating hand of government was either useless or hurtful. The nature of a government, its spirit, maxims, and laws, with respect to trade, are among those constant moral causes which influence its general results, and when it has by accident taken a wrong direction, assist in bringing it back to its natural course. This is everywhere admitted by all writers upon the subject; nor is there one who has asserted a contrary doctrine.

Trade may be said to have taken its rise in England under the auspices of Elizabeth, and its rapid progress there is in a great measure to be ascribed to the fostering care of government in that and succeeding reigns.

From a different spirit in the government, with superior advantages, France was much later in commercial improvements; nor would her trade have been at this time in so prosperous a condition, had it not been for the abilities and indefatigable endeavors of the great Colbert. He laid the foundation of the French commerce, and taught the way to his successors to enlarge and improve it. The establishment of the woollen manufacture in a kingdom where nature seemed to have denied the means, is one, among many proofs, how much may be effected in favor of commerce by the attention and patronage of a wise administration.

The number of useful edicts passed by Louis XIV., and since his time, in spite of frequent interruptions from the jealous enmity of

Great Britain, has advanced that of France to a degree which has excited the envy and astonishment of its neighbors.

The Dutch, who may justly be allowed a pre-eminence in the knowledge of trade, have ever made it an essential object of state. Their commercial regulations are more rigid and numerous than those of any other country; and it is by a judicious and unremitted vigilance of government that they have been able to extend their traffic to a degree so much beyond their natural and comparative advantages.

Perhaps it may be thought that the power of regulation will be best placed in the governments of the several States, and that a general superintendence is unnecessary. If the States had distinct interests, were unconnected with each other, their own governments would then be the proper, and could be the only, depositories of such a power; but as they are parts of a whole, with a common interest in trade, as in other things, there ought to be a common direction in that as in all other matters. It is easy to conceive that many cases may occur in which it would be beneficial to all the States to encourage or suppress a particular branch of trade, while it would be detrimental to either to attempt it without the concurrence of the rest, and where the experiment would probably be left untried for fear of a want of that concurrence.

No mode can be so convenient as a source of revenue to the United States. It is agreed that imposts on trade, when not immoderate, or improperly laid, are one of the most eligible species of taxation. They fall in a great measure upon articles not of absolute necessity, and being partly transferred to the price of the commodity, are so far imperceptibly paid by the consumer. It is therefore that mode which may be exercised by the Federal Government with least exception or disgust. Congress can easily possess all the information necessary to impose the duties with judgment, and the collection can without difficulty be made by their own officers.

They can have no temptation to abuse this power, because the motive of revenue will check its own extremes. Experience has shown that moderate duties are more productive than high ones. When they are low, a nation can trade abroad on better terms, its imports and exports will be larger, the duties will be regularly paid, and arising on a greater quantity of commodities, will yield more in the aggregate than when they are so high as to operate either as a prohibition, or as an inducement to evade them by illicit practices.

It is difficult to assign any good reason why Congress should be more liable to abuse the powers with which they are entrusted than the State Assemblies. The frequency of the election of the members is a full security against a dangerous ambition, and the rotation established by the Confederation makes it impossible for any state, by continuing the same men, who may put themselves at the head of a prevailing faction, to maintain for any length of time an undue influence in the national councils. It is to be presumed that Congress will be in general better composed for abilities, as well as for integrity, than any assembly on the continent.

But to take away any temptation from a cabal to load particular articles, which are the principal objects of commerce to particular States, with a too great proportion of duties, to ease the others in the general distribution of expense, let all the duties, whether for regulation or revenue, raised in each State, be credited to that State, and let it, in like manner, be charged for all the bounties paid within itself for the encouragement of agriculture, manufactures, or trade. This expedient will remove the temptation; for as the quotas of the respective States are to be determined by a standard of land, agreeable to the eighth article of the Confederation, each will have so much the less to contribute otherwise, as it pays more on its commerce. An objection has been made in a late instance to this principle. It has been urged that as the consumer pays the duty, those States which are not equally well situated for foreign commerce, and which consume a great part of the imports of their neighbors, will become contributors to a part of their taxes. This objection is rather specious than solid.

The maxim, that the consumer pays the duty, has been admitted in theory with too little reserve; frequently contradicted in practice. It is true, the merchant will be unwilling to let the duty be a deduction from his profits, if the state of the market will permit him to incorporate it with the price of his commodity. But this is often not practicable. It turns upon the quantity of goods at market in proportion to the demand. When the latter exceeds the former, and the competition is among the buyers, the merchant can easily increase his price, and make his customers pay the duty. When the reverse is the case, and the competition is among the sellers, he must then content himself with smaller profits and lose the value of the duty, or at least a part of it. When a nation has a flourishing and well-settled trade, this more commonly happens than may be imagined, and it will, many times, be found that the duty is divided between the merchant and the consumer.

Besides this consideration which greatly diminishes the force of the objection, there is another which entirely destroys it. There is a strong reciprocal influence between the prices of all commodities in a State, by which they, sooner or later, attain a pretty exact balance and proportion to each other. If the immediate productions of the soil rise, the manufacturer will have more for his manufacture, the merchant for his goods; and the same will happen with whatever class the increase of price begins. If duties are laid upon the imports in one State, by which the prices of foreign articles are raised, the products of land and labor within that State will take a proportionate rise; and if a part of those articles are consumed in a neighboring State, it will have the same influence there as at home. The importing State must allow an advanced price upon the commodities which it receives in exchange from its neighbor, in a ratio to the increased price of the article it sells. To know, then, which is the gainer or loser, we must examine how the general balance of trade stands between them. If the importing State takes more of the commodities of its neighbor than it gives in exchange, that will be the loser by the reciprocal augmentation of prices; it will be the gainer if it takes less, and neither will gain or lose if the barter is carried on upon equal terms. The balance of trade, and consequently the gain, or loss, in this respect, will be governed more by the relative industry and frugality of the parties than by their relative advantages for foreign commerce.

Between separate nations this reasoning will not apply with full force, because a multitude of local and extraneous circumstances may counteract the principle; but from the intimate connections of these States, the similitude of governments, situations, customs, manners, political and commercial causes will have nearly the same operation in the intercourse between the States, as in that between the different parts of the same State. If this should be controverted, the objection drawn from the hypothesis of the consumer paying the duty must fall at the same time; for as far as this is true it is as much confined in its application to a State within itself as the doctrine of a reciprocal proportion of prices.

General principles in subjects of this nature ought always to be advanced with caution; in an experimental analysis there are found such a number of exceptions as tend to render them very doubtful; and in questions which affect the existence and collective happiness of these States, all nice and abstract distinctions should give way to plainer interests, and to more obvious and simple rules of conduct.

But the objection which has been urged ought to have no weight on another account. Which are the States that have not sufficient advantages for foreign commerce, and that will not in time be their own carriers? Connecticut and Jersey are the least maritime of the whole; yet the Sound which washes the coast of Connecticut has an easy outlet to the ocean, affords a number of harbors and bays very commodious for trading vessels. New London may be a receptacle for merchantmen of almost any burthen; and the fine rivers with which the State is intersected, by facilitating the transportation of commodities to and from every part, are extremely favorable both to its domestic and foreign trade.

Jersey, by way of Amboy, has a shorter communication with the ocean than the city of New York. Prince's Bay, which may serve as an outport to it, will admit and shelter in winter and summer vessels of any size. Egg Harbor, on its southern coast, is not to be despised. The Delaware may be made as subservient to its commerce as to that of Pennsylvania, Gloucester, Burlington, and Trenton, being all conveniently situated on that river. The United Provinces, with inferior advantages of position to either of these States, have for centuries held the first rank among commercial nations.

The want of large trading cities has been sometimes objected as an obstacle to the commerce of these States; but this is a temporary deficiency that will repair itself with the increase of population and riches. The reason that the States in question have hitherto carried on little foreign trade, is that they have found it equally beneficial to purchase the commodities imported by their neighbors. If the imposts on trade should work an inconvenience to them, it will soon cease by making it their interest to trade abroad.

It is too much characteristic of our national temper to be ingenious in finding out and magnifying the minutest disadvantages, and to reject measures of evident utility, even of necessity, to avoid trivial and sometimes imaginary evils. We seem not to reflect that in human society there is scarcely any plan, however salutary to the whole and to every part, by the share each has in the common prosperity, but in one way, or another, and under particular circumstances, will operate more to the benefit of some parts than of others. Unless we can overcome this narrow disposition and learn to estimate measures by their general tendencies, we shall never be a great or a happy people, if we remain a people at all.

NO. VI

July 4, 1782.

Let us see what will be the consequences of not authorizing the Federal Government to regulate the trade of these States. Besides the want of revenue and of power, besides the immediate risk to our independence and the dangers of all the future evils of a precarious Union, besides the deficiency of a wholesome concert and provident superintendence to advance the general prosperity of trade, the direct consequence will be that the landed interest and the laboring poor will in the first place fall a sacrifice to the trading interest, and the whole eventually to a bad system of policy made necessary by the want of such regulating power.

Each State will be afraid to impose duties on its commerce, lest the other States, not doing the same, should enjoy greater advantages than itself, by being able to afford native commodities cheaper abroad and foreign commodities cheaper at home.

A part of the evils resulting from this would be a loss to the revenue of those moderate duties which, without being injurious to commerce, are allowed to be the most agreeable species of taxes to the people. Articles of foreign luxury, while they would contribute nothing to the income of the State, being less dear by an exemption from duties, would have a more extensive consumption.

Many branches of trade, hurtful to the common interest, would be continued for want of proper checks and discouragements. As revenues must be found to satisfy the public exigencies in peace and in war, too great a proportion of taxes will fall directly upon land, and upon the necessaries of life—the produce of that land. The influence of these evils will be to render landed property fluctuating and less valuable; to oppress the poor by raising the prices of necessaries; to injure commerce by encouraging the consumption of foreign luxuries, by increasing the value of labor, by lessening the quantity of home productions, enhancing their prices at foreign markets, of course obstructing their sale, and enabling other nations to supplant us.

Particular caution ought at present to be observed in this country not to burthen the soil itself and its productions with heavy impositions, because the quantity of unimproved land will invite the husbandman to abandon old settlements for new, and the disproportion of our population for some time to come will necessarily make labor dear, to reduce which, and not to increase it, ought to be a capital object of our policy.

Easy duties, therefore, on commerce, especially on imports, ought to lighten the burthens which will unavoidably fall upon land. Though it may be said that, on the principle of a reciprocal influence of prices, whereon the taxes are laid in the first instance, they will in the end be borne by all classes, yet it is of the greatest importance that no one should sink under the immediate pressure. The great art is to distribute the public burthens well, and not suffer them, either first or last, to fall too heavily on parts of the community, else distress and disorder must ensue; a shock given to any part of the political machine vibrates through the whole.

As a sufficient revenue could not be raised from trade to answer the public purposes, other articles have been proposed. A moderate land and poll tax, being of easy and unexpensive collection, and leaving nothing to discretion, are the simplest and best that could be devised.

It is to be feared that the avarice of many of the landholders will be opposed to a perpetual tax upon land, however moderate. They will ignorantly hope to shift the burthens of the national expense from themselves to others—a disposition as iniquitous as it is fruitless. The public necessities must be satisfied; this can only be done by the contributions of the whole society. Particular classes are neither able nor will they be willing to pay for the protection and security of the others, and where so selfish a spirit discovers itself in any member, the rest of the community will unite to compel it to do its duty.

Indeed, many theorists in political economy have held that all taxes, wherever they originate, fall upon land, and have therefore been of opinion that it would be best to draw the whole revenue of the state immediately from that source, to avoid the expense of a more diversified collection, and the accumulations which will be heaped, in their several stages, upon the primitive sums, advanced in those stages, which are imposed on our trade. But though it has been demonstrated that this theory has been carried to an extreme impracticable in fact, yet it is evident, in tracing the matter, that a large part of all taxes, however remotely laid, will, by an insensible circulation, come at last to settle upon land—the source of most of the materials employed in commerce.

It appears, from calculation made by the ablest master of political arithmetic, about sixty years ago, that the yearly product of all the lands in England amounted to £42,000,000 sterling, and the whole annual consumption at that period, of foreign as well as domestic commodities, did not exceed £49,000,000, and the surplus of the exportation above the importation £2,000,000, on which sums arise all the revenues, in whatever shape, which go into the Treasury. It is easy to infer from this how large a part of them must, directly or indirectly, be derived from land.

Nothing can be more mistaken than the collision and rivalship which almost always subsist between the landed and trading interests, for the truth is they are so inseparably interwoven that one cannot be injured without injury nor benefited without benefit to the other. Oppress trade, lands sink in value; make it flourish, their value rises. Incumber husbandry, trade declines; encourage agriculture, commerce revives. The progress of this mutual reaction might be easily delineated, but it is too obvious to every man who turns his thoughts, however superficially, upon the subject to require it. It is only to be regretted that it is too often lost sight of when the seductions of some immediate advantage or exemption tempt us to sacrifice the future to the present.

But perhaps the class is more numerous of those who, not unwilling to bear their share of public burthens, are yet averse to the idea of perpetuity, as if there ever would arrive a period when the state would cease to want revenues and taxes become unnecessary. It is of importance to unmask this delusion, and open the eyes of the people to the truth. It is paying too great a tribute to the idol of popularity, to flatter so injurious and so visionary an expectation. The error is too gross to be tolerated anywhere but in the cottage of the peasant. Should we meet with it in the Senate-house, we must lament the ignorance or despise the hypocrisy on which it is ingrafted. Expense is in the present state of things entailed upon all governments; though, if we continue united, we shall be hereafter less exposed to wars by land than most other countries; yet while we have powerful neighbors on either extremity, and our frontier is embraced by savages whose alliance they may without difficulty command, we cannot, in prudence, dispense with the usual precautions for our interior security. As a commercial people, maritime power must be a primary object of our attention, and a navy cannot be created or maintained without ample revenues. The nature of our popular institutions requires a numerous magistracy, for whom competent provision must be made, or we may be certain our affairs will always be committed to improper hands, and experience will teach us that no government costs so much as a bad one.

We may preach, till we are tired of the theme, the necessity of disinterestedness in republics, without making a single proselyte. The virtuous declaimer will neither persuade himself nor any other person to be content with a double mess of pottage, instead of a reasonable stipend for his services. We might as soon reconcile ourselves to the Spartan community of goods and wives, to their iron coin, their long beards, or their black broth. There is a total dissimilarity in the circumstances as well as the manners of society among us, and it is as ridiculous to seek for models in the small ages of Greece and Rome, as it would be to go in quest of them among the Hottentots and Laplanders.

The public, for the different purposes that have been mentioned, must always have large demands upon its constituents, and the only question is, whether these shall be satisfied by annual grants perpetually renewed, by a perpetual grant once for all, or by a compound of permanent and occasional supplies. The last is the wisest course. The Federal Government should neither be independent nor too much dependent. It should neither be raised above responsibility or control, nor should it want the means of maintaining its own weight, authority, dignity, and credit. To this end, permanent funds are indispensable, but they ought to be of such a nature and so moderate in their amount as never to be inconvenient. Extraordinary supplies can be the objects of extraordinary emergencies, and in that salutary medium will consist our true wisdom.

It would seem as if no mode of taxation could be relished but the worst of all modes, which now prevails—by assessment. Every proposal for a specific tax is sure to meet with opposition. It has been objected to a poll tax at a fixed rate, that it will be unequal, and the rich will pay no more than the poor. In the form in which it has been offered in these papers, the poor, properly speaking, are not comprehended, though it is true that beyond the exclusion of the indigent the tax has no reference to the proportion of property, but it should be remembered that it is impossible to devise any specific tax that will operate equally on the whole community. It must be the province of the Legislature to hold the scales with a judicious hand and balance one by another. The rich must be made to pay for their luxuries, which is the only proper way of taxing their superior wealth.

Do we imagine that our assessments operate equally? Nothing can be more contrary to the fact. Wherever a discretionary power is lodged in any set of men over the property of their neighbors, they will abuse it; their passions, prejudices, partialities, dislikes, will have the principal lead in measuring the abilities of those over whom their power extends; and assessors will ever be a set of petty tyrants, too unskilful, if honest, to be possessed of so delicate a trust, and too seldom honest to give them the excuse of want of skill.

The genius of liberty reprobates every thing arbitrary or discretionary in taxation. It exacts that every man, by a definite and general rule, should know what proportion of his property the state demands; whatever liberty we may boast in theory, it cannot exist in fact while assessments continue.

The admission of them among us is a new proof how often human conduct reconciles the most glaring opposites; in the present case, the most vicious practice of despotic governments with the freest constitutions and the greatest love of liberty.

The establishment of permanent funds would not only answer the public purposes infinitely better than temporary supplies, but it would be the most effectual way of easing the people.

With this basis for procuring credit, the amount of present taxes might be greatly diminished. Large sums of money might be borrowed abroad at a low interest, and introduced into the country, to defray the current expenses and pay the public debts; which would not only lessen the demand for immediate supplies, but would throw more money into circulation, and furnish the people with greater means of paying the taxes,

Though it be a just rule that we ought not to run in debt to avoid present expense, so far as our faculties extend, yet the propriety of doing it cannot be disputed when it is apparent that these are incompetent to the public necessities. Efforts beyond our abilities can only tend to individual distress and national disappointment. The product of the three foregoing articles will be as little as can be required to enable Congress to pay their debts and restore order into their finances. In addition to them:

The disposal of the unlocated lands will hereafter be a valuable source of revenue and an immediate one of credit. As it may be liable to the same condition with the duties on trade—that is, the product of the sales within each State to be credited to that State—and as the rights of jurisdiction are not infringed, it seems to be susceptible of no reasonable objection.

Mines in every country constitute a branch of revenue. In this, where nature has so richly impregnated the bowels of the earth, they may in time become a valuable one; and as they require the care and attention of government to bring them to perfection, this care and a share in the profits of it will very properly devolve upon Congress. All the precious metals should absolutely be the property of the

Federal Government, and with respect to the others it should have a discretionary power of reserving, in the nature of a tax, such part as it may judge not inconsistent with the encouragement due to so important an object. This is rather a future than a present resource.

The reason of allowing Congress to appoint its own officers of the customs, collectors of the taxes, and military officers of every rank, is to create in the interior of each State a mass of influence in favor of the Federal Government. The great danger has been shown to be that it will not have power enough to defend itself and preserve the Union, not that it will ever become formidable to the general liberty; a mere regard to the interests of the Confederacy will never be a principle sufficiently active to crush the ambition and intrigues of different members. Force cannot effect it. A contest of arms will seldom be between the common sovereign and a single refractory member, but between distinct combinations of the several parts against each other. A sympathy of situations will be apt to produce associates to the disobedient. The application of force is always disagreeable— the issue uncertain. It will be wise to obviate the necessity of it, by interesting such a number of individuals in each State in support of the Federal Government as will be counterpoised to the ambition of others, and will make it difficult for them to unite the people in opposition to the first and necessary measures of the Union.

There is something noble and magnificent in the perspective of a great Federal Republic, closely linked in the pursuit of a common interest, tranquil and prosperous at home, respectable abroad; but there is something proportionably diminutive and contemptible in the prospect of a number of petty States, with the appearance only of union, jarring, jealous, and perverse, without any determined direction, fluctuating and unhappy at home, weak and insignificant by their dissensions in the eyes of other nations.

Happy America, if those to whom thou hast intrusted the guardianship of thy infancy know how to provide for thy future repose, but miserable and undone, if their negligence or ignorance permits the spirit of discord to erect her banner on the ruins of thy tranquillity!

3

Letter to George Washington, "The Critical Opportunity," July 13, 1787

Midway through the Philadelphia Constitutional Convention in 1787, Alexander Hamilton left Philadelphia and did some traveling. This put him in contact with people in different parts of the colonies, and he took this opportunity to write a very fascinating letter to George Washington. It reveals both how important Hamilton thought the final result of the Convention would be for the new nation as well as his hopes and concerns about the outcome.

Hamilton expresses some cautious good news about what he had heard on the street. There were some people opposed to the kind of Constitution that Hamilton and Washington wanted—people who wanted the Convention to fail. Nevertheless, Hamilton was more optimistic than he had been that some version of the more progressive plan for the Constitution would emerge and win the delegates' approval.

Early in the letter, Hamilton writes, "I am more and more convinced that this is the critical opportunity for establishing the prosperity of this country on a solid foundation." Later on, deep concern bordering on genuine fear reemerges from the shadows: "I fear that we shall let slip the golden opportunity of rescuing the American empire from disunion anarchy and misery." When this letter was written, there was still a long way to go. The Convention was in the middle of their work, and then would come the battle for ratification by the states.

[New York, July 3, 1787]

Dr. Sir.

In my passage through the Jerseys and since my arrival here I have taken particular pains to discover the public sentiment and I am more and more convinced that this is the critical opportunity for establishing the prosperity of this country on a solid foundation. I have conversed with men of information not only of this City but from different parts of the state; and they agree that there has been an astonishing revolution for the better in the minds of the people. The prevailing apprehension among thinking men is that the Convention, from a fear of shocking the popular opinion, will not go far enough. They seem to be convinced that a strong well mounted government will better suit the popular palate than one of a different complexion. Men in office are indeed taking all possible pains to give an unfavourable impression of the Convention; but the current seems to be running strongly the other way.

A plain but sensible man, in a conversation I had with him yesterday, expressed himself nearly in this manner. The people begin to be convinced that their "excellent form of government" as they have been used to call it, will not answer their purpose; and that they must substitute something not very remote from that which they have lately quitted.

These appearances though they will not warrant a conclusion that the people are yet ripe for such a plan as I advocate, yet serve to prove that there is no reason to despair of their adopting one equally energetic, if the Convention should think proper to propose it. They serve to prove that we ought not to allow too much weight to objections drawn from the supposed repugnancy of the people to an efficient constitution. I confess I am more and more inclined to believe that former habits of thinking are regaining their influence with more rapidity than is generally imagined.

Not having compared ideas with you, Sir, I cannot judge how far our sentiments agree; but as I persuade myself the genuineness of my representations will receive credit with you, my anxiety for the event of the deliberations of the Convention induces me to make this communication of what appears to be the tendency of the public mind. I own to you Sir that I am seriously and deeply distressed at the aspect of the Councils which prevailed when I left Philadelphia. I fear that we shall let slip the golden opportunity of rescuing the American empire from disunion anarchy and misery. No motley or feeble measure can answer the end or will finally receive the public support. Decision is true wisdom and will be not less reputable to the Convention than salutary to the community.

I shall of necessity remain here ten or twelve days; if I have reason to believe that my attendance at Philadelphia will not be mere waste of time, I shall after that period rejoin the Convention.

I remain with sincere esteem Dr Sir   Yr. Obed serv*

A Hamilton

July 3d. 87
General Washington

---

*Dear Sir, Your Obedient Servant

4

Conjecture about the New Constitution, September 17–30, 1787

Alexander Hamilton apparently wrote this tantalizing essay toward the end of September 1787, as the work of the Philadelphia Convention was drawing to a close. It is part of the voluminous Hamilton papers that have come down to us, but it is not known what he planned to do with it. It does not appear in any known letter or newspaper contribution, but it could have been a rough draft of one or the other of these. It could have been a draft of something like one of *The Federalist Papers*, which he found himself hard at work on soon enough.

Like the letter to George Washington in July 1787, this document shows Hamilton's state of mind when everything was up in the air. In the middle of the essay, he writes, "In this view of the subject it is difficult to form any judgment whether the plan will be adopted or rejected. It must be essentially [a] matter of conjecture. The present appearances and all other circumstances considered the probability seems to be on the side of its adoption."

In Hamilton's view, the Constitution would have a lot going for it, once the details were ironed out. Despite the prestige brought to the project by Washington's immense popularity, the widespread belief among many—especially in the North and among those in business and commerce—was that the Articles were insufficient and had amply proved themselves to be so. But there would always be those who wanted the constitutional project to fail—people who held state offices and who might lose power because of it; people who didn't want their plans, questionable or otherwise, upset by an effective national government; and people who saw the Constitution as a plan to raise an aristocracy above everyone else. Hamilton supposes that people with property to defend would probably welcome the new national government, suggesting that people without property might not feel the same. At this moment, it seemed unsettled, with the long battle for ratification still to come. The best guess is that Hamilton was gearing up for that battle when he wrote these paragraphs.

[September 17–30, 1787]

The new constitution has in favour of its success these circumstances—a very great weight of influence of the persons who framed it, particularly in the universal popularity of General Washington—the good will of the commercial interest throughout the states which will give all its efforts to the establishment of a government capable of regulating protecting and extending the commerce of the Union—the good will of most men of property in the several states who wish a government of the union able to protect them against domestic violence and the depredations which the democratic spirit is apt to make on property; and who are besides anxious for the respectability of the nation—the hopes of the Creditors of the United States that a general government possessing the means of doing it will pay the debt of the Union—a strong belief in the people at large of the insufficiency of the present confederation to preserve the existence of the Union and of the necessity of the union to their safety and prosperity; of course a strong desire of a change and a predisposition to receive well the propositions of the Convention.

Against its success is to be put the dissent of two or three important men in the Convention; who will think their characters pleged to defeat the plan—the influence of many *inconsiderable* men in possession of considerable offices under the state governments who will fear a diminution of their consequence, power and emolument by the establishment of the general government and who can hope for nothing there—the influence of some *considerable* men in office possessed of talents and popularity who partly from the same motives and partly from a desire of *playing a part* in a convulsion for their own aggrandisement will oppose the quiet adoption of the new government—(some considerable men out of office, from motives of ⟨am⟩bition may be disposed to act the same part)—add ⟨to⟩ these causes the disinclination of the people to taxes, and of course to a strong government—the opposition of all men much in debt who will not wish to see a government established one object of which is to restrain the means of cheating Creditors—the democratical jealousy of the people which may be alarmed at the appearance of institutions that may seem calculated to place the power of the community in few hands and to raise a few individuals to stations of great preeminence—and the influence of some foreign powers who from different motives will not wish to see an energetic government established throughout the states.

In this view of the subject it is difficult to form any judgment whether the plan will be adopted or rejected. It must be essentially [a] matter of conjecture. The present appearances and all other circumstances considered the probability seems to be on the side of its adoption.

But the causes operating against its adoption are powerful and there will be nothing astonishing in the Contrary.

If it do not finally obtain, it is probable the discussion of the question will beget such struggles animosities and heats in the community that this circumstance conspiring with the *real necessity* of an essential change in our present situation will produce civil war. Should this happen, whatever parties prevail it is probable governments very different from the present in their principles will be established. A dismemberment of the Union and monarchies in different portions of it may be expected. It may however happen that no civil war will take place; but several republican confederacies be established between different combinations of the particular states.

A reunion with Great Britain, from universal disgust at a state of commotion, is not impossible, though not much to be feared. The most plausible shape of such a business would be the establishment of a son of the present monarch in the supreme government of this country with a family compact.

If the government be adopted, it is probable general Washington will be the President of the United States. This will insure a wise choice of men to administer the government and a good administration. A good administration will conciliate the confidence and affection of the people and perhaps enable the government to acquire more consistency than the proposed constitution seems to promise for so great a Country. It may then triumph altogether over the state governments and reduce them to an intire subordination, dividing the larger states into smaller districts. The *organs* of the general government may also acquire additional strength.

If this should not be the case, in the course of a few years, it is probable that the contests about the boundaries of power between the particular governments and the general government and the *momentum* of the larger states in such contests will produce a dissolution of the Union. This after all seems to be the most likely result.

But it is almost arrogance in so complicated a subject, depending so intirely on the incalculable fluctuations of the human passions, to attempt even a conjecture about the event.

It will be Eight or Nine months before any certain judgment can be formed respecting the adoption of the Plan.

5

The Federalist Papers, October 1787–May 1788

Speaking only once at the Philadelphia Convention of 1787, albeit for six hours, Alexander Hamilton largely worked behind the scenes while the details of the Constitution were debated and drafted. He took a leading role in arguing for ratification by the states once the Constitution was completed and signed by the Convention's delegates. His primary effort was writing fifty-one of the eighty-five essays that became known as *The Federalist Papers*, which were written between October 1787 and May 1788. James Madison and John Jay wrote the other essays. The first seventy-seven were published in two New York newspapers, *The New-York Packet* and *The Independent Journal*, and the final eight were added to the first book edition, published in 1788. Jay wrote several of the earliest essays and then took a long hiatus because of his ill health.

The essays were often written on the fly to meet newspaper deadlines, and the three authors barely had any time to consult each other. Nevertheless, over two hundred years later, they stand as the essential achievement of American political philosophy and the definitive expression of Hamilton's political thought. They are still referred to and quoted in Supreme Court decisions as evidence of the Founding Fathers' thinking and intentions on various issues. The essays were all signed with the pseudonym "Publius" to honor a sixth century BCE Roman statesman and general, Publius Valerius Publicola, who, according to the ancient historian Plutarch, saved the Roman republic from tyranny more than once. He was considered a founder of the Roman republic by the American founders, who saw themselves playing an equivalent role for America.

It would be an error to see *The Federalist Papers* as *the* crucial voice that turned the tide for ratification of the Constitution. They were certainly one of the voices, but they were published at first in only two New York newspapers, although they were picked up, somewhat haphazardly, by other papers in New York and other states. They first appeared collected in book form in two volumes, in March and May 1788, while the ratification debate was going on. This was a time when books were generally printed in small numbers and didn't circulate widely. The relevance of *The Federalist Papers* today lies largely in what they tell us about the political philosophy of Hamilton and his colleagues. Hamilton's authorship of his essays was only made public after his death in 1804, although some newspaper readers might have suspected they were his creations.

The title commonly used today, *The Federalist Papers*, was created in the twentieth century. The original title of the newspaper articles was *The Federalist*. The 1788 book, published by John and Andrew McLean in New York, was titled *The Federalist: A Collection of Essays Written in Favour of the New Constitution*. A small number of deluxe copies of the 1788 book edition were printed on special thick paper. In 1990, George Washington's copy of this edition sold at an auction for almost one and a half million dollars. When Washington received this copy, he wrote, "When the transient circumstances and fugitive performances which attended this Crisis shall have disappeared, That Work [*The Federalist*] will merit the Notice of Posterity; because in it are candidly and ably discussed the principles of freedom and the topics of government, which will be always interesting to mankind so long as they shall be connected in Civil Society."

The following essays from *The Federalist Papers* are included:

No. 1: General Introduction
No. 6: Concerning Dangers from Dissensions Between the States
No. 8: The Consequences of Hostilities Between the States
No. 9: The Union as a Safeguard Against Domestic Faction and Insurrection
No. 12: The Utility of the Union in Respect to Revenue
No. 15: The Insufficiency of the Present Confederation to Preserve the Union
No. 23: The Necessity of a Government as Energetic as the One Proposed to the Preservation of the Union
No. 29: Concerning the Militia

No. 1: General Introduction

After an unequivocal experience of the inefficacy of the subsisting federal government, you are called upon to deliberate on a new Constitution for the United States of America. The subject speaks its own importance; comprehending in its consequences nothing less than the existence of the UNION, the safety and welfare of the parts of which it is composed, the fate of an empire in many respects the most interesting in the world. It has been frequently remarked that it seems to have been reserved to the people of this country, by their conduct and example, to decide the important question, whether societies of men are really capable or not of establishing good government from reflection and choice, or whether they are forever destined to depend for their political constitutions on accident and force. If there be any truth in the remark, the crisis at which we are arrived may with propriety be regarded as the era in which that decision is to be made; and a wrong election of the part we shall act may, in this view, deserve to be considered as the general misfortune of mankind.

This idea will add the inducements of philanthropy to those of patriotism, to heighten the solicitude which all considerate and good men must feel for the event. Happy will it be if our choice should be directed by a judicious estimate of our true interests, unperplexed and unbiased by considerations not connected with the public good. But this is a thing more ardently to be wished than seriously to be expected. The plan offered to our deliberations affects too many particular interests, innovates upon too many local institutions, not to involve in its discussion a variety of objects foreign to its merits, and of views, passions, and prejudices little favorable to the discovery of truth.

Among the most formidable of the obstacles which the new Constitution will have to encounter may readily be distinguished the obvious interest of a certain class of men in every State to resist all changes which may hazard a diminution of the power, emolument, and consequence of the offices they hold under the State establishments; and the perverted ambition of another class of men, who will either hope to aggrandize themselves by the confusions of their country, or will flatter themselves with fairer prospects of elevation from the subdivision of the empire into several partial confederacies than from its union under one government.

It is not, however, my design to dwell upon observations of this nature. I am well aware that it would be disingenuous to resolve indiscriminately the opposition of any set of men (merely because their situations might subject them to suspicion) into interested or ambitious views. Candor will oblige us to admit that even such men may be actuated by upright intentions; and it cannot be doubted that much of the opposition which has made its appearance, or may hereafter make its appearance, will spring from sources, blameless at least if not respectable—the honest errors of minds led astray by preconceived jealousies and fears. So numerous indeed and so powerful are the causes which serve to give a false bias to the judgment, that we, upon many occasions, see wise and good men on the wrong as well as on the right side of questions of the first magnitude to society. This circumstance, if duly attended to, would furnish a lesson of moderation to those who are ever so thoroughly persuaded of their being in the right in any controversy. And a further reason for caution, in this respect, might be drawn from the reflection that we are not always sure that those who advocate the truth are influenced by purer principles than their antagonists. Ambition, avarice, personal animosity, party opposition, and many other motives not more laudable than these, are apt to operate as well upon those who support as those who oppose the right side of a question. Were there not even these inducements to moderation, nothing could be more ill-judged than that intolerant spirit which has at all times characterized political parties. For in politics, as in religion, it is equally absurd to aim at making proselytes by fire and sword. Heresies in either can rarely be cured by persecution.

And yet, however just these sentiments will be allowed to be, we have already sufficient indications that it will happen in this as in all former cases of great national discussion. A torrent of angry and malignant passions will be let loose. To judge from the conduct of the opposite parties, we shall be led to conclude that they will mutually hope to evince the justness of their opinions, and to increase the number of their converts by the loudness of their declamations and by the bitterness of their invectives. An enlightened zeal for the energy and efficiency of government will be stigmatized as the offspring of a temper fond of despotic power and hostile to the principles of liberty. An over-scrupulous jealousy of danger to the rights of the people, which is more commonly the fault of the head than of the heart, will be represented as mere pretense and artifice, the stale bait for popularity at the expense of public good. It will be forgotten, on the one hand, that jealousy is the usual concomitant of violent love, and that the noble enthusiasm of liberty is too apt to be infected with a spirit of narrow and illiberal distrust. On the other hand, it will be equally forgotten that the vigor of government is essential to the security of liberty; that, in the contemplation of a sound and well-informed judgment, their interests can never be separated; and that a dangerous ambition more often lurks behind the specious mask of zeal for the rights of the people than under the forbidding appearance of zeal for the firmness and efficiency of government. History will teach us that the former has been found a much more certain road to the introduction of despotism than the latter, and that of those men who have overturned the liberties of republics, the greatest number have begun their career by paying an obsequious court to the people, commencing demagogues and ending tyrants.

In the course of the preceding observations, I have had an eye, my fellow-citizens, to putting you upon your guard against all attempts, from whatever quarter, to influence your decision in a matter of the utmost moment to your welfare by any impressions other than those which may result from the evidence of truth. You will, no doubt, at the same time have collected from the general scope of them that they proceed from a source not unfriendly to the new Constitution. Yes, my countrymen, I own to you that after having given it an attentive consideration, I am clearly of opinion it is your interest to adopt it. I am convinced that this is the safest course for your liberty, your dignity, and your happiness. I affect not reserves which I do not feel. I will not amuse you with an appearance of deliberation when I have decided. I frankly acknowledge to you my convictions, and I will freely lay before you the reasons on which they are founded. The consciousness of good intentions disdains ambiguity. I shall not, however, multiply professions on this head. My motives must remain in the depository of my own breast. My arguments will be open to all and may be judged of by all. They shall at least be offered in a spirit which will not disgrace the cause of truth.

I propose, in a series of papers, to discuss the following interesting particulars:—*The utility of the UNION to your political prosperity—The insufficiency of the present Confederation to preserve that Union—The necessity of a government at least equally energetic with the one proposed, to the attainment of this object—The conformity of the proposed Constitution to the true principles of republican government—Its analogy to your own State constitution—*and lastly, *The additional security which its adoption* *will afford to the preservation of that species of government, to liberty, and to property.*

In the progress of this discussion I shall endeavor to give a satisfactory answer to all the objections which shall have made their appearance that may seem to have any claim to your attention.

It may perhaps be thought superfluous to offer arguments to prove the utility of the UNION, a point, no doubt, deeply engraved on the hearts of the great body of the people in every State, and one which, it may be imagined, has no adversaries. But the fact is that we already hear it whispered in the private circles of those who oppose the new Constitution, that the thirteen States are of too great extent for any general system, and that we must of necessity resort to separate confederacies of distinct portions of the whole.* This doctrine will, in all probability, be gradually propagated, till it has votaries enough to countenance an open avowal of it. For nothing can be more evident to those who are able to take an enlarged view of the subject than the alternative of an adoption of the new Constitution or a dismemberment of the Union. It will therefore be of use to begin by examining the advantages of that Union, the certain evils, and the probable dangers, to which every State will be exposed from its dissolution. This shall accordingly constitute the subject of my next address.

PUBLIUS

---

*The same idea, tracing the arguments to their consequences, is held out in several of the late publications against the new Constitution.

No. 6: Concerning Dangers
from Dissensions Between the States

The three last numbers of this paper have been dedicated to an enumeration of the dangers to which we should be exposed, in a state of disunion, from the arms and arts of foreign nations. I shall now proceed to delineate dangers of a different and, perhaps, still more alarming kind—those which will in all probability flow from dissensions between the States themselves and from domestic factions and convulsions. These have been already in some instances slightly anticipated; but they deserve a more particular and more full investigation.

A man must be far gone in Utopian speculations who can seriously doubt that if these States should either be wholly disunited, or only united in partial confederacies, the subdivisions into which they might be thrown would have frequent and violent contests with each other. To presume a want of motives for such contests as an argument against their existence would be to forget that men are ambitious, vindictive, and rapacious. To look for a continuation of harmony between a number of independent, unconnected sovereignties situated in the same neighborhood would be to disregard the uniform course of human events, and to set at defiance the accumulated experience of ages.

The causes of hostility among nations are innumerable. There are some which have a general and almost constant operation upon the collective bodies of society. Of this description are the love of power or the desire of pre-eminence and dominion—the jealousy of power, or the desire of equality and safety. There are others which have a more circumscribed though an equally operative influence within their spheres. Such are the rivalships and competitions of commerce between commercial nations. And there are others, not less numerous than either of the former, which take their origin entirely in private passions; in the attachments, enmities, interests, hopes, and fears of leading individuals in the communities of which they are members. Men of this class, whether the favorites of a king or of a people, have in too many instances abused the confidence they possessed; and assuming the pretext of some public motive, have not scrupled to sacrifice the national tranquillity to personal advantage or personal gratification.

The celebrated Pericles, in compliance with the resentment of a prostitute,* at the expense of much of the blood and treasure of his countrymen, attacked, vanquished, and destroyed the city of the *Samnians*. The same man, stimulated by private pique against the *Megarensians*,† another nation of Greece, or to avoid a prosecution with which he was threatened as an accomplice in a supposed theft of the statuary of Phidias,‡ or to get rid of the accusations prepared to be brought against him for dissipating the funds of the state in the purchase of popularity,§ or from a combination of all these causes, was the primitive author of that famous and fatal war, distinguished in the Grecian annals by the name of the *Peloponnesian war*, which, after various vicissitudes, intermissions, and renewals, terminated in the ruin of the Athenian commonwealth.

The ambitious cardinal, who was prime minister to Henry VIII, permitting his vanity to aspire to the triple crown,¶ entertained hopes of succeeding in the acquisition of that splendid prize by the influence of the Emperor Charles V. To secure the favor and interest of this enterprising and powerful monarch, he precipitated England into a war with France, contrary to the plainest dictates of policy, and at the hazard of the safety and independence, as well of the kingdom over which he presided by his counsels as of Europe in general. For if there ever was a sovereign who bid fair to realize the project of universal monarchy, it was the Emperor Charles V, of whose intrigues Wolsey was at once the instrument and the dupe.

The influence which the bigotry of one female,** the petulancies of another,†† and the cabals of a third,‡‡ had in the contemporary policy, ferments, and pacifications of a considerable part of Europe, are topics that have been too often descanted upon not to be generally known.

To multiply examples of the agency of personal considerations in the production of great national events, either foreign or domestic, according to their direction, would be an unnecessary waste of time. Those who have but a superficial acquaintance with the sources from

---

*Aspasia, *vide* Plutarch's *Life of Pericles*.

†*Ibid*.

‡*Ibid*. Phidias was supposed to have stolen some public gold, with the connivance of Pericles, for the embellishment of the statue of Minerva.

§*Ibid*.

¶Worn by the popes.

**Madame de Maintenon.

††Duchess of Marlborough.

‡‡Madame de Pompadour.

which they are to be drawn will themselves recollect a variety of instances; and those who have a tolerable knowledge of human nature will not stand in need of such lights to form their opinion either of the reality or extent of that agency. Perhaps, however, a reference, tending to illustrate the general principle, may with propriety be made to a case which has lately happened among ourselves. If Shays had not been a *desperate debtor,* it is much to be doubted whether Massachusetts would have been plunged into a civil war.

But notwithstanding the concurring testimony of experience, in this particular, there are still to be found visionary or designing men, who stand ready to advocate the paradox of perpetual peace between the States, though dismembered and alienated from each other. The genius of republics (say they) is pacific; the spirit of commerce has a tendency to soften the manners of men, and to extinguish those inflammable humors which have so often kindled into wars. Commercial republics, like ours, will never be disposed to waste themselves in ruinous contentions with each other. They will be governed by mutual interest, and will cultivate a spirit of mutual amity and concord.

Is it not (we may ask these projectors in politics) the true interest of all nations to cultivate the same benevolent and philosophic spirit? If this be their true interest, have they in fact pursued it? Has it not, on the contrary, invariably been found that momentary passions, and immediate interests, have a more active and imperious control over human conduct than general or remote considerations of policy, utility, or justice? Have republics in practice been less addicted to war than monarchies? Are not the former administered by *men* as well as the latter? Are there not aversions, predilections, rivalships, and desires of unjust acquisitions that affect nations as well as kings? Are not popular assemblies frequently subject to the impulses of rage, resentment, jealousy, avarice, and of other irregular and violent propensities? Is it not well known that their determinations are often governed by a few individuals in whom they place confidence, and are, of course, liable to be tinctured by the passions and views of those individuals? Has commerce hitherto done any thing more than change the objects of war? Is not the love of wealth as domineering and enterprising a passion as that of power or glory? Have there not been as many wars founded upon commercial motives since that has become the prevailing system of nations, as were before occasioned by the cupidity of territory or dominion? Has not the spirit of commerce, in many instances, administered new incentives to the appetite, both for the one and for the other? Let experience, the least fallible guide of human opinions, be appealed to for an answer to these inquiries.

Sparta, Athens, Rome, and Carthage were all republics; two of them, Athens and Carthage, of the commercial kind. Yet were they as often engaged in wars, offensive and defensive, as the neighboring monarchies of the same times. Sparta was little better than a well-regulated camp; and Rome was never sated of carnage and conquest.

Carthage, though a commercial republic, was the aggressor in the very war that ended in her destruction. Hannibal had carried her arms into the heart of Italy and to the gates of Rome, before Scipio, in turn, gave him an overthrow in the territories of Carthage and made a conquest of the commonwealth.

Venice, in later times, figured more than once in wars of ambition, till, becoming an object to the other Italian states, Pope Julius the Second found means to accomplish that formidable league,* which gave a deadly blow to the power and pride of this haughty republic.

The provinces of Holland, till they were overwhelmed in debts and taxes, took a leading and conspicuous part in the wars of Europe. They had furious contests with England for the dominion of the sea, and were among the most persevering and most implacable of the opponents of Louis XIV.

In the government of Britain the representatives of the people compose one branch of the national legislature. Commerce has been for ages the predominant pursuit of that country. Few nations, nevertheless, have been more frequently engaged in war; and the wars in which that kingdom has been engaged have, in numerous instances, proceeded from the people.

There have been, if I may so express it, almost as many popular as royal wars. The cries of the nation and the importunities of their representatives have, upon various occasions, dragged their monarchs into war, or continued them in it, contrary to their inclinations, and sometimes contrary to the real interests of the state. In that memorable struggle for superiority between the rival houses of *Austria* and *Bourbon,* which so long kept Europe in a flame, it is well known that the antipathies of the English against the French, seconding the ambition,

---

*The League of Cambray, comprehending the Emperor, the King of France, the King of Aragon, and most of the Italian princes and states.

or rather the avarice, of a favorite leader,* protracted the war beyond the limits marked out by sound policy, and for a considerable time in opposition to the views of the court.

The wars of these two last-mentioned nations have in a great measure grown out of commercial considerations—the desire of supplanting and the fear of being supplanted, either in particular branches of traffic or in the general advantages of trade and navigation, and sometimes even the more culpable desire of sharing in the commerce of other nations without their consent.

The last war but two between Britain and Spain sprang from the attempts of the English merchants to prosecute an illicit trade with the Spanish Main. These unjustifiable practices on their part produced severity on the part of the Spaniards towards the subjects of Great Britain which were not more justifiable, because they exceeded the bounds of a just retaliation and were chargeable with inhumanity and cruelty. Many of the English who were taken on the Spanish coast were sent to dig in the mines of Potosi; and by the usual progress of a spirit of resentment, the innocent were, after a while, confounded with the guilty in indiscriminate punishment. The complaints of the merchants kindled a violent flame throughout the nation, which soon after broke out in the House of Commons, and was communicated from that body to the ministry. Letters of reprisal were granted, and a war ensued, which in its consequences overthrew all the alliances that but twenty years before had been formed with sanguine expectations of the most beneficial fruits.

From this summary of what has taken place in other countries, whose situations have borne the nearest resemblance to our own, what reason can we have to confide in those reveries which would seduce us into an expectation of peace and cordiality between the members of the present confederacy, in a state of separation? Have we not already seen enough of the fallacy and extravagance of those idle theories which have amused us with promises of an exemption from the imperfections, the weaknesses, and the evils incident to society in every shape? Is it not time to awake from the deceitful dream of a golden age and to adopt as a practical maxim for the direction of our political conduct that we, as well as the other inhabitants of the globe, are yet remote from the happy empire of perfect wisdom and perfect virtue?

---

*The Duke of Marlborough.

Let the point of extreme depression to which our national dignity and credit have sunk, let the inconveniences felt everywhere from a lax and ill administration of government, let the revolt of a part of the State of North Carolina, the late menacing disturbances in Pennsylvania, and the actual insurrections and rebellions in Massachusetts, declare——!

So far is the general sense of mankind from corresponding with the tenets of those who endeavor to lull asleep our apprehensions of discord and hostility between the States, in the event of disunion, that it has from long observation of the progress of society become a sort of axiom in politics that vicinity, or nearness of situation, constitutes nations' natural enemies. An intelligent writer expresses himself on this subject to this effect: "NEIGHBORING NATIONS, [says he] are naturally ENEMIES of each other, unless their common weakness forces them to league in a CONFEDERATE REPUBLIC, and their constitution prevents the differences that neighborhood occasions, extinguishing that secret jealousy which disposes all states to aggrandize themselves at the expense of their neighbors."* This passage, at the same time, points out the EVIL and suggests the REMEDY.

PUBLIUS

Vide Principes des Négociations par l'Abbé de Mably.

No. 8: The Consequences of Hostilities Between the States

Assuming it therefore as an established truth that the several States, in case of disunion, or such combinations of them as might happen to be formed out of the wreck of the general Confederacy, would be subject to those vicissitudes of peace and war, of friendship and enmity with each other, which have fallen to the lot of all neighboring nations not united under one government, let us enter into a concise detail of some of the consequences that would attend such a situation.

War between the States, in the first period of their separate existence, would be accompanied with much greater distresses than it commonly is in those countries where regular military establishments have long obtained. The disciplined armies always kept on foot on the continent of Europe, though they bear a malignant aspect to liberty and economy, have, notwithstanding, been productive of the signal advantage of rendering sudden conquests impracticable, and of preventing that rapid desolation which used to mark the progress of war prior to their introduction. The art of fortification has contributed to the same ends. The nations of Europe are encircled with chains of fortified places, which mutually obstruct invasion. Campaigns are wasted in reducing two or three frontier garrisons to gain admittance into an enemy's country. Similar impediments occur at every step to exhaust the strength and delay the progress of an invader. Formerly an invading army would penetrate into the heart of a neighboring country almost as soon as intelligence of its approach could be received; but now a comparatively small force of disciplined troops, acting on the defensive, with the aid of posts, is able to impede, and finally to frustrate, the enterprises of one much more considerable. The history of war in that quarter of the globe is no longer a history of nations subdued and empires overturned, but of towns taken and retaken, of battles that decide nothing, of retreats more beneficial than victories, of much effort and little acquisition.

In this country the scene would be altogether reversed. The jealousy of military establishments would postpone them as long as possible. The want of fortifications, leaving the frontiers of one State open to another, would facilitate inroads. The populous States would, with little difficulty, overrun their less populous neighbors. Conquests would be as easy to be made as difficult to be retained. War, therefore, would be desultory and predatory. PLUNDER and devastation ever march in the train of irregulars. The calamities of individuals would make the principal figure in the events which would characterize our military exploits.

This picture is not too highly wrought; though, I confess, it would not long remain a just one. Safety from external danger is the most powerful director of national conduct. Even the ardent love of liberty will, after a time, give way to its dictates. The violent destruction of life and property incident to war, the continual effort and alarm attendant on a state of continual danger, will compel nations the most attached to liberty to resort for repose and security to institutions which have a tendency to destroy their civil and political rights. To be more safe, they at length become willing to run the risk of being less free.

The institutions chiefly alluded to are STANDING ARMIES and the correspondent appendages of military establishments. Standing armies, it is said, are not provided against in the new Constitution; and it is thence inferred that they may exist under it. This inference, from the very form of the proposition, is, at best, problematical and uncertain.* But standing armies, it may be replied, must inevitably result from a dissolution of the Confederacy. Frequent war and constant apprehension, which require a state of as constant preparation, will infallibly produce them. The weaker States, or confederacies, would first have recourse to them to put themselves upon an equality with their more potent neighbors. They would endeavor to supply the inferiority of population and resources by a more regular and effective system of defense, by disciplined troops, and by fortifications. They would, at the same time, be necessitated to strengthen the executive arm of government, in doing which their constitutions would acquire a progressive direction towards monarchy. It is of the nature of war to increase the executive at the expense of the legislative authority.

The expedients which have been mentioned would soon give the States, or confederacies, that made use of them a superiority over their neighbors. Small states, or states of less natural strength, under vigorous governments, and with the assistance of disciplined armies, have often triumphed over large states, or states of greater natural strength, which have been destitute of these advantages. Neither the pride nor the safety of the more important States, or confederacies,

---

*This objection will be fully examined in its proper place, and it will be shown that the only rational precaution which could have been taken on this subject has been taken; and a much better one than is to be found in any constitution that has been heretofore framed in America, most of which contain no guard at all on this subject.

would permit them long to submit to this mortifying and adventitious superiority. They would quickly resort to means similar to those by which it had been effected, to reinstate themselves in their lost pre-eminence. Thus we should, in a little time, see established in every part of this country the same engines of despotism which have been the scourge of the old world. This, at least, would be the natural course of things; and our reasonings will be the more likely to be just in proportion as they are accommodated to this standard.

These are not vague inferences drawn from supposed or speculative defects in a Constitution, the whole power of which is lodged in the hands of a people, or their representatives and delegates, but they are solid conclusions, drawn from the natural and necessary progress of human affairs.

It may, perhaps, be asked, by way of objection to this, why did not standing armies spring up out of the contentions which so often distracted the ancient republics of Greece? Different answers, equally satisfactory, may be given to this question. The industrious habits of the people of the present day, absorbed in the pursuits of gain and devoted to the improvements of agriculture and commerce, are incompatible with the condition of a nation of soldiers, which was the true condition of the people of those republics. The means of revenue, which have been so greatly multiplied by the increase of gold and silver and of the arts of industry, and the science of finance, which is the offspring of modern times, concurring with the habits of nations, have produced an entire revolution in the system of war, and have rendered disciplined armies, distinct from the body of the citizens, the inseparable companion of frequent hostility.

There is a wide difference, also, between military establishments in a country seldom exposed by its situation to internal invasions, and in one which is often subject to them and always apprehensive of them. The rulers of the former can have no good pretext, if they are even so inclined, to keep on foot armies so numerous as must of necessity be maintained in the latter. These armies being, in the first case, rarely if at all called into activity for interior defense, the people are in no danger of being broken to military subordination. The laws are not accustomed to relaxation in favor of military exigencies; the civil state remains in full vigor, neither corrupted, nor confounded with the principles or propensities of the other state. The smallness of the army renders the natural strength of the community an overmatch for it; and the citizens, not habituated to look up to the military power for protection, or to submit to its oppressions, neither love nor fear the soldiery; they view them with a spirit of jealous acquiescence in a necessary evil and stand ready to resist a power which they suppose may be exerted to the prejudice of their rights.

The army under such circumstances may usefully aid the magistrate to suppress a small faction, or an occasional mob, or insurrection; but it will be unable to enforce encroachments against the united efforts of the great body of the people.

In a country in the predicament last described, the contrary of all this happens. The perpetual menacings of danger oblige the government to be always prepared to repel it; its armies must be numerous enough for instant defense. The continual necessity for their services enhances the importance of the soldier, and proportionably degrades the condition of the citizen. The military state becomes elevated above the civil. The inhabitants of territories, often the theater of war, are unavoidably subjected to frequent infringements on their rights, which serve to weaken their sense of those rights; and by degrees the people are brought to consider the soldiery not only as their protectors but as their superiors. The transition from this disposition to that of considering them masters is neither remote nor difficult; but it is very difficult to prevail upon a people under such impressions to make a bold or effectual resistance to usurpations supported by the military power.

The kingdom of Great Britain fails within the first description. An insular situation, and a powerful marine, guarding it in a great measure against the possibility of foreign invasion, supersede the necessity of a numerous army within the kingdom. A sufficient force to make head against a sudden descent, till the militia could have time to rally and embody, is all that has been deemed requisite. No motive of national policy has demanded, nor would public opinion have tolerated, a larger number of troops upon its domestic establishment. There has been, for a long time past, little room for the operation of the other causes, which have been enumerated as the consequences of internal war. This peculiar felicity of situation has, in a great degree, contributed to preserve the liberty which that country to this day enjoys, in spite of the prevalent venality and corruption. If, on the contrary, Britain had been situated on the continent, and had been compelled, as she would have been, by that situation, to make her military establishments at home coextensive with those of the other great powers of Europe, she, like them, would in all probability be, at this day, a victim to the absolute power of a single man. 'Tis possible, though not easy, that the people of that island may be enslaved from other causes; but it cannot be by the prowess of an army so inconsiderable as that which has been usually kept up within the kingdom.

If we are wise enough to preserve the Union we may for ages enjoy an advantage similar to that of an insulated situation. Europe is at a great distance from us. Her colonies in our vicinity will be likely to continue too much disproportioned in strength to be able to give us any dangerous annoyance. Extensive military establishments cannot, in this position, be necessary to our security. But if we should be disunited, and the integral parts should either remain separated, or, which is most probable, should be thrown together into two or three confederacies, we should be, in a short course of time, in the predicament of the continental powers of Europe—our liberties would be a prey to the means of defending ourselves against the ambition and jealousy of each other.

This is an idea not superficial nor futile, but solid and weighty. It deserves the most serious and mature consideration of every prudent and honest man of whatever party. If such men will make a firm and solemn pause, and meditate dispassionately on the importance of this interesting idea; if they will contemplate it in all its attitudes, and trace it to all its consequences, they will not hesitate to part with trivial objections to a Constitution, the rejection of which would in all probability put a final period to the Union. The airy phantoms that flit before the distempered imaginations of some of its adversaries would quickly give place to the more substantial prospects of dangers, real, certain, and formidable.

PUBLIUS

No. 9: The Union as a Safeguard Against Domestic Faction and Insurrection

A firm Union will be of the utmost moment to the peace and liberty of the States as a barrier against domestic faction and insurrection. It is impossible to read the history of the petty republics of Greece and Italy without feeling sensations of horror and disgust at the distractions with which they were continually agitated, and at the rapid succession of revolutions by which they were kept in a state of perpetual vibration between the extremes of tyranny and anarchy. If they exhibit occasional calms, these only serve as short-lived contrasts to the furious storms that are to succeed. If now and then intervals of felicity open themselves to view, we behold them with a mixture of regret, arising from the reflection that the pleasing scenes before us are soon to be overwhelmed by the tempestuous waves of sedition and party rage. If momentary rays of glory break forth from the gloom, while they dazzle us with a transient and fleeting brilliancy, they at the same time admonish us to lament that the vices of government should pervert the direction and tarnish the luster of those bright talents and exalted endowments for which the favored soils that produced them have been so justly celebrated.

From the disorders that disfigure the annals of those republics the advocates of despotism have drawn arguments, not only against the forms of republican government, but against the very principles of civil liberty. They have decried all free government as inconsistent with the order of society, and have indulged themselves in malicious exultation over its friends and partisans. Happily for mankind, stupendous fabrics reared on the basis of liberty, which have flourished for ages, have, in a few glorious instances, refuted their gloomy sophisms. And, I trust, America will be the broad and solid foundation of other edifices, not less magnificent, which will be equally permanent monuments of their errors.

But it is not to be denied that the portraits they have sketched of republican government were too just copies of the originals from which they were taken. If it had been found impracticable to have devised models of a more perfect structure, the enlightened friends to liberty would have been obliged to abandon the cause of that species of government as indefensible. The science of politics, however, like most other sciences, has received great improvement. The efficacy of various principles is now well understood, which were either not known at all, or imperfectly known to the ancients. The regular distribution of power into distinct departments; the introduction of legislative balances and checks; the institution of courts composed of judges holding their offices during good behavior; the representation of the people in the legislature by deputies of their own election: these are wholly new discoveries, or have made their principal progress towards perfection in modern times. They are means, and powerful means, by which the excellencies of republican government may be retained and its imperfections lessened or avoided. To this catalogue of circumstances that tend to the amelioration of popular systems of civil government, I shall venture, however novel it may appear to some, to add one more, on a principle which has been made the foundation of an objection to the new Constitution; I mean the ENLARGEMENT of the ORBIT within which such systems are to revolve, either in respect to the dimensions of a single State, or to the consolidation of several smaller States into one great Confederacy. The latter is that which immediately concerns the object under consideration. It will, however, be of use to examine the principle in its application to a single State, which shall be attended to in another place.

The utility of a Confederacy, as well to suppress faction and to guard the internal tranquillity of States as to increase their external force and security, is in reality not a new idea. It has been practised upon in different countries and ages, and has received the sanction of the most applauded writers on the subjects of politics. The opponents of the PLAN proposed have, with great assiduity, cited and circulated the observations of Montesquieu on the necessity of a contracted territory for a republican government. But they seem not to have been apprised of the sentiments of that great man expressed in another part of his work, nor to have adverted to the consequences of the principle to which they subscribe with such ready acquiescence.

When Montesquieu recommends a small extent for republics, the standards he had in view were of dimensions far short of the limits of almost every one of these States. Neither Virginia, Massachusetts, Pennsylvania, New York, North Carolina, nor Georgia can by any means be compared with the models from which he reasoned and to which the terms of his description apply. If we therefore take his ideas on this point as the criterion of truth, we shall be driven to the alternative either of taking refuge at once in the arms of monarchy, or of splitting ourselves into an infinity of little, jealous, clashing, tumultuous commonwealths, the wretched nurseries of unceasing discord and the miserable objects of universal pity or contempt.

Some of the writers who have come forward on the other side of the question seem to have been aware of the dilemma; and have even been bold enough to hint at the division of the larger States as a desirable thing. Such an infatuated policy, such a desperate expedient, might, by the multiplication of petty offices, answer the views of men who possess not qualifications to extend their influence beyond the narrow circles of personal intrigue, but it could never promote the greatness or happiness of the people of America.

Referring the examination of the principle itself to another place, as has been already mentioned, it will be sufficient to remark here that, in the sense of the author who has been most emphatically quoted upon the occasion, it would only dictate a reduction of the SIZE of the more considerable MEMBERS of the Union, but would not militate against their being all comprehended in one confederate government. And this is the true question, in the discussion of which we are at present interested.

So far are the suggestions of Montesquieu from standing in opposition to a general Union of the States that he explicitly treats of a CONFEDERATE REPUBLIC as the expedient for extending the sphere of popular government and reconciling the advantages of monarchy with those of republicanism.

"It is very probable" (says he*) "that mankind would have been obliged at length to live constantly under the government of a SINGLE PERSON, had they not contrived a kind of constitution that has all the internal advantages of a republican, together with the external force of a monarchical, government. I mean a CONFEDERATE REPUBLIC.

"This form of government is a convention by which several smaller *states* agree to become members of a larger *one*, which they intend to form. It is a kind of assemblage of societies that constitute a new one, capable of increasing, by means of new associations, till they arrive to such a degree of power as to be able to provide for the security of the united body.

"A republic of this kind, able to withstand an external force, may support itself without any internal corruptions. The form of this society prevents all manner of inconveniences.

"If a single member should attempt to usurp the supreme authority, he could not be supposed to have an equal authority and credit in all the confederate states. Were he to have too great influence over one, this would alarm the rest. Were he to subdue a part, that which

---

**Spirit of Laws, Vol. I., Book IX., Chap. I.

would still remain free might oppose him with forces independent of those which he had usurped, and overpower him before he could be settled in his usurpation.

"Should a popular insurrection happen in one of the confederate states, the others are able to quell it. Should abuses creep into one part, they are reformed by those that remain sound. The state may be destroyed on one side, and not on the other; the confederacy may be dissolved, and the confederates preserve their sovereignty.

"As this government is composed of small republics, it enjoys the internal happiness of each; and with respect to its external situation, it is possessed, by means of the association, of all the advantages of large monarchies."

I have thought it proper to quote at length these interesting passages, because they contain a luminous abridgment of the principal arguments in favor of the Union, and must effectually remove the false impressions which a misapplication of other parts of the work was calculated to produce. They have, at the same time, an intimate connection with the more immediate design of this paper, which is to illustrate the tendency of the Union to repress domestic faction and insurrection.

A distinction, more subtle than accurate, has been raised between a *confederacy* and a *consolidation* of the States. The essential characteristic of the first is said to be the restriction of its authority to the members in their collective capacities, without reaching to the individuals of whom they are composed. It is contended that the national council ought to have no concern with any object of internal administration. An exact equality of suffrage between the members has also been insisted upon as a leading feature of a confederate government. These positions are, in the main, arbitrary; they are supported neither by principle nor precedent. It has indeed happened that governments of this kind have generally operated in the manner which the distinction, taken notice of, supposes to be inherent in their nature; but there have been in most of them extensive exceptions to the practice, which serve to prove, as far as example will go, that there is no absolute rule on the subject. And it will be clearly shown, in the course of this investigation, that as far as the principle contended for has prevailed, it has been the cause of incurable disorder and imbecility in the government.

The definition of a *confederate republic* seems simply to be "an assemblage of societies," or an association of two or more states into one state. The extent, modifications, and objects of the federal authority are mere matters of discretion. So long as the separate organization of the members be not abolished; so long as it exists, by a constitutional necessity, for local purposes; though it should be in perfect subordination to the general authority of the union, it would still be, in fact and in theory, an association of states, or a confederacy. The proposed Constitution, so far from implying an abolition of the State governments, makes them constituent parts of the national sovereignty, by allowing them a direct representation in the Senate, and leaves in their possession certain exclusive and very important portions of sovereign power. This fully corresponds, in every rational import of the terms, with the idea of a federal government.

In the Lycian confederacy, which consisted of twenty-three CITIES, or republics, the largest were entitled to *three* votes in the COMMON COUNCIL, those of the middle class to *two*, and the smallest to *one*. The COMMON COUNCIL had the appointment of all the judges and magistrates of the respective CITIES. This was certainly the most delicate species of interference in their internal administration; for if there be any thing that seems exclusively appropriated to the local jurisdictions, it is the appointment of their own officers. Yet Montesquieu, speaking of this association, says: "Were I to give a model of an excellent Confederate Republic, it would be that of Lycia." Thus we perceive that the distinctions insisted upon were not within the contemplation of this enlightened civilian; and we shall be led to conclude that they are the novel refinements of an erroneous theory.

PUBLIUS

No. 12: The Utility of the Union in Respect to Revenue

The effects of Union upon the commercial prosperity of the States have been sufficiently delineated. Its tendency to promote the interests of revenue will be the subject of our present inquiry.

The prosperity of commerce is now perceived and acknowledged by all enlightened statesmen to be the most useful as well as the most productive source of national wealth, and has accordingly become a primary object of their political cares. By multiplying the means of gratification, by promoting the introduction and circulation of the precious metals, those darling objects of human avarice and enterprise, it serves to vivify and invigorate all the channels of industry and to make them flow with greater activity and copiousness. The assiduous merchant, the laborious husbandman, the active mechanic, and the industrious manufacturer—all orders of men look forward with eager expectation and growing alacrity to this pleasing reward of their toils. The often-agitated question between agriculture and commerce has from indubitable experience received a decision which has silenced the rivalship that once subsisted between them, and has proved, to the entire satisfaction of their friends, that their interests are intimately blended and interwoven. It has been found in various countries that in proportion as commerce has flourished land has risen in value. And how could it have happened otherwise? Could that which procures a freer vent for the products of the earth, which furnishes new incitements to the cultivators of land, which is the most powerful instrument in increasing the quantity of money in a state—could that, in fine, which is the faithful handmaid of labor and industry in every shape fail to augment the value of that article, which is the prolific parent of far the greatest part of the objects upon which they are exerted? It is astonishing that so simple a truth should ever have had an adversary; and it is one among a multitude of proofs how apt a spirit of ill-informed jealousy, or of too great abstraction and refinement, is to lead men astray from the plainest paths of reason and conviction.

The ability of a country to pay taxes must always be proportioned in a great degree to the quantity of money in circulation and to the celerity with which it circulates. Commerce, contributing to both these objects, must of necessity render the payment of taxes easier and facilitate the requisite supplies to the treasury. The hereditary dominions of the Emperor of Germany contain a great extent of fertile, cultivated, and populous territory, a large proportion of which is situated in mild and luxuriant climates. In some parts of this territory are to be found the best gold and silver mines in Europe. And yet from the want of the fostering influence of commerce that monarch can boast but slender revenues. He has several times been compelled to owe obligations to the pecuniary succors of other nations for the preservation of his essential interests, and is unable, upon the strength of his own resources, to sustain a long or continued war.

But it is not in this aspect of the subject alone that Union will be seen to conduce to the purposes of revenue. There are other points of view in which its influence will appear more immediate and decisive. It is evident from the state of the country, from the habits of the people, from the experience we have had on the point itself that it is impracticable to raise any very considerable sums by direct taxation. Tax laws have in vain been multiplied; new methods to enforce the collection have in vain been tried; the public expectation has been uniformly disappointed, and the treasuries of the States have remained empty. The popular system of administration inherent in the nature of popular government, coinciding with the real scarcity of money incident to a languid and mutilated state of trade, has hitherto defeated every experiment for extensive collections, and has at length taught the different legislatures the folly of attempting them.

No person acquainted with what happens in other countries will be surprised at this circumstance. In so opulent a nation as that of Britain, where direct taxes from superior wealth must be much more tolerable, and from the vigor of the government, much more practicable than in America, far the greatest part of the national revenue is derived from taxes of the indirect kind, from imposts and from excises. Duties on imported articles form a large branch of this latter description.

In America it is evident that we must a long time depend for the means of revenue chiefly on such duties. In most parts of it excises must be confined within a narrow compass. The genius of the people will ill brook the inquisitive and peremptory spirit of excise laws. The pockets of the farmers, on the other hand, will reluctantly yield but scanty supplies in the unwelcome shape of impositions on their houses and lands; and personal property is too precarious and invisible a fund to be laid hold of in any other way than by the imperceptible agency of taxes on consumption.

If these remarks have any foundation, that state of things which will best enable us to improve and extend so valuable a resource must be the best adapted to our political welfare. And it cannot admit of a serious doubt that this state of things must rest on the basis of a general Union. As far as this would be conducive to the interests of commerce, so far it must tend to the extension of the revenue to be drawn from that source. As far as it would contribute to rendering regulations for the collection of the duties more simple and efficacious, so far it must serve to answer the purposes of making the same rate of duties more productive and of putting it into the power of the government to increase the rate without prejudice to trade.

The relative situation of these States; the number of rivers with which they are intersected and of bays that wash their shores; the facility of communication in every direction; the affinity of language and manners; the familiar habits of intercourse—all these are circumstances that would conspire to render an illicit trade between them a matter of little difficulty and would insure frequent evasions of the commercial regulations of each other. The separate States, or confederacies, would be necessitated by mutual jealousy to avoid the temptations to that kind of trade by the lowness of their duties. The temper of our governments for a long time to come would not permit those rigorous precautions by which the European nations guard the avenues into their respective countries, as well by land as by water; and which, even there, are found insufficient obstacles to the adventurous stratagems of avarice.

In France there is an army of patrols (as they are called) constantly employed to secure her fiscal regulations against the inroads of the dealers in contraband. Mr. Neckar computes the number of these patrols at upwards of twenty thousand. This proves the immense difficulty in preventing that species of traffic where there is an inland communication and shows in a strong light the disadvantages with which the collection of duties in this country would be encumbered, if by disunion the States should be placed in a situation with respect to each other resembling that of France with respect to her neighbors. The arbitrary and vexatious powers with which the patrols are necessarily armed would be intolerable in a free country.

If, on the contrary, there be but one government pervading all the States, there will be, as to the principal part of our commerce, but ONE SIDE to guard—the ATLANTIC COAST. Vessels arriving directly from foreign countries, laden with valuable cargoes, would rarely choose to hazard themselves to the complicated and critical perils which would attend attempts to unlade prior to their coming into port. They would have to dread both the dangers of the coast and of detection, as well after as before their arrival at the places of their final destination. An ordinary degree of vigilance would be competent to the prevention of any material infractions upon the rights of the revenue. A few armed vessels, judiciously stationed at the entrances of our ports, might at small expense be made useful sentinels of the laws. And the government having the same interests to provide against violations everywhere, the co-operation of its measures in each State would have a powerful tendency to render them effectual. Here also we should preserve, by Union, an advantage which nature holds out to us and which would be relinquished by separation. The United States lie at a great distance from Europe and at a considerable distance from all other places with which they would have extensive connections of foreign trade. The passage from them to us, in a few hours or in a single night, as between the coasts of France and Britain, and of other neighboring nations, would be impracticable. This is a prodigious security against a direct contraband with foreign countries; but a circuitous contraband to one State through the medium of another would be both easy and safe. The difference between a direct importation from abroad, and an indirect importation through the channel of a neighboring State, in small parcels according to time and opportunity, with the additional facilities of inland communication, must be palpable to every man of discernment.

It is therefore evident that one national government would be able at much less expense to extend the duties on imports beyond comparison, further than would be practicable to the States separately, or to any partial confederacies. Hitherto, I believe, it may safely be asserted that these duties have not upon an average exceeded in any State three percent. In France they are estimated at about fifteen percent, and in Britain the proportion is still greater. There seems to be nothing to hinder their being increased in this country to at least treble their present amount. The single article of ardent spirits under federal regulation might be made to furnish a considerable revenue. Upon a ratio to the importation into this State, the whole quantity imported into the United States may at a low computation be estimated at four millions of gallons, which, at a shilling per gallon, would produce two hundred thousand pounds. That article would well bear this rate of duty; and if it should tend to diminish the consumption of it, such an effect would be equally favorable to the agriculture, to the economy, to the morals, and to the health of the society. There is, perhaps, nothing so much a subject of national extravagance as this very article.

What will be the consequence if we are not able to avail ourselves of the resource in question in its full extent? A nation cannot long exist without revenue. Destitute of this essential support, it must resign its independence and sink into the degraded condition of a province. This is an extremity to which no government will of choice accede. Revenue, therefore, must be had at all events. In this country if the principal part be not drawn from commerce, it must fall with oppressive weight upon land. It has been already intimated that excises in their true signification are too little in unison with the feelings of the people to admit of great use being made of that mode of taxation; nor, indeed, in the States where almost the sole employment is agriculture are the objects proper for excise sufficiently numerous to permit very ample collections in that way. Personal estate (as has been before remarked), from the difficulty of tracing it, cannot be subjected to large contributions by any other means than by taxes on consumption. In populous cities it may be enough the subject of conjecture to occasion the oppression of individuals, without much aggregate benefit to the State; but beyond these circles it must, in a great measure, escape the eye and the hand of the tax-gatherer. As the necessities of the State, nevertheless, must be satisfied in some mode or other, the defect of other resources must throw the principal weight of the public burdens on the possessors of land. And as on the other hand the wants of the government can never obtain an adequate supply, unless all the sources of revenue are open to its demands, the finances of the community, under such embarrassments, cannot be put into a situation consistent with its respectability or its security. Thus we shall not even have the consolations of a full treasury to atone for the oppression of that valuable class of the citizens who are employed in the cultivation of the soil. But public and private distress will keep pace with each other in gloomy concert and unite in deploring the infatuation of those counsels which led to disunion.

PUBLIUS

No. 15: The Insufficiency of the Present Confederation to Preserve the Union

In the course of the preceding papers I have endeavored, my fellow-citizens, to place before you in a clear and convincing light the importance of Union to your political safety and happiness. I have unfolded to you a complication of dangers to which you would be exposed, should you permit that sacred knot which binds the people of America together to be severed or dissolved by ambition or by avarice, by jealousy or by misrepresentation. In the sequel of the inquiry through which I propose to accompany you, the truths intended to be inculcated will receive further confirmation from facts and arguments hitherto unnoticed. If the road over which you will still have to pass should in some places appear to you tedious or irksome, you will recollect that you are in quest of information on a subject the most momentous which can engage the attention of a free people, that the field through which you have to travel is in itself spacious, and that the difficulties of the journey have been unnecessarily increased by the mazes with which sophistry has beset the way. It will be my aim to remove the obstacles to your progress in as compendious a manner as it can be done, without sacrificing utility to dispatch.

In pursuance of the plan which I have laid down for the discussion of the subject, the point next in order to be examined is the "insufficiency of the present Confederation to the preservation of the Union." It may perhaps be asked what need there is of reasoning or proof to illustrate a position which is not either controverted or doubted, to which the understandings and feelings of all classes of men assent, and which in substance is admitted by the opponents as well as by the friends of the new Constitution. It must in truth be acknowledged that, however these may differ in other respects, they in general appear to harmonize in this sentiment at least: that there are material imperfections in our national system and that something is necessary to be done to rescue us from impending anarchy. The facts that support this opinion are no longer objects of speculation. They have forced themselves upon the sensibility of the people at large, and have at length extorted from those, whose mistaken policy has had the principal share in precipitating the extremity at which we are arrived, a reluctant confession of the reality of those defects in the scheme of our federal government which have been long pointed out and regretted by the intelligent friends of the Union.

We may indeed with propriety be said to have reached almost the last stage of national humiliation. There is scarcely anything that can wound the pride or degrade the character of an independent nation which we do not experience. Are there engagements to the performance of which we are held by every tie respectable among men? These are the subjects of constant and unblushing violation. Do we owe debts to foreigners and to our own citizens contracted in a time of imminent peril for the preservation of our political existence? These remain without any proper or satisfactory provision for their discharge. Have we valuable territories and important posts in the possession of a foreign power which, by express stipulations, ought long since to have been surrendered? These are still retained to the prejudice of our interests, not less than of our rights. Are we in a condition to resent or to repel the aggression? We have neither troops, nor treasury, nor government.* Are we even in a condition to remonstrate with dignity? The just imputations on our own faith in respect to the same treaty ought first to be removed. Are we entitled by nature and compact to a free participation in the navigation of the Mississippi? Spain excludes us from it. Is public credit an indispensable resource in time of public danger? We seem to have abandoned its cause as desperate and irretrievable. Is commerce of importance to national wealth? Ours is at the lowest point of declension. Is respectability in the eyes of foreign powers a safeguard against foreign encroachments? The imbecility of our government even forbids them to treat with us. Our ambassadors abroad are the mere pageants of mimic sovereignty. Is a violent and unnatural decrease in the value of land a symptom of national distress? The price of improved land in most parts of the country is much lower than can be accounted for by the quantity of waste land at market, and can only be fully explained by that want of private and public confidence, which are so alarmingly prevalent among all ranks and which have a direct tendency to depreciate property of every kind. Is private credit the friend and patron of industry? That most useful kind which relates to borrowing and lending is reduced within the narrowest limits, and this still more from an opinion of insecurity than from a scarcity of money. To shorten an enumeration of particulars which can afford neither pleasure nor instruction, it may in general

---

*"I mean for the Union."

be demanded, what indication is there of national disorder, poverty, and insignificance that could befall a community so peculiarly blessed with natural advantages as we are, which does not form a part of the dark catalogue of our public misfortunes?

This is the melancholy situation to which we have been brought by those very maxims and counsels which would now deter us from adopting the proposed Constitution; and which, not content with having conducted us to the brink of a precipice, seem resolved to plunge us into the abyss that awaits us below. Here, my countrymen, impelled by every motive that ought to influence an enlightened people, let us make a firm stand for our safety, our tranquillity, our dignity, our reputation. Let us at last break the fatal charm which has too long seduced us from the paths of felicity and prosperity.

It is true, as has been before observed, that facts too stubborn to be resisted have produced a species of general assent to the abstract proposition that there exist material defects in our national system; but the usefulness of the concession on the part of the old adversaries of federal measures is destroyed by a strenuous opposition to a remedy upon the only principles that can give it a chance of success. While they admit that the government of the United States is destitute of energy, they contend against conferring upon it those powers which are requisite to supply that energy. They seem still to aim at things repugnant and irreconcilable; at an augmentation of federal authority without a diminution of State authority; at sovereignty in the Union and complete independence in the members. They still, in fine, seem to cherish with blind devotion the political monster of an *imperium in imperio*. This renders a full display of the principal defects of the Confederation necessary in order to show that the evils we experience do not proceed from minute or partial imperfections, but from fundamental errors in the structure of the building, which cannot be amended otherwise than by an alteration in the first principles and main pillars of the fabric.

The great and radical vice in the construction of the existing Confederation is in the principle of LEGISLATION for STATES or GOVERNMENTS, in their CORPORATE or COLLECTIVE CAPACITIES, and as contradistinguished from the INDIVIDUALS of whom they consist. Though this principle does not run through all the powers delegated to the Union, yet it pervades and governs those on which the efficacy of the rest depends. Except as to the rule of apportionment, the United States have an indefinite discretion to make requisitions for men and money; but they have no authority to raise either by regulations extending to the individual citizens of America. The consequence of this is that though in theory their resolutions concerning those objects are laws constitutionally binding on the members of the Union, yet in practice they are mere recommendations which the States observe or disregard at their option.

It is a singular instance of the capriciousness of the human mind that after all the admonitions we have had from experience on this head, there should still be found men who object to the new Constitution for deviating from a principle which has been found the bane of the old and which is in itself evidently incompatible with the idea of GOVERNMENT; a principle, in short, which, if it is to be executed at all, must substitute the violent and sanguinary agency of the sword to the mild influence of the magistracy.

There is nothing absurd or impracticable in the idea of a league or alliance between independent nations for certain defined purposes precisely stated in a treaty regulating all the details of time, place, circumstance, and quantity, leaving nothing to future discretion, and depending for its execution on the good faith of the parties. Compacts of this kind exist among all civilized nations, subject to the usual vicissitudes of peace and war, of observance and nonobservance, as the interests or passions of the contracting powers dictate. In the early part of the present century there was an epidemical rage in Europe for this species of compacts, from which the politicians of the times fondly hoped for benefits which were never realized. With a view to establishing the equilibrium of power and the peace of that part of the world, all the resources of negotiations were exhausted, and triple and quadruple alliances were formed; but they were scarcely formed before they were broken, giving an instructive but afflicting lesson to mankind how little dependence is to be placed on treaties which have no other sanction than the obligations of good faith, and which oppose general considerations of peace and justice to the impulse of any immediate interest or passion.

If the particular States in this country are disposed to stand in a similar relation to each other, and to drop the project of a general DISCRETIONARY SUPERINTENDENCE, the scheme would indeed be pernicious and would entail upon us all the mischiefs which have been enumerated under the first head; but it would have the merit of being, at least, consistent and practicable. Abandoning all views towards a confederate government, this would bring us to a simple alliance offensive and defensive; and would place us in a situation to be alternate friends and enemies of each other, as our mutual jealousies and rivalships, nourished by the intrigues of foreign nations, should prescribe to us.

But if we are unwilling to be placed in this perilous situation; if we still will adhere to the design of a national government, or, which is the same thing, of a superintending power under the direction of a common council, we must resolve to incorporate into our plan those ingredients which may be considered as forming the characteristic difference between a league and a government; we must extend the authority of the Union to the persons of the citizens—the only proper objects of government.

Government implies the power of making laws. It is essential to the idea of a law that it be attended with a sanction; or, in other words, a penalty or punishment for disobedience. If there be no penalty annexed to disobedience, the resolutions or commands which pretend to be laws will, in fact, amount to nothing more than advice or recommendation. This penalty, whatever it may be, can only be inflicted in two ways: by the agency of the courts and ministers of justice, or by military force; by the COERCION of the magistracy, or by the COERCION of arms. The first kind can evidently apply only to men; the last kind must of necessity be employed against bodies politic, or communities, or States. It is evident that there is no process of a court by which the observance of the laws can in the last resort be enforced. Sentences may be denounced against them for violations of their duty; but these sentences can only be carried into execution by the sword. In an association where the general authority is confined to the collective bodies of the communities that compose it, every breach of the laws must involve a state of war; and military execution must become the only instrument of civil obedience. Such a state of things can certainly not deserve the name of government, nor would any prudent man choose to commit his happiness to it.

There was a time when we were told that breaches by the States of the regulations of the federal authority were not to be expected; that a sense of common interest would preside over the conduct of the respective members, and would beget a full compliance with all the constitutional requisitions of the Union. This language, at the present day, would appear as wild as a great part of what we now hear from the same quarter will be thought, when we shall have received further lessons from that best oracle of wisdom, experience. It at all times betrayed an ignorance of the true springs by which human conduct is actuated, and belied the original inducements to the establishment of civil power. Why has government been instituted at all? Because the passions of men will not conform to the dictates of reason and justice without constraint. Has it been found that bodies of men act with more rectitude or greater disinterestedness than individuals? The contrary of this has been inferred by all accurate observers of the conduct of mankind; and the inference is founded upon obvious reasons. Regard to reputation has a less active influence when the infamy of a bad action is to be divided among a number than when it is to fall singly upon one. A spirit of faction, which is apt to mingle its poison in the deliberations of all bodies of men, will often hurry the persons of whom they are composed into improprieties and excesses for which they would blush in a private capacity.

In addition to all this, there is in the nature of sovereign power an impatience of control that disposes those who are invested with the exercise of it to look with an evil eye upon all external attempts to restrain or direct its operations. From this spirit it happens that in every political association which is formed upon the principle of uniting in a common interest a number of lesser sovereignties, there will be found a kind of eccentric tendency in the subordinate or inferior orbs by the operation of which there will be a perpetual effort in each to fly off from the common center. This tendency is not difficult to be accounted for. It has its origin in the love of power. Power controlled or abridged is almost always the rival and enemy of that power by which it is controlled or abridged. This simple proposition will teach us how little reason there is to expect that the persons intrusted with the administration of the affairs of the particular members of a confederacy will at all times be ready with perfect good humor and an unbiased regard to the public weal to execute the resolutions or decrees of the general authority. The reverse of this results from the constitution of man.

If, therefore, the measures of the Confederacy cannot be executed without the intervention of the particular administrations, there will be little prospect of their being executed at all. The rulers of the respective members, whether they have a constitutional right to do it or not, will undertake to judge of the propriety of the measures themselves. They will consider the conformity of the thing proposed or required to their immediate interests or aims; the momentary conveniences or inconveniences that would attend its adoption. All this will be done; and in a spirit of interested and suspicious scrutiny, without that knowledge of national circumstances and reasons of state, which is essential to a right judgment, and with that strong predilection in favor of local objects, which can hardly fail to mislead the decision. The same process must be repeated in every member of which the body is constituted; and the execution of the plans, framed by the councils of the whole, will always fluctuate on the discretion of the ill-informed and prejudiced opinion of every part. Those who have been conversant in the proceedings of popular assemblies; who have seen how difficult it often is, when there is no exterior pressure of circumstances, to bring them to harmonious resolutions on important points, will readily conceive how impossible it must be to induce a number of such assemblies, deliberating at a distance from each other, at different times and under different impressions, long to co-operate in the same views and pursuits.

In our case the concurrence of thirteen distinct sovereign wills is requisite under the Confederation to the complete execution of every important measure that proceeds from the Union. It has happened as was to have been foreseen. The measures of the Union have not been executed; and the delinquencies of the States have step by step matured themselves to an extreme, which has, at length, arrested all the wheels of the national government and brought them to an awful stand. Congress at this time scarcely possess the means of keeping up the forms of administration, till the States can have time to agree upon a more substantial substitute for the present shadow of a federal government. Things did not come to this desperate extremity at once. The causes which have been specified produced at first only unequal and disproportionate degrees of compliance with the requisitions of the Union. The greater deficiencies of some States furnished the pretext of example and the temptation of interest to the complying, or to the least delinquent States. Why should we do more in proportion than those who are embarked with us in the same political voyage? Why should we consent to bear more than our proper share of the common burden? There were suggestions which human selfishness could not withstand, and which even speculative men, who looked forward to remote consequences, could not without hesitation combat. Each State yielding to the persuasive voice of immediate interest or convenience has successively withdrawn its support, till the frail and tottering edifice seems ready to fall upon our heads and to crush us beneath its ruins.

PUBLIUS

No. 23: The Necessity of a Government as Energetic as the One Proposed to the Preservation of the Union

The necessity of a Constitution, at least equally energetic with the one proposed, to the preservation of the Union, is the point at the examination of which we are now arrived.

This inquiry will naturally divide itself into three branches—the objects to be provided for by a federal government, the quantity of power necessary to the accomplishment of those objects, the persons upon whom that power ought to operate. Its distribution and organization will more properly claim our attention under the succeeding head.

The principal purposes to be answered by union are these—the common defense of the members; the preservation of the public peace, as well against internal convulsions as external attacks; the regulation of commerce with other nations and between the States; the superintendence of our intercourse, political and commercial, with foreign countries.

The authorities essential to the common defense are these: to raise armies; to build and equip fleets; to prescribe rules for the government of both; to direct their operations; to provide for their support. These powers ought to exist without limitation, *because it is impossible to foresee or to define the extent and variety of national exigencies, and the correspondent extent and variety of the means which may be necessary to satisfy them.* The circumstances that endanger the safety of nations are infinite, and for this reason no constitutional shackles can wisely be imposed on the power to which the care of it is committed. This power ought to be coextensive with all the possible combinations of such circumstances; and ought to be under the direction of the same councils which are appointed to preside over the common defense.

This is one of those truths which to a correct and unprejudiced mind carries its own evidence along with it, and may be obscured, but cannot be made plainer by argument or reasoning. It rests upon axioms as simple as they are universal; the *means* ought to be proportioned to the *end;* the persons from whose agency the attainment of any *end* is expected ought to possess the *means* by which it is to be attained.

Whether there ought to be a federal government intrusted with the care of the common defense is a question in the first instance open to discussion; but the moment it is decided in the affirmative, it will follow that that government ought to be clothed with all the powers requisite to complete execution of its trust. And unless it can be shown that the circumstances which may affect the public safety are reducible within certain determinate limits; unless the contrary of this position can be fairly and rationally disputed, it must be admitted as a necessary consequence that there can be no limitation of that authority which is to provide for the defense and protection of the community in any matter essential to its efficacy—that is, in any matter essential to the *formation, direction,* or *support* of the NATIONAL FORCES.

Defective as the present Confederation has been proved to be, this principle appears to have been fully recognized by the framers of it; though they have not made proper or adequate provision for its exercise. Congress have an unlimited discretion to make requisitions of men and money; to govern the army and navy; to direct their operations. As their requisitions are made constitutionally binding upon the States, who are in fact under the most solemn obligations to furnish the supplies required of them, the intention evidently was that the United States should command whatever resources were by them judged requisite to the "common defense and general welfare." It was presumed that a sense of their true interests, and a regard to the dictates of good faith, would be found sufficient pledges for the punctual performance of the duty of the members to the federal head.

The experiment has, however, demonstrated that this expectation was ill-founded and illusory; and the observations made under the last head will, I imagine, have sufficed to convince the impartial and discerning that there is an absolute necessity for an entire change in the first principles of the system; that if we are in earnest about giving the Union energy and duration we must abandon the vain project of legislating upon the States in their collective capacities; we must extend the laws of the federal government to the individual citizens of America; we must discard the fallacious scheme of quotas and requisitions as equally impracticable and unjust. The result from all this is that the Union ought to be invested with full power to levy troops; to build and equip fleets; and to raise the revenues which will be required for the formation and support of an army and navy in the customary and ordinary modes practiced in other governments.

If the circumstances of our country are such as to demand a compound instead of a simple, a confederate instead of a sole, government, the essential point which will remain to be adjusted will be to discriminate the OBJECTS, as far as it can be done, which shall appertain to the different provinces or departments of power; allowing to each the most ample authority for fulfilling the objects committed to its charge. Shall the Union be constituted the guardian of the common safety? Are fleets and armies and revenues necessary to this purpose? The government of the Union must be empowered to pass all laws, and to make all regulations which have relation to them. The same must be the case in respect to commerce, and to every other matter to which its jurisdiction is permitted to extend. Is the administration of justice between the citizens of the same State the proper department of the local governments? These must possess all the authorities which are connected with this object, and with every other that may be allotted to their particular cognizance and direction. Not to confer in each case a degree of power commensurate to the end would be to violate the most obvious rules of prudence and propriety, and improvidently to trust the great interests of the nation to hands which are disabled from managing them with vigor and success.

Who so likely to make suitable provisions for the public defense as that body to which the guardianship of the public safety is confided; which, as the center of information, will best understand the extent and urgency of the dangers that threaten; as the representative of the WHOLE, will feel itself most deeply interested in the preservation of every part; which, from the responsibility implied in the duty assigned to it, will be most sensibly impressed with the necessity of proper exertions; and which, by the extension of its authority throughout the States, can alone establish uniformity and concert in the plans and measures by which the common safety is to be secured? Is there not a manifest inconsistency in devolving upon the federal government the care of the general defense and leaving in the State governments the *effective* powers by which it is to be provided for? Is not a want of co-operation the infallible consequence of such a system? And will not weakness, disorder, an undue distribution of the burdens and calamities of war, an unnecessary and intolerable increase of expense, be its natural and inevitable concomitants? Have we not had unequivocal experience of its effects in the course of the revolution which we have just achieved?

Every view we may take of the subject, as candid inquirers after truth, will serve to convince us that it is both unwise and dangerous to deny the federal government an unconfined authority in respect to all those objects which are intrusted to its management. It will indeed deserve the most vigilant and careful attention of the people to see that it be modeled in such a manner as to admit of its being safely vested with the requisite powers. If any plan which has been, or may be, offered to our consideration should not, upon a dispassionate inspection, be found to answer this description, it ought to be rejected. A government, the constitution of which renders it unfit to be trusted with all the powers which a free people *ought to delegate to any government*, would be an unsafe and improper depositary of the NATIONAL INTERESTS. Wherever THESE can with propriety be confided, the co-incident powers may safely accompany them. This is the true result of all just reasoning upon the subject. And the adversaries of the plan promulgated by the convention would have given a better impression of their candor if they had confined themselves to showing that the internal structure of the proposed government was such as to render it unworthy of the confidence of the people. They ought not to have wandered into inflammatory declamations and unmeaning cavils about the extent of the powers. The POWERS are not too extensive for the OBJECTS of federal administration, or, in other words, for the management of our NATIONAL INTERESTS; nor can any satisfactory argument be framed to show that they are chargeable with such an excess. If it be true, as has been insinuated by some of the writers on the other side, that the difficulty arises from the nature of the thing, and that the extent of the country will not permit us to form a government in which such ample powers can safely be reposed, it would prove that we ought to contract our views, and resort to the expedient of separate confederacies, which will move within more practicable spheres. For the absurdity must continually stare us in the face of confiding to a government the direction of the most essential national interests, without daring to trust it to the authorities which are indispensable to their proper and efficient management. Let us not attempt to reconcile contradictions, but firmly embrace a rational alternative.

I trust, however, that the impracticability of one general system cannot be shown. I am greatly mistaken if anything of weight has yet been advanced of this tendency; and I flatter myself that the observations which have been made in the course of these papers have served to place the reverse of that position in as clear a light as any matter still in the womb of time and experience is susceptible of. This, at all events, must be evident, that the very difficulty itself, drawn from the extent of the country, is the strongest argument in favor of an energetic government; for any other can certainly never preserve the Union of so large an empire. If we embrace the tenets of those who oppose the adoption of the proposed Constitution as the standard of our political creed we cannot fail to verify the gloomy doctrines which predict the impracticability of a national system pervading the entire limits of the present Confederacy.

PUBLIUS

No. 29: Concerning the Militia

The power of regulating the militia and of commanding its services in times of insurrection and invasion are natural incidents to the duties of superintending the common defense, and of watching over the internal peace of the Confederacy.

It requires no skill in the science of war to discern that uniformity in the organization and discipline of the militia would be attended with the most beneficial effects, whenever they were called into service for the public defense. It would enable them to discharge the duties of the camp and of the field with mutual intelligence and concert—an advantage of peculiar moment in the operations of an army; and it would fit them much sooner to acquire the degree of proficiency in military functions which would be essential to their usefulness. This desirable uniformity can only be accomplished by confiding the regulation of the militia to the direction of the national authority. It is, therefore, with the most evident propriety that the plan of the convention proposes to empower the Union "to provide for organizing, arming, and disciplining the militia, and for governing such part of them as may be employed in the service of the United States, *reserving to the States respectively the appointment of the officers, and the authority of training the militia according to the discipline prescribed by Congress.*"

Of the different grounds which have been taken in opposition to this plan there is none that was so little to have been expected, or is so untenable in itself, as the one from which this particular provision has been attacked. If a well-regulated militia be the most natural defense of a free country, it ought certainly to be under the regulation and at the disposal of that body which is constituted the guardian of the national security. If standing armies are dangerous to liberty, an efficacious power over the militia in the same body ought, as far as possible, to take away the inducement and the pretext to such unfriendly institutions. If the federal government can command the aid of the militia in those emergencies which call for the military arm in support of the civil magistrate, it can the better dispense with the employment of a different kind of force. If it cannot avail itself of the former, it will be obliged to recur to the latter. To render an army unnecessary will be a more certain method of preventing its existence than a thousand prohibitions upon paper.

In order to cast an odium upon the power of calling forth the militia to execute the laws of the Union, it has been remarked that there is nowhere any provision in the proposed Constitution for requiring the aid of the POSSE COMITATUS to assist the magistrate in the execution of his duty; whence it has been inferred that military force was intended to be his only auxiliary. There is a striking incoherence in the objections which have appeared, and sometimes even from the same quarter, not much calculated to inspire a very favorable opinion of the sincerity or fair dealing of their authors. The same persons who tell us in one breath that the powers of the federal government will be despotic and unlimited, inform us in the next that it has not authority sufficient even to call out the POSSE COMITATUS. The latter, fortunately, is as much short of the truth as the former exceeds it. It would be absurd to doubt that a right to pass all laws *necessary* and *proper* to execute its declared powers would include that of requiring the assistance of the citizens to the officers who may be intrusted with the execution of those laws, as it would be to believe that a right to enact laws necessary and proper for the imposition and collection of taxes would involve that of varying the rules of descent and of the alienation of landed property, or of abolishing the trial by jury in cases relating to it. It being therefore evident that the supposition of a want of power to require the aid of the POSSE COMITATUS is entirely destitute of color, it will follow that the conclusion which has been drawn from it, in its application to the authority of the federal government over the militia, is as uncandid as it is illogical. What reason could there be to infer that force was intended to be the sole instrument of authority, merely because there is a power to make use of it when necessary? What shall we think of the motives which could induce men of sense to reason in this extraordinary manner? How shall we prevent a conflict between charity and conviction?

By a curious refinement upon the spirit of republican jealousy, we are even taught to apprehend danger from the militia itself in the hands of the federal government. It is observed that select corps may be formed, composed of the young and the ardent, who may be rendered subservient to the views of arbitrary power. What plan for the regulation of the militia may be pursued by the national government is impossible to be foreseen. But so far from viewing the matter in the same light with those who object to select corps as dangerous, were the Constitution ratified and were I to deliver my sentiments to a member of the federal legislature on the subject of a militia establishment, I should hold to him, in the substance, the following discourse:

"The project of disciplining all the militia of the United States is as futile as it would be injurious if it were capable of being carried into execution. A tolerable expertness in military movements is a business that requires time and practice. It is not a day, nor a week nor even a month, that will suffice for the attainment of it. To oblige the great body of the yeomanry and of the other classes of the citizens to be under arms for the purpose of going through military exercises and evolutions, as often as might be necessary to acquire the degree of perfection which would entitle them to the character of a well-regulated militia, would be a real grievance to the people and a serious public inconvenience and loss. It would form an annual deduction from the productive labor of the country to an amount which, calculating upon the present numbers of the people, would not fall far short of a million pounds. To attempt a thing which would abridge the mass of labor and industry to so considerable an extent would be unwise: and the experiment, if made, could not succeed, because it would not long be endured. Little more can reasonably be aimed at with respect to the people at large than to have them properly armed and equipped; and in order to see that this be not neglected, it will be necessary to assemble them once or twice in the course of a year.

"But though the scheme of disciplining the whole nation must be abandoned as mischievous or impracticable; yet it is a matter of the utmost importance that a well-digested plan should, as soon as possible, be adopted for the proper establishment of the militia. The attention of the government ought particularly to be directed to the formation of a select corps of moderate size, upon such principles as will really fit it for service in case of need. By thus circumscribing the plan, it will be possible to have an excellent body of well-trained militia ready to take the field whenever the defense of the State shall require it. This will not only lessen the call for military establishments, but if circumstances should at any time oblige the government to form an army of any magnitude, that army can never be formidable to the liberties of the people while there is a large body of citizens, little if at all inferior to them in discipline and the use of arms, who stand ready to defend their own rights and those of their fellow-citizens. This appears to me the only substitute that can be devised for a standing army, and the best possible security against it, if it should exist."

Thus differently from the adversaries of the proposed Constitution should I reason on the same subject, deducing arguments of safety from the very sources which they represent as fraught with danger and perdition. But how the national legislature may reason on the point is a thing which neither they nor I can foresee.

There is something so far-fetched and so extravagant in the idea of danger to liberty from the militia that one is at a loss whether to treat it with gravity or with raillery; whether to consider it as a mere trial of skill, like the paradoxes of rhetoricians; as a disingenuous artifice to instil prejudices at any price; or as the serious offspring of political fanaticism. Where in the name of common sense are our fears to end if we may not trust our sons, our brothers, our neighbors, our fellow-citizens? What shadow of danger can there be from men who are daily mingling with the rest of their countrymen and who participate with them in the same feelings, sentiments, habits, and interests? What reasonable cause of apprehension can be inferred from a power in the Union to prescribe regulations for the militia and to command its services when necessary, while the particular States are to have the *sole and exclusive appointment of the officers?* If it were possible seriously to indulge a jealousy of the militia upon any conceivable establishment under the federal government, the circumstance of the officers being in the appointment of the States ought at once to extinguish it. There can be no doubt that this circumstance will always secure to them a preponderating influence over the militia.

In reading many of the publications against the Constitution, a man is apt to imagine that he is perusing some ill-written tale or romance, which, instead of natural and agreeable images, exhibits to the mind nothing but frightful and distorted shapes—

"Gorgons, Hydras, and Chimeras dire;"

discoloring and disfiguring whatever it represents, and transforming everything it touches into a monster.

A sample of this is to be observed in the exaggerated and improbable suggestions which have taken place respecting the power of calling for the services of the militia. That of New Hampshire is to be marched to Georgia, of Georgia to New Hampshire, of New York to Kentucky, and of Kentucky to Lake Champlain. Nay, the debts due to the French and Dutch are to be paid in militiamen instead of Louis d'ors and ducats. At one moment there is to be a large army to lay prostrate the liberties of the people; at another moment the militia of Virginia are to be dragged from their homes five or six hundred miles to tame the republican contumacy of Massachusetts; and that of Massachusetts is to be transported an equal distance to subdue the refractory haughtiness of the aristocratic Virginians. Do the persons who rave at this rate imagine that their art or their eloquence can impose any conceits or absurdities upon the people of America for infallible truths?

If there should be an army to be made use of as the engine of despotism, what need of the militia? If there should be no army, whither would the militia, irritated at being required to undertake a distant and distressing expedition for the purpose of riveting the chains of slavery upon a part of their countrymen, direct their course, but to the seat of the tyrants, who had meditated so foolish as well as so wicked a project to crush them in their imagined entrenchments of power, and to make them an example of the just vengeance of an abused and incensed people? Is this the way in which usurpers stride to dominion over a numerous and enlightened nation? Do they begin by exciting the detestation of the very instruments of their intended usurpations? Do they usually commence their career by wanton and disgustful acts of power, calculated to answer no end, but to draw upon themselves universal hatred and execration? Are suppositions of this sort the sober admonitions of discerning patriots to a discerning people? Or are they the inflammatory ravings of chagrined incendiaries or distempered enthusiasts? If we were even to suppose the national rulers actuated by the most ungovernable ambition, it is impossible to believe that they would employ such preposterous means to accomplish their designs.

In times of insurrection, or invasion, it would be natural and proper that the militia of a neighboring State should be marched into another, to resist a common enemy, or to guard the republic against the violence of faction or sedition. This was frequently the case in respect to the first object in the course of the late war; and this mutual succor is, indeed, a principal end of our political association. If the power of affording it be placed under the direction of the Union, there will be no danger of a supine and listless inattention to the dangers of a neighbor till its near approach had superadded the incitements of self-preservation to the too feeble impulses of duty and sympathy.

PUBLIUS

No. 30: Concerning the General Power of Taxation

It has been already observed that the federal government ought to possess the power of providing for the support of the national forces; in which proposition was intended to be included the expense of raising troops, of building and equipping fleets, and all other expenses in any wise connected with military arrangements and operations. But these are not the only objects to which the jurisdiction of the Union in respect to revenue must necessarily be empowered to extend. It must embrace a provision for the support of the national civil list; for the payment of the national debts contracted, or that may be contracted; and, in general, for all those matters which will call for disbursements out of the national treasury. The conclusion is that there must be interwoven in the frame of the government a general power of taxation, in one shape or another.

Money is, with propriety, considered as the vital principle of the body politic; as that which sustains its life and motion and enables it to perform its most essential functions. A complete power, therefore, to procure a regular and adequate supply of revenue, as far as the resources of the community will permit, may be regarded as an indispensable ingredient in every constitution. From a deficiency in this particular, one of two evils must ensue: either the people must be subjected to continual plunder, as a substitute for a more eligible mode of supplying the public wants, or the government must sink into a fatal atrophy, and, in a short course of time, perish.

In the Ottoman or Turkish empire the sovereign, though in other respects absolute master of the lives and fortunes of his subjects, has no right to impose a new tax. The consequence is that he permits the bashaws or governors of provinces to pillage the people at discretion, and, in turn, squeezes out of them the sums of which he stands in need to satisfy his own exigencies and those of the state. In America, from a like cause, the government of the Union has gradually dwindled into a state of decay, approaching nearly to annihilation. Who can doubt that the happiness of the people in both countries would be promoted by competent authorities in the proper hands to provide the revenues which the necessities of the public might require?

The present Confederation, feeble as it is, intended to repose in the United States an unlimited power of providing for the pecuniary wants of the Union. But proceeding upon an erroneous principle, it has been done in such a manner as entirely to have frustrated the intention. Congress, by the articles which compose that compact (as has already been stated), are authorized to ascertain and call for any sums of money necessary in their judgment to the service of the United States; and their requisitions, if conformable to the rule of apportionment, are in every constitutional sense obligatory upon the States. These have no right to question the propriety of the demand; no discretion beyond that of devising the ways and means of furnishing the sums demanded. But though this be strictly and truly the case; though the assumption of such a right would be an infringement of the articles of Union; though it may seldom or never have been avowedly claimed, yet in practice it has been constantly exercised and would continue to be so, as long as the revenues of the Confederacy should remain dependent on the intermediate agency of its members. What the consequences of this system have been is within the knowledge of every man the least conversant in our public affairs, and has been abundantly unfolded in different parts of these inquiries. It is this which affords ample cause of mortification to ourselves, and of triumph to our enemies.

What remedy can there be for this situation, but in a change of the system which has produced it—in a change of the fallacious and delusive system of quotas and requisitions? What substitute can there be imagined for this *ignis fatuus* in finance, but that of permitting the national government to raise its own revenues by the ordinary methods of taxation authorized in every well-ordered constitution of civil government? Ingenious men may declaim with plausibility on any subject; but no human ingenuity can point out any other expedient to rescue us from the inconveniences and embarrassments naturally resulting from defective supplies of the public treasury.

The more intelligent adversaries of the new Constitution admit the force of this reasoning; but they qualify their admission by a distinction between what they call *internal* and *external* taxation. The former they would reserve to the State governments; the latter, which they explain into commercial imposts, or rather duties on imported articles, they declare themselves willing to concede to the federal head. This distinction, however, would violate that fundamental maxim of good sense and sound policy, which dictates that every POWER ought to be proportionate to its OBJECT; and would still leave the general government in a kind of tutelage to the State governments, inconsistent with every idea of vigor or efficiency. Who can pretend that commercial imposts are, or would be, alone equal to the present and future exigencies of the Union? Taking into the account the existing debt, foreign and domestic, upon any plan of extinguishment which a man moderately impressed with the importance of public justice and public credit could approve, in addition to the establishments which all parties will acknowledge to be necessary, we could not reasonably flatter ourselves that this resource alone, upon the most improved scale, would even suffice for its present necessities. Its future necessities admit not of calculation or limitation; and upon the principle more than once adverted to the power of making provision for them as they arise ought to be equally unconfined. I believe it may be regarded as a position warranted by the history of mankind that, *in the usual progress of things, the necessities of a nation, in every stage of its existence, will be found at least equal to its resources.*

To say that deficiencies may be provided for by requisitions upon the States is on the one hand to acknowledge that this system cannot be depended upon, and on the other hand to depend upon it for every thing beyond a certain limit. Those who have carefully attended to its vices and deformities as they have been exhibited by experience or delineated in the course of these papers must feel an invincible repugnancy to trusting the national interests in any degree to its operation. Its inevitable tendency, whenever it is brought into activity, must be to enfeeble the Union, and sow the seeds of discord and contention between the federal head and its members, and between the members themselves. Can it be expected that the deficiencies would be better supplied in this mode than the total wants of the Union have heretofore been supplied in the same mode? It ought to be recollected that if less will be required from the States, they will have proportionably less means to answer the demand. If the opinions of those who contend for the distinction which has been mentioned were to be received as evidence of truth, one would be led to conclude that there was some known point in the economy of national affairs at which it would be safe to stop and to say: Thus far the ends of public happiness will be promoted by supplying the wants of government, and all beyond this is unworthy of our care or anxiety. How is it possible that a government half supplied and always necessitous can fulfil the purposes of its institution, can provide for the security, advance the prosperity, or support the reputation of the commonwealth? How can it ever possess either energy or stability, dignity or credit, confidence at home or respectability abroad? How can its administration be anything else than a succession of expedients temporizing, impotent, disgraceful? How will it be able to avoid a frequent sacrifice of its engagements to immediate necessity? How can it undertake or execute any liberal or enlarged plans of public good?

Let us attend to what would be the effects of this situation in the very first war in which we should happen to be engaged. We will presume, for argument's sake, that the revenue arising from the impost duties answers the purposes of a provision for the public debt and of a peace establishment for the Union. Thus circumstanced, a war breaks out. What would be the probable conduct of the government in such an emergency? Taught by experience that proper dependence could not be placed on the success of requisitions, unable by its own authority to lay hold of fresh resources, and urged by considerations of national danger, would it not be driven to the expedient of diverting the funds already appropriated from their proper objects to the defense of the State? It is not easy to see how a step of this kind could be avoided; and if it should be taken, it is evident that it would prove the destruction of public credit at the very moment that it was becoming essential to the public safety. To imagine that at such a crisis credit might be dispensed with would be the extreme of infatuation. In the modern system of war, nations the most wealthy are obliged to have recourse to large loans. A country so little opulent as ours must feel this necessity in a much stronger degree. But who would lend to a government that prefaced its overtures for borrowing by an act which demonstrated that no reliance could be placed on the steadiness of its measures for paying? The loans it might be able to procure would be as limited in their extent as burdensome in their conditions. They would be made upon the same principles that usurers commonly lend to bankrupt and fraudulent debtors—with a sparing hand and at enormous premiums.

It may perhaps be imagined that from the scantiness of the resources of the country the necessity of diverting the established funds in the case supposed would exist, though the national government should possess an unrestrained power of taxation. But two considerations will serve to quiet all apprehension on this head: one is that we are sure the resources of the community, in their full extent, will be brought into activity for the benefit of the Union; the other is that whatever deficiencies there may be can without difficulty be supplied by loans.

The power of creating new funds upon new objects of taxation by its own authority would enable the national government to borrow as far as its necessities might require. Foreigners, as well as the citizens of America, could then reasonably repose confidence in its engagements; but to depend upon a government that must itself depend upon thirteen other governments for the means of fulfilling its contracts, when once its situation is clearly understood, would require a degree of credulity not often to be met with in the pecuniary transactions of mankind, and little reconcilable with the usual sharp-sightedness of avarice.

Reflections of this kind may have trifling weight with men who hope to see realized in America the halcyon scenes of the poetic or fabulous age; but to those who believe we are likely to experience a common portion of the vicissitudes and calamities which have fallen to the lot of other nations, they must appear entitled to serious attention. Such men must behold the actual situation of their country with painful solicitude, and deprecate the evils which ambition or revenge might, with too much facility, inflict upon it.

PUBLIUS

No. 33: The Same Subject Continued

The residue of the argument against the provisions of the Constitution in respect to taxation is ingrafted upon the following clauses. The last clause of the eighth section of the first article authorizes the national legislature "to make all laws which shall be *necessary* and *proper* for carrying into execution *the powers* by that Constitution vested in the government of the United States, or in any department or officer thereof"; and the second clause of the sixth article declares that "the Constitution and the laws of the United States made *in pursuance thereof* and the treaties made by their authority shall be the *supreme law* of the land, anything in the constitution or laws of any State to the contrary notwithstanding."

These two clauses have been the source of much virulent invective and petulant declamation against the proposed Constitution. They have been held up to the people in all the exaggerated colors of misrepresentation as the pernicious engines by which their local governments were to be destroyed and their liberties exterminated; as the hideous monster whose devouring jaws would spare neither sex nor age, nor high nor low, nor sacred nor profane; and yet, strange as it may appear, after all this clamor, to those who may not have happened to contemplate them in the same light, it may be affirmed with perfect confidence that the constitutional operation of the intended government would be precisely the same if these clauses were entirely obliterated as if they were repeated in every article. They are only declaratory of a truth which would have resulted by necessary and unavoidable implication from the very act of constituting a federal government and vesting it with certain specified powers. This is so clear a proposition, that moderation itself can scarcely listen to the railings which have been so copiously vented against this part of the plan, without emotions that disturb its equanimity.

What is a power but the ability or faculty of doing a thing? What is the ability to do a thing but the power of employing the *means* necessary to its execution? What is a LEGISLATIVE power but a power of making LAWS? What are the *means* to execute a LEGISLATIVE power but LAWS? What is the power of laying and collecting taxes but a *legislative power,* or a power of *making laws* to lay and collect taxes? What are the proper means of executing such a power but *necessary* and *proper* laws?

This simple train of inquiry furnishes us at once with a test of the true nature of the clause complained of. It conducts us to this palpable truth that a power to lay and collect taxes must be a power to pass all laws *necessary* and *proper* for the execution of that power; and what does the unfortunate and calumniated provision in question do more than declare the same truth, to wit, that the national legislature to whom the power of laying and collecting taxes had been previously given might, in the execution of that power, pass all laws *necessary* and *proper* to carry it into effect? I have applied these observations thus particularly to the power of taxation, because it is the immediate subject under consideration and because it is the most important of the authorities proposed to be conferred upon the Union. But the same process will lead to the same result in relation to all other powers declared in the Constitution. And it is *expressly* to execute these powers that the sweeping clause, as it has been affectedly called, authorizes the national legislature to pass all *necessary* and *proper* laws. If there be anything exceptionable, it must be sought for in the specific powers upon which this general declaration is predicated. The declaration itself, though it may be chargeable with tautology or redundancy, is at least perfectly harmless.

But SUSPICION may ask, Why then was it introduced? The answer is that it could only have been done for greater caution, and to guard against all cavilling refinements in those who might hereafter feel a disposition to curtail and evade the legitimate authorities of the Union. The Convention probably foresaw what it has been a principal aim of these papers to inculcate, that the danger which most threatens our political welfare is that the State governments will finally sap the foundations of the Union; and might therefore think it necessary, in so cardinal a point, to leave nothing to construction. Whatever may have been the inducement to it, the wisdom of the precaution is evident from the cry which has been raised against it; as that very cry betrays a disposition to question the great and essential truth which it is manifestly the object of that provision to declare.

But it may be again asked, Who is to judge of the *necessity* and *propriety* of the laws to be passed for executing the powers of the Union? I answer first that this question arises as well and as fully upon the simple grant of those powers as upon the declaratory clause; and I answer in the second place that the national government, like every other, must judge, in the first instance, of the proper exercise of its powers, and its constituents in the last. If the federal government should overpass the just bounds of its authority and make a tyrannical use of its powers, the people, whose creature it is, must appeal to the standard they have formed, and take such measures to redress the injury done to the Constitution as the exigency may suggest and prudence justify. The propriety of a law, in a constitutional light, must always be determined by the nature of the powers upon which it is founded. Suppose, by some forced constructions of its authority (which, indeed, cannot easily be imagined), the federal legislature should attempt to vary the law of descent in any State, would it not be evident that in making such an attempt it had exceeded its jurisdiction and infringed upon that of the State? Suppose, again, that upon the pretense of an interference with its revenues, it should undertake to abrogate a land tax imposed by the authority of a State; would it not be equally evident that this was an invasion of that concurrent jurisdiction in respect to this species of tax, which its Constitution plainly supposes to exist in the State governments? If there ever should be a doubt on this head, the credit of it will be entirely due to those reasoners who, in the imprudent zeal of their animosity to the plan of the convention, have labored to envelop it in a cloud calculated to obscure the plainest and simplest truths.

But it is said that the laws of the Union are to be the *supreme law* of the land. What inference can be drawn from this, or what would they amount to, if they were not to be supreme? It is evident they would amount to nothing. A LAW, by the very meaning of the term, includes supremacy. It is a rule which those to whom it is prescribed are bound to observe. This results from every political association. If individuals enter into a state of society the laws of that society must be the supreme regulator of their conduct. If a number of political societies enter into a larger political society, the laws which the latter may enact, pursuant to the powers intrusted to it by its constitution, must necessarily be supreme over those societies and the individuals of whom they are composed. It would otherwise be a mere treaty, dependent on the good faith of the parties, and not a government, which is only another word for POLITICAL POWER AND SUPREMACY. But it will not follow from this doctrine that acts of the larger society which are *not pursuant* to its constitutional powers, but which are invasions of the residuary authorities of the smaller societies, will become the supreme law of the land. These will be merely acts of usurpation, and will deserve to be treated as such. Hence we perceive that the clause which declares the supremacy of the laws of the Union, like the one we have just before considered, only declares a truth which flows immediately and necessarily from the institution of a federal government. It will not, I presume, have escaped observation that it *expressly* confines this supremacy to laws made *pursuant to the Constitution*; which I mention merely as an instance of caution in the convention; since that limitation would have been to be understood, though it had not been expressed.

Though a law, therefore, for laying a tax for the use of the United States would be supreme in its nature and could not legally be opposed or controlled, yet a law for abrogating or preventing the collection of a tax laid by the authority of a State (unless upon imports and exports) would not be the supreme law of the land, but a usurpation of power not granted by the Constitution. As far as an improper accumulation of taxes on the same object might tend to render the collection difficult or precarious, this would be a mutual inconvenience, not arising from a superiority or defect of power on either side, but from an injudicious exercise of power by one or the other in a manner equally disadvantageous to both. It is to be hoped and presumed, however, that mutual interest would dictate a concert in this respect which would avoid any material inconvenience. The inference from the whole is that the individual States would, under the proposed Constitution, retain an independent and uncontrollable authority to raise revenue to any extent of which they may stand in need, by every kind of taxation, except duties on imports and exports. It will be shown in the next paper that this *concurrent jurisdiction* in the article of taxation was the only admissible substitute for an entire subordination, in respect to this branch of power, of the State authority to that of the Union.

PUBLIUS

No. 35: The Same Subject Continued

Before we proceed to examine any other objections to an indefinite power of taxation in the Union, I shall make one general remark; which is that if the jurisdiction of the national government in the article of revenue should be restricted to particular objects, it would naturally occasion an undue proportion of the public burdens to fall upon those objects. Two evils would spring from this source: the oppression of particular branches of industry; and an unequal distribution of the taxes, as well among the several States as among the citizens of the same State.

Suppose, as has been contended for, the federal power of taxation were to be confined to duties on imports, it is evident that the government, for want of being able to command other resources, would frequently be tempted to extend these duties to an injurious excess. There are persons who imagine that it can never be the case; since the higher they are, the more it is alleged they will tend to discourage an extravagant consumption to produce a favorable balance of trade and to promote domestic manufactures. But all extremes are pernicious in various ways. Exorbitant duties on imported articles would serve to beget a general spirit of smuggling; which is always prejudicial to the fair trader, and eventually to the revenue itself: they tend to render other classes of the community tributary in an improper degree to the manufacturing classes, to whom they give a premature monopoly of the markets; they sometimes force industry out of its more natural channels into others in which it flows with less advantage; and in the last place, they oppress the merchant, who is often obliged to pay them himself without any retribution from the consumer. When the demand is equal to the quantity of goods at market, the consumer generally pays the duty; but when the markets happen to be overstocked, a great proportion falls upon the merchant, and sometimes not only exhausts his profits, but breaks in upon his capital. I am apt to think that a division of the duty, between the seller and the buyer, more often happens than is commonly imagined. It is not always possible to raise the price of a commodity in exact proportion to every additional imposition laid upon it. The merchant especially, in a country of small commercial capital, is often under a necessity of keeping prices down in order to make a more expeditious sale.

The maxim that the consumer is the payer is so much oftener true than the reverse of the proposition, that it is far more equitable that the duties on imports should go into a common stock than that they should redound to the exclusive benefit of the importing States. But it is not so generally true as to render it equitable that those duties should form the only national fund. When they are paid by the merchant they operate as an additional tax upon the importing State, whose citizens pay their proportion of them in the character of consumers. In this view they are productive of inequality among the States; which inequality would be increased with the increased extent of the duties. The confinement of the national revenues to this species of imposts would be attended with inequality, from a different cause, between the manufacturing and the non-manufacturing States. The States which can go furthest towards the supply of their own wants by their own manufactures will not, according to their numbers or wealth, consume so great a proportion of imported articles as those States which are not in the same favorable situation. They would not, therefore, in this mode alone contribute to the public treasury in a ratio to their abilities. To make them do this it is necessary that recourse be had to excises, the proper objects of which are particular kinds of manufactures. New York is more deeply interested in these considerations than such of her citizens as contend for limiting the power of the Union to external taxation may be aware of. New York is an importing State, and from a greater disproportion between her population and territory is less likely, than some other States, speedily to become in any considerable degree a manufacturing State. She would, of course, suffer in a double light from restraining the jurisdiction of the Union to commercial imposts.

So far as these observations tend to inculcate a danger of the import duties being extended to an injurious extreme it may be observed, conformably to a remark made in another part of these papers, that the interest of the revenue itself would be a sufficient guard against such an extreme. I readily admit that this would be the case as long as other resources were open; but if the avenues to them were closed, HOPE, stimulated by necessity, might beget experiments, fortified by rigorous precautions and additional penalties, which, for a time, might have the intended effect, till there had been leisure to contrive expedients to elude these new precautions. The first success would be apt to inspire false opinions, which it might require a long course of subsequent experience to correct. Necessity, especially in politics, often occasions false hopes, false reasonings, and a system of measures correspondingly erroneous. But even if this supposed excess should not be a consequence of the limitation of the federal power of taxation, the inequalities spoken of would still ensue, though not in the same degree, from the other causes that have been noticed. Let us now return to the examination of objections.

One which, if we may judge from the frequency of its repetition, seems most to be relied on, is that the House of Representatives is not sufficiently numerous for the reception of all the different classes of citizens in order to combine the interests and feelings of every part of the community, and to produce a true sympathy between the representative body and its constituents. This argument presents itself under a very specious and seducing form; and is well calculated to lay hold of the prejudices of those to whom it is addressed. But when we come to dissect it with attention, it will appear to be made up of nothing but fair-sounding words. The object it seems to aim at is, in the first place, impracticable, and in the sense in which it is contended for, is unnecessary. I reserve for another place the discussion of the question which relates to the sufficiency of the representative body in respect to numbers, and shall content myself with examining here the particular use which has been made of a contrary supposition in reference to the immediate subject of our inquiries.

The idea of an actual representation of all classes of the people by persons of each class is altogether visionary. Unless it were expressly provided in the Constitution that each different occupation should send one or more members, the thing would never take place in practice. Mechanics and manufacturers will always be inclined, with few exceptions, to give their votes to merchants in preference to persons of their own professions or trades. Those discerning citizens are well aware that the mechanic and manufacturing arts furnish the materials of mercantile enterprise and industry. Many of them, indeed, are immediately connected with the operations of commerce. They know that the merchant is their natural patron and friend; and they are aware that however great the confidence they may justly feel in their own good sense, their interests can be more effectually promoted by the merchant than by themselves. They are sensible that their habits in life have not been such as to give them those acquired endowments, without which in a deliberative assembly the greatest natural abilities are for the most part useless; and that the influence and weight and superior acquirements of the merchants render them more equal to a contest with any spirit which might happen to infuse itself into the public councils, unfriendly to the manufacturing and trading interests. These considerations and many others that might be mentioned prove, and experience confirms it, that artisans and manufacturers will commonly be disposed to bestow their votes upon merchants and those whom they recommend. We must therefore consider merchants as the natural representatives of all these classes of the community.

With regard to the learned professions, little need be observed; they truly form no distinct interest in society, and according to their situation and talents, will be indiscriminately the objects of the confidence and choice of each other and of other parts of the community.

Nothing remains but the landed interest; and this in a political view, and particularly in relation to taxes, I take to be perfectly united from the wealthiest landlord to the poorest tenant. No tax can be laid on land which will not affect the proprietor of millions of acres as well as the proprietor of a single acre. Every landholder will therefore have a common interest to keep the taxes on land as low as possible; and common interest may always be reckoned upon as the surest bond of sympathy. But if we even could suppose a distinction of interest between the opulent landholder and the middling farmer, what reason is there to conclude that the first would stand a better chance of being deputed to the national legislature than the last? If we take fact as our guide, and look into our own senate and assembly, we shall find that moderate proprietors of land prevail in both; nor is this less the case in the senate, which consists of a smaller number than in the assembly, which is composed of a greater number. Where the qualifications of the electors are the same, whether they have to choose a small or a large number, their votes will fall upon those in whom they have most confidence; whether these happen to be men of large fortunes, or of moderate property, or of no property at all.

It is said to be necessary that all classes of citizens should have some of their own number in the representative body in order that their feelings and interests may be the better understood and attended to. But we have seen that this will never happen under any arrangement that leaves the votes of the people free. Where this is the case, the representative body, with too few exceptions to have any influence on the spirit of the government, will be composed of landholders, merchants, and men of the learned professions. But where is the danger that the interests and feelings of the different classes of citizens will not be understood or attended to by these three descriptions of men? Will not the landholder know and feel whatever will promote or injure the interest of landed property? And will he not, from his own interest in that species of property, be sufficiently prone to resist every attempt to prejudice or encumber it? Will not the merchant understand and be disposed to cultivate, as far as may be proper, the interests of the mechanic and manufacturing arts to which his commerce is so nearly allied? Will not the man of the learned profession, who will feel a neutrality to the rivalships between the different branches of industry, be likely to prove an impartial arbiter between them, ready to promote either, so far as it shall appear to him conducive to the general interests of the society?

If we take into the account the momentary humors or dispositions which may happen to prevail in particular parts of the society, and to which a wise administration will never be inattentive, is the man whose situation leads to extensive inquiry and information less likely to be a competent judge of their nature, extent, and foundation than one whose observation does not travel beyond the circle of his neighbors and acquaintances? Is it not natural that a man who is a candidate for the favor of the people, and who is dependent on the suffrages of his fellow-citizens for the continuance of his public honors, should take care to inform himself of their dispositions and inclinations and should be willing to allow them their proper degree of influence upon his conduct? This dependence, and the necessity of being bound, himself and his posterity, by the laws to which he gives his assent are the true, and they are the strong chords of sympathy between the representative and the constituent.

There is no part of the administration of government that requires extensive information and a thorough knowledge of the principles of political economy so much as the business of taxation. The man who understands those principles best will be least likely to resort to oppressive expedients, or to sacrifice any particular class of citizens to the procurement of revenue. It might be demonstrated that the most productive system of finance will always be the least burdensome. There can be no doubt that in order to have a judicious exercise of the power of taxation, it is necessary that the person in whose hands it is should be acquainted with the general genius, habits, and modes of thinking of the people at large, and with the resources of the country. And this is all that can be reasonably meant by a knowledge of the interests and feelings of the people. In any other sense the proposition has either no meaning, or an absurd one. And in that sense let every considerate citizen judge for himself where the requisite qualification is most likely to be found.

PUBLIUS

No. 67: The Executive Department

The constitution of the executive department of the proposed government claims next our attention.

There is hardly any part of the system which could have been attended with greater difficulty in the arrangement of it than this; and there is, perhaps, none which has been inveighed against with less candor or criticized with less judgment.

Here the writers against the Constitution seem to have taken pains to signalize their talent of misrepresentation. Calculating upon the aversion of the people to monarchy, they have endeavored to enlist all their jealousies and apprehensions in opposition to the intended President of the United States; not merely as the embryo, but as the full-grown progeny of that detested parent. To establish the pretended affinity, they have not scrupled to draw resources even from the regions of fiction. The authorities of a magistrate, in few instances greater, in some instances less, than those of a governor of New York, have been magnified into more than royal prerogatives. He has been decorated with attributes superior in dignity and splendor to those of a king of Great Britain. He has been shown to us with the diadem sparkling on his brow and the imperial purple flowing in his train. He has been seated on a throne surrounded with minions and mistresses, giving audience to the envoys of foreign potentates in all the supercilious pomp of majesty. The images of Asiatic despotism and voluptuousness have scarcely been wanting to crown the exaggerated scene. We have been almost taught to tremble at the terrific visages of murdering janizaries, and to blush at the unveiled mysteries of a future seraglio.

Attempts so extravagant as these to disfigure or, it might rather be said, to metamorphose the object, render it necessary to take an accurate view of its real nature and form: in order as well to ascertain its true aspect and genuine appearance, as to unmask the disingenuity and expose the fallacy of the counterfeit resemblances which have been so insidiously, as well as industriously, propagated.

In the execution of this task there is no man who would not find it an arduous effort either to behold with moderation or to treat with seriousness the devices, not less weak than wicked, which have been contrived to pervert the public opinion in relation to the subject. They so far exceed the usual though unjustifiable licenses of party artifice, that even in a disposition the most candid and tolerant, they must force the sentiments which favor an indulgent construction of the conduct of political adversaries to give place to a voluntary and unreserved indignation. It is impossible not to bestow the imputation of deliberate imposture and deception upon the gross pretense of a similitude between a king of Great Britain and a magistrate of the character marked out for that of the President of the United States. It is still more impossible to withhold that imputation from the rash and barefaced expedients which have been employed to give success to the attempted imposition.

In one instance, which I cite as a sample of the general spirit, the temerity has proceeded so far as to ascribe to the President of the United States a power which by the instrument reported is *expressly* alloted to the executives of the individual States. I mean the power of filling casual vacancies in the Senate.

This bold experiment upon the discernment of his countrymen has been hazarded by a writer who (whatever may be his real merit) has had no inconsiderable share in the applauses of his party;[*] and who, upon his false and unfounded suggestion, has built a series of observations equally false and unfounded. Let him now be confronted with the evidence of the fact, and let him, if he be able, justify or extenuate the shameful outrage he has offered to the dictates of truth and to the rules of fair dealing.

The second clause of the second section of the second article empowers the President of the United States "to nominate, and by and with the advice and consent of the Senate, to appoint ambassadors, other public ministers and consuls, judges of the Supreme Court, and all other *officers* of the United States whose appointments are not in the Constitution *otherwise provided for,* and *which shall be established by law.*" Immediately after this clause follows another in these words: "The President shall have power to fill up all vacancies that may happen *during the recess of the Senate,* by granting commissions which shall *expire at the end of their next session.*" It is from this last provision that the pretended power of the President to fill vacancies in the Senate has been deduced. A slight attention to the connection of the clauses and to the obvious meaning of the terms will satisfy us that the deduction is not even colorable.

The first of these two clauses, it is clear, only provides a mode for appointing such officers "whose appointments are *not otherwise provided for* in the Constitution, and which *shall be established by law";* of course

---

[*]See CATO, No. V.

it cannot extend to the appointment of senators, whose appointments are *otherwise provided for* in the Constitution,* and who are *established by the Constitution,* and will not require a future establishment by law. This position will hardly be contested.

The last of these two clauses, it is equally clear, cannot be understood to comprehend the power of filling vacancies in the Senate, for the following reasons:—*First.* The relation in which that clause stands to the other, which declares the general mode of appointing officers of the United States, denotes it to be nothing more than a supplement to the other for the purpose of establishing an auxiliary method of appointment, in cases to which the general method was inadequate. The ordinary power of appointment is confided to the President and Senate *jointly,* and can therefore only be exercised during the session of the Senate; but as it would have been improper to oblige this body to be continually in session for the appointment of officers, and as vacancies might happen *in their recess,* which it might be necessary for the public service to fill without delay, the succeeding clause is evidently intended to authorize the President, *singly,* to make temporary appointments "during the recess of the Senate, by granting commissions which shall expire at the end of their next session." *Second.* If this clause is to be considered as supplementary to the one which precedes, the *vacancies* of which it speaks must be construed to relate to the "officers" described in the preceding one; and this, we have seen, excludes from its description the members of the Senate. *Third.* The time within which the power is to operate "during the recess of the Senate," and the duration of the appointments "to the end of the next session" of that body, conspire to elucidate the sense of the provision which, if it had been intended to comprehend senators, would naturally have referred the temporary power of filling vacancies to the recess of the State legislatures, who are to make the permanent appointments, and not to the recess of the national Senate, who are to have no concern in those appointments; and would have extended the duration in office of the temporary senators to the next session of the legislature of the State, in whose representation the vacancies had happened, instead of making it to expire at the end of the ensuing session of the national Senate. The circumstances of the body authorized to make the permanent appointments would, of course, have governed the modification of a power which related to the temporary appointments; and as the national Senate is the body

---

*Article 1, Section 3, Clause 1.

whose situation is alone contemplated in the clause upon which the suggestion under examination has been founded, the vacancies to which it alludes can only be deemed to respect those officers in whose appointment that body has a concurrent agency with the President. But *lastly,* the first and second clauses of the third section of the first article not only obviate all possibility of doubt, but destroy the pretext of misconception. The former provides that "the Senate of the United States shall be composed of two senators from each State, chosen *by the legislature thereof* for six years"; and the latter directs that "if vacancies in that body should happen by resignation or otherwise, *during the recess of the legislature of* ANY STATE, the executive THEREOF may make temporary appointments until the *next meeting of the legislature,* which shall then fill such vacancies." Here is an express power given, in clear and unambiguous terms, to the State executives to fill casual vacancies in the Senate by temporary appointments; which not only invalidates the supposition that the clause before considered could have been intended to confer that power upon the President of the United States, but proves that this supposition, destitute as it is even of the merit of plausibility, must have originated in an intention to deceive the people, too palpable to be obscured by sophistry, too atrocious to be palliated by hypocrisy.

I have taken the pains to select this instance of misrepresentation and to place it in a clear and strong light, as an unequivocal proof of the unwarrantable arts which are practised to prevent a fair and impartial judgment of the real merits of the Constitution submitted to the consideration of the people. Nor have I scrupled, in so flagrant a case, to allow myself a severity of animadversion little congenial with the general spirit of these papers. I hesitate not to submit it to the decision of any candid and honest adversary of the proposed government whether language can furnish epithets of too much asperity for so shameless and so prostitute an attempt to impose on the citizens of America.

PUBLIUS

No. 70: The Executive Department
Further Considered

There is an idea, which is not without its advocates, that a vigorous executive is inconsistent with the genius of republican government. The enlightened well-wishers to this species of government must at least hope that the supposition is destitute of foundation; since they can never admit its truth, without at the same time admitting the condemnation of their own principles. Energy in the executive is a leading character in the definition of good government. It is essential to the protection of the community against foreign attacks; it is not less essential to the steady administration of the laws; to the protection of property against those irregular and high-handed combinations which sometimes interrupt the ordinary course of justice; to the security of liberty against the enterprises and assaults of ambition, of faction, and of anarchy. Every man the least conversant in Roman history knows how often that republic was obliged to take refuge in the absolute power of a single man, under the formidable title of dictator, as well against the intrigues of ambitious individuals who aspired to the tyranny, and the seditions of whole classes of the community whose conduct threatened the existence of all government, as against the invasions of external enemies who menaced the conquest and destruction of Rome.

There can be no need, however, to multiply arguments or examples on this head. A feeble executive implies a feeble execution of the government. A feeble execution is but another phrase for a bad execution; and a government ill executed, whatever it may be in theory, must be, in practice, a bad government.

Taking it for granted, therefore, that all men of sense will agree in the necessity of an energetic executive, it will only remain to inquire, what are the ingredients which constitute this energy? How far can they be combined with those other ingredients which constitute safety in the republican sense? And how far does this combination characterize the plan which has been reported by the convention?

The ingredients which constitute energy in the executive are unity; duration; an adequate provision for its support; and competent powers.

The ingredients which constitute safety in the republican sense are a due dependence on the people, and a due responsibility.

Those politicians and statesmen who have been the most celebrated for the soundness of their principles and for the justness of their views have declared in favor of a single executive and a numerous legislature. They have, with great propriety, considered energy as the most necessary qualification of the former, and have regarded this as most applicable to power in a single hand; while they have, with equal propriety, considered the latter as best adapted to deliberation and wisdom, and best calculated to conciliate the confidence of the people and to secure their privileges and interests.

That unity is conducive to energy will not be disputed. Decision, activity, secrecy, and dispatch will generally characterize the proceedings of one man in a much more eminent degree than the proceedings of any greater number; and in proportion as the number is increased, these qualities will be diminished.

This unity may be destroyed in two ways: either by vesting the power in two or more magistrates of equal dignity and authority, or by vesting it ostensibly in one man, subject in whole or in part to the control and co-operation of others, in the capacity of counselors to him. Of the first, the two consuls of Rome may serve as an example; of the last, we shall find examples in the constitutions of several of the States. New York and New Jersey, if I recollect right, are the only States which have intrusted the executive authority wholly to single men.* Both these methods of destroying the unity of the executive have their partisans; but the votaries of an executive council are the most numerous. They are both liable, if not to equal, to similar objections, and may in most lights be examined in conjunction.

The experience of other nations will afford little instruction on this head. As far, however, as it teaches anything, it teaches us not to be enamored of plurality in the executive. We have seen that the Achaeans, on an experiment of two Praetors, were induced to abolish one. The Roman history records many instances of mischiefs to the republic from the dissensions between the consuls, and between the military tribunes, who were at times substituted for the consuls. But it gives us no specimens of any peculiar advantages derived to the state from the circumstance of the plurality of those magistrates. That the dissensions between them were not more frequent or more fatal is matter of astonishment, until we advert to the singular position in which the republic was almost continually placed, and to the prudent policy pointed out by the circumstances of the state, and

---

*New York has no council except for the single purpose of appointing to offices; New Jersey has a council whom the governor may consult. But I think, from the terms of the Constitution, their resolutions do not bind him.

pursued by the consuls, of making a division of the government between them. The patricians engaged in a perpetual struggle with the plebeians for the preservation of their ancient authorities and dignities; the consuls, who were generally chosen out of the former body, were commonly united by the personal interest they had in the defense of the privileges of their order. In addition to this motive of union, after the arms of the republic had considerably expanded the bounds of its empire, it became an established custom with the consuls to divide the administration between themselves by lot—one of them remaining at Rome to govern the city and its environs, the other taking command in the more distant provinces. This expedient must no doubt have had great influence in preventing those collisions and rivalships which might otherwise have embroiled the peace of the republic.

But quitting the dim light of historical research, and attaching ourselves purely to the dictates of reason and good sense, we shall discover much greater cause to reject than to approve the idea of plurality in the executive, under any modification whatever.

Whenever two or more persons are engaged in any common enterprise or pursuit, there is always danger of difference of opinion. If it be a public trust or office in which they are clothed with equal dignity and authority, there is peculiar danger of personal emulation and even animosity. From either, and especially from all these causes, the most bitter dissensions are apt to spring. Whenever these happen, they lessen the respectability, weaken the authority, and distract the plans and operations of those whom they divide. If they should unfortunately assail the supreme executive magistracy of a country, consisting of a plurality of persons, they might impede or frustrate the most important measures of the government in the most critical emergencies of the state. And what is still worse, they might split the community into the most violent and irreconcilable factions, adhering differently to the different individuals who composed the magistracy.

Men often oppose a thing merely because they have had no agency in planning it, or because it may have been planned by those whom they dislike. But if they have been consulted, and have happened to disapprove, opposition then becomes, in their estimation, an indispensable duty of self-love. They seem to think themselves bound in honor, and by all the motives of personal infallibility, to defeat the success of what has been resolved upon contrary to their sentiments. Men of upright, benevolent tempers have too many opportunities of remarking, with horror, to what desperate lengths this disposition is sometimes carried and how often the great interests of society are sacrificed to the vanity, to the conceit, and to the obstinacy of individuals, who have credit enough to make their passions and their caprices interesting to mankind. Perhaps the question now before the public may, in its consequences, afford melancholy proofs of the effects of this despicable frailty, or rather detestable vice, in the human character.

Upon the principles of a free government, inconveniences from the source just mentioned must necessarily be submitted to in the formation of the legislature; but it is unnecessary, and therefore unwise, to introduce them into the constitution of the executive. It is here too that they may be most pernicious. In the legislature, promptitude of decision is oftener an evil than a benefit. The differences of opinion, and the jarring of parties in that department of the government, though they may sometimes obstruct salutary plans, yet often promote deliberation and circumspection, and serve to check excesses in the majority. When a resolution too is once taken, the opposition must be at an end. That resolution is a law, and resistance to it punishable. But no favorable circumstances palliate or atone for the disadvantages of dissension in the executive department. Here they are pure and unmixed. There is no point at which they cease to operate. They serve to embarrass and weaken the execution of the plan or measure to which they relate, from the first step to the final conclusion of it. They constantly counteract those qualities in the executive which are the most necessary ingredients in its composition—vigor and expedition, and this without any counterbalancing good. In the conduct of war, in which the energy of the executive is the bulwark of the national security, everything would be to be apprehended from its plurality.

It must be confessed that these observations apply with principal weight to the first case supposed—that is, to a plurality of magistrates of equal dignity and authority, a scheme, the advocates for which are not likely to form a numerous sect; but they apply, though not with equal yet with considerable weight to the project of a council, whose concurrence is made constitutionally necessary to the operations of the ostensible executive. An artful cabal in that council would be able to distract and to enervate the whole system of administration. If no such cabal should exist, the mere diversity of views and opinions would alone be sufficient to tincture the exercise of the executive authority with a spirit of habitual feebleness and dilatoriness.

But one of the weightiest objections to a plurality in the executive, and which lies as much against the last as the first plan is that it tends to conceal faults and destroy responsibility. Responsibility is of two kinds—to censure and to punishment. The first is the more important of the two, especially in an elective office. Men in public trust will much oftener act in such a manner as to render them unworthy of being any longer trusted, than in such a manner as to make them obnoxious to legal punishment. But the multiplication of the executive adds to the difficulty of detection in either case. It often becomes impossible, amidst mutual accusations, to determine on whom the blame or the punishment of a pernicious measure, or series of pernicious measures, ought really to fall. It is shifted from one to another with so much dexterity, and under such plausible appearances, that the public opinion is left in suspense about the real author. The circumstances which may have led to any national miscarriage or misfortune are sometimes so complicated that where there are a number of actors who may have had different degrees and kinds of agency, though we may clearly see upon the whole that there has been mismanagement, yet it may be impracticable to pronounce to whose account the evil which may have been incurred is truly chargeable.

"I was overruled by my council. The council were so divided in their opinions that it was impossible to obtain any better resolution on the point." These and similar pretexts are constantly at hand, whether true or false. And who is there that will either take the trouble or incur the odium of a strict scrutiny into the secret springs of the transaction? Should there be found a citizen zealous enough to undertake the unpromising task, if there happened to be a collusion between the parties concerned, how easy it is to clothe the circumstances with so much ambiguity as to render it uncertain what was the precise conduct of any of those parties.

In the single instance in which the governor of this State is coupled with a council—that is, in the appointment to offices, we have seen the mischiefs of it in the view now under consideration. Scandalous appointments to important offices have been made. Some cases, indeed, have been so flagrant that ALL PARTIES have agreed in the impropriety of the thing. When inquiry has been made, the blame has been laid by the governor on the members of the council, who, on their part, have charged it upon his nomination; while the people remain altogether at a loss to determine by whose influence their interests have been committed to hands so unqualified and so manifestly improper. In tenderness to individuals, I forbear to descend to particulars.

It is evident from these considerations that the plurality of the executive tends to deprive the people of the two greatest securities they can have for the faithful exercise of any delegated power, *first,* the restraints of public opinion, which lose their efficacy, as well on account of the division of the censure attendant on bad measures among a number as on account of the uncertainty on whom it ought to fall; and, *second,* the opportunity of discovering with facility and clearness the misconduct of the persons they trust, in order either to their removal from office or to their actual punishment in cases which admit of it.

In England, the king is a perpetual magistrate; and it is a maxim which has obtained for the sake of the public peace that he is unaccountable for his administration, and his person sacred. Nothing, therefore, can be wiser in that kingdom than to annex to the king a constitutional council, who may be responsible to the nation for the advice they give. Without this, there would be no responsibility whatever in the executive department—an idea inadmissible in a free government. But even there the king is not bound by the resolutions of his council, though they are answerable for the advice they give. He is the absolute master of his own conduct in the exercise of his office and may observe or disregard the counsel given to him at his sole discretion.

But in a republic where every magistrate ought to be personally responsible for his behavior in office, the reason which in the British Constitution dictates the propriety of a council not only ceases to apply, but turns against the institution. In the monarchy of Great Britain, it furnishes a substitute for the prohibited responsibility of the Chief Magistrate which serves in some degree as a hostage to the national justice for his good behavior. In the American republic, it would serve to destroy, or would greatly diminish, the intended and necessary responsibility of the Chief Magistrate himself.

The idea of a council to the executive, which has so generally obtained in the State constitutions, has been derived from that maxim of republican jealousy which considers power as safer in the hands of a number of men than of a single man. If the maxim should be admitted to be applicable to the case, I should contend that the advantage on that side would not counterbalance the numerous disadvantages on the opposite side. But I do not think the rule at all applicable to the executive power. I clearly concur in opinion, in this particular, with a writer whom the celebrated Junius pronounces to be "deep, solid, and ingenious," that "the executive power is more easily confined when it is one";* that it is far more safe there should

---

*De Lolme.

be a single object for the jealousy and watchfulness of the people; and, in a word, that all multiplication of the executive is rather dangerous than friendly to liberty.

A little consideration will satisfy us that the species of security sought for in the multiplication of the executive is unattainable. Numbers must be so great as to render combination difficult or they are rather a source of danger than of security. The united credit and influence of several individuals must be more formidable to liberty than the credit and influence of either of them separately. When power, therefore, is placed in the hands of so small a number of men as to admit of their interests and views being easily combined in a common enterprise, by an artful leader, it becomes more liable to abuse, and more dangerous when abused, than if it be lodged in the hands of one man, who, from the very circumstance of his being alone, will be more narrowly watched and more readily suspected, and who cannot unite so great a mass of influence as when he is associated with others. The decemvirs of Rome, whose name denotes their number,* were more to be dreaded in their usurpation than any ONE of them would have been. No person would think of proposing an executive much more numerous than that body; from six to a dozen have been suggested for the number of the council. The extreme of these numbers is not too great for an easy combination; and from such a combination America would have more to fear than from the ambition of any single individual. A council to a magistrate, who is himself responsible for what he does, are generally nothing better than a clog upon his good intentions, are often the instruments and accomplices of his bad, and are almost always a cloak to his faults.

I forbear to dwell upon the subject of expense; though it be evident that if the council should be numerous enough to answer the principal end aimed at by the institution, the salaries of the members, who must be drawn from their homes to reside at the seat of government, would form an item in the catalogue of public expenditures too serious to be incurred for an object of equivocal utility.

I will only add that, prior to the appearance of the Constitution, I rarely met with an intelligent man from any of the States who did not admit, as the result of experience, that the UNITY of the executive of this State was one of the best of the distinguishing features of our Constitution.

PUBLIUS

---

*Ten

No. 71: The Duration in Office of the Executive

Duration in office has been mentioned as the second requisite to the energy of the executive authority. This has relation to two objects: to the personal firmness of the executive magistrate in the employment of his constitutional powers, and to the stability of the system of administration which may have been adopted under his auspices. With regard to the first, it must be evident that the longer the duration in office, the greater will be the probability of obtaining so important an advantage. It is a general principle of human nature that a man will be interested in whatever he possesses, in proportion to the firmness or precariousness of the tenure by which he holds it; will be less attached to what he holds by a momentary or uncertain title, than to what he enjoys by a durable or certain title; and, of course, will be willing to risk more for the sake of the one than for the sake of the other. This remark is not less applicable to a political privilege, or honor, or trust, than to any article of ordinary property. The inference from it is that a man acting in the capacity of chief magistrate, under a consciousness that in a very short time he *must* lay down his office, will be apt to feel himself too little interested in it to hazard any material censure or perplexity from the independent exertion of his powers, or from encountering the ill-humors, however transient, which may happen to prevail, either in a considerable part of the society itself, or even in a predominant faction in the legislative body. If the case should only be that he *might* lay it down, unless continued by a new choice, and if he should be desirous of being continued, his wishes, conspiring with his fears, would tend still more powerfully to corrupt his integrity, or debase his fortitude. In either case, feebleness and irresolution must be the characteristics of the station.

There are some who would be inclined to regard the servile pliancy of the executive to a prevailing current, either in the community or in the legislature, as its best recommendation. But such men entertain very crude notions, as well of the purposes for which government was instituted, as of the true means by which the public happiness may be promoted. The republican principle demands that the deliberate sense of the community should govern the conduct of those to whom they intrust the management of their affairs; but it does not require an unqualified complaisance to every sudden breeze of passion, or to every transient impulse which the people may receive from the arts of men, who flatter their prejudices to betray their interests. It is a just observation that the people commonly *intend* the PUBLIC GOOD. This often applies to their very errors. But their good sense would despise the adulator who should pretend that they always *reason right* about the *means* of promoting it. They know from experience that they sometimes err; and the wonder is that they so seldom err as they do, beset as they continually are by the wiles of parasites and sycophants, by the snares of the ambitious, the avaricious, the desperate, by the artifices of men who possess their confidence more than they deserve it, and of those who seek to possess rather than to deserve it. When occasions present themselves in which the interests of the people are at variance with their inclinations, it is the duty of the persons whom they have appointed to be the guardians of those interests to withstand the temporary delusion in order to give them time and opportunity for more cool and sedate reflection. Instances might be cited in which a conduct of this kind has saved the people from very fatal consequences of their own mistakes, and has procured lasting monuments of their gratitude to the men who had courage and magnanimity enough to serve them at the peril of their displeasure.

But however inclined we might be to insist upon an unbounded complaisance in the executive to the inclinations of the people, we can with no propriety contend for a like complaisance to the humors of the legislature. The latter may sometimes stand in opposition to the former, and at other times the people may be entirely neutral. In either supposition, it is certainly desirable that the executive should be in a situation to dare to act his own opinion with vigor and decision.

The same rule which teaches the propriety of a partition between the various branches of power teaches likewise that this partition ought to be so contrived as to render the one independent of the other. To what purpose separate the executive or the judiciary from the legislative, if both the executive and the judiciary are so constituted as to be at the absolute devotion of the legislative? Such a separation must be merely nominal, and incapable of producing the ends for which it was established. It is one thing to be subordinate to the laws, and another to be dependent on the legislative body. The first comports with, the last violates, the fundamental principles of good government; and, whatever may be the forms of the Constitution, unites all power in the same hands. The tendency of the legislative authority to absorb every other has been fully displayed and illustrated by examples in some preceding numbers. In governments purely republican, this tendency is almost irresistible. The representatives of the people, in a popular assembly, seem sometimes to fancy that they are the people themselves, and betray strong symptoms of impatience and disgust at the least sign of opposition from any other quarter; as if the exercise of its rights, by either the executive or judiciary, were a breach of their privilege and an outrage to their dignity. They often appear disposed to exert an imperious control over the other departments; and as they commonly have the people on their side, they always act with such momentum as to make it very difficult for the other members of the government to maintain the balance of the Constitution.

It may perhaps be asked how the shortness of the duration in office can affect the independence of the executive on the legislature, unless the one were possessed of the power of appointing or displacing the other. One answer to this inquiry may be drawn from the principle already remarked—that is, from the slender interest a man is apt to take in a short-lived advantage, and the little inducement it affords him to expose himself, on account of it, to any considerable inconvenience or hazard. Another answer, perhaps more obvious, though not more conclusive, will result from the consideration of the influence of the legislative body over the people, which might be employed to prevent the re-election of a man who, by an upright resistance to any sinister project of that body, should have made himself obnoxious to its resentment.

It may be asked also whether a duration of four years would answer the end proposed; and if it would not, whether a less period, which would at least be recommended by greater security against ambitious designs, would not, for that reason, be preferable to a longer period which was, at the same time, too short for the purpose of inspiring the desired firmness and independence of the magistrate.

It cannot be affirmed that a duration of four years, or any other limited duration, would completely answer the end proposed; but it would contribute towards it in a degree which would have a material influence upon the spirit and character of the government. Between the commencement and termination of such a period there would always be a considerable interval in which the prospect of annihilation would be sufficiently remote not to have an improper effect upon the conduct of a man endowed with a tolerable portion of fortitude; and in which he might reasonably promise himself that there would be time enough before it arrived to make the community sensible of the propriety of the measures he might incline to pursue. Though it be probable that, as he approached the moment when the public were, by a new election, to signify their sense of his conduct, his confidence, and with it his firmness, would decline; yet both the one and the other would derive support from the opportunities which his previous continuance in the station had afforded him, of establishing himself in the esteem and goodwill of his constituents. He might, then, hazard with safety, in proportion to the proofs he had given of his wisdom and integrity, and to the title he had acquired to the respect and attachment of his fellow-citizens. As on the one hand, a duration of four years will contribute to the firmness of the executive in a sufficient degree to render it a very valuable ingredient in the composition, so, on the other, it is not long enough to justify any alarm for the public liberty. If a British House of Commons, from the most feeble beginnings, *from the mere power of assenting or disagreeing to the imposition of a new tax,* have, by rapid strides, reduced the prerogatives of the crown and the privileges of the nobility within the limits they conceived to be compatible with the principles of a free government, while they raised themselves to the rank and consequence of a co-equal branch of the legislature; if they have been able, in one instance, to abolish both the royalty and the aristocracy, and to overturn all the ancient establishments, as well in the Church as State; if they have been able, on a recent occasion, to make the monarch tremble at the prospect of an innovation* attempted by them, what would be to be feared from an elective magistrate of four years' duration with the confined authorities of a President of the United States? What, but that he might be unequal to the task which the Constitution assigns him? I shall only add that if his duration be such as to leave a doubt of his firmness, that doubt is inconsistent with a jealousy of his encroachments.

PUBLIUS

---

*This was the case with respect to Mr. Fox's India bill, which was carried in the House of Commons and rejected in the House of Lords, to the entire satisfaction, as it is said, of the people.

No. 73: The Provision for the Support of the Executive, and the Veto Power

The third ingredient towards constituting the vigor of the executive authority is an adequate provision for its support. It is evident that without proper attention to this article, the separation of the executive from the legislative department would be merely nominal and nugatory. The legislature, with a discretionary power over the salary and emoluments of the Chief Magistrate, could render him as obsequious to their will as they might think proper to make him. They might, in most cases, either reduce him by famine, or tempt him by largesses, to surrender at discretion his judgment to their inclinations. These expressions, taken in all the latitude of the terms, would no doubt convey more than is intended. There are men who could neither be distressed nor won into a sacrifice of their duty; but this stern virtue is the growth of few soils; and in the main it will be found that a power over a man's support is a power over his will. If it were necessary to confirm so plain a truth by facts, examples would not be wanting, even in this country, of the intimidation or seduction of the executive by the terrors or allurements of the pecuniary arrangements of the legislative body.

It is not easy, therefore, to commend too highly the judicious attention which has been paid to this subject in the proposed Constitution. It is there provided that "The President of the United States shall, at stated times, receive for his services a compensation *which shall neither be increased nor diminished during the period for which he shall have been elected,* and he *shall not receive within that period any other emolument* from the United States, or any of them." It is impossible to imagine any provision which would have been more eligible than this. The legislature, on the appointment of a President, is once for all to declare what shall be the compensation for his services during the time for which he shall have been elected. This done, they will have no power to alter it, either by increase or diminution, till a new period of service by a new election commences. They can neither weaken his fortitude by operating on his necessities, nor corrupt his integrity by appealing to his avarice. Neither the Union, nor any of its members, will be at liberty to give, nor will he be at liberty to receive, any other emolument than that which may have been determined by the first act. He can, of course, have no pecuniary inducement to renounce or desert the independence intended for him by the Constitution.

The last of the requisites to energy which have been enumerated are competent powers. Let us proceed to consider those which are proposed to be vested in the President of the United States.

The first thing that offers itself to our observation is the qualified negative of the President upon the acts or resolutions of the two houses of the legislature; or, in other words, his power of returning all bills with objections to have the effect of preventing their becoming laws, unless they should afterwards be ratified by two thirds of each of the component members of the legislative body.

The propensity of the legislative department to intrude upon the rights, and to absorb the powers, of the other departments has been already more than once suggested. The insufficiency of a mere parchment delineation of the boundaries of each has also been remarked upon; and the necessity of furnishing each with constitutional arms for its own defense has been inferred and proved. From these clear and indubitable principles results the propriety of a negative, either absolute or qualified, in the executive upon the acts of the legislative branches. Without the one or the other, the former would be absolutely unable to defend himself against the depredations of the latter. He might gradually be stripped of his authorities by successive resolutions or annihilated by a single vote. And in the one mode or the other, the legislative and executive powers might speedily come to be blended in the same hands. If even no propensity had ever discovered itself in the legislative body to invade the rights of the executive, the rules of just reasoning and theoretic propriety would of themselves teach us that the one ought not to be left to the mercy of the other but ought to possess a constitutional and effectual power of self-defense.

But the power in question has a further use. It not only serves as a shield to the executive, but it furnishes an additional security against the enaction of improper laws. It establishes a salutary check upon the legislative body, calculated to guard the community against the effects of faction, precipitancy, or of any impulse unfriendly to the public good, which may happen to influence a majority of that body.

The propriety of a negative has, upon some occasions, been combated by an observation that it was not to be presumed a single man would possess more virtue and wisdom than a number of men; and that unless this presumption should be entertained, it would be improper to give the executive magistrate any species of control over the legislative body.

But this observation, when examined, will appear rather specious than solid. The propriety of the thing does not turn upon the supposition of superior wisdom or virtue in the executive, but upon the supposition that the legislature will not be infallible; that the love of power may sometimes betray it into a disposition to encroach upon the rights of other members of the government; that a spirit of faction may sometimes pervert its deliberations; that impressions of the moment may sometimes hurry it into measures which itself, on maturer reflection, would condemn. The primary inducement to conferring the power in question upon the executive is to enable him to defend himself; the secondary one is to increase the chances in favor of the community against the passing of bad laws, through haste, inadvertence, or design. The oftener the measure is brought under examination, the greater the diversity in the situations of those who are to examine it, the less must be the danger of those errors which flow from want of due deliberation, or of those missteps which proceed from the contagion of some common passion or interest. It is far less probable that culpable views of any kind should infect all the parts of the government at the same moment and in relation to the same object than that they should by turns govern and mislead every one of them.

It may perhaps be said that the power of preventing bad laws includes that of preventing good ones; and may be used to the one purpose as well as to the other. But this objection will have little weight with those who can properly estimate the mischiefs of that inconstancy and mutability in the laws, which form the greatest blemish in the character and genius of our governments. They will consider every institution calculated to restrain the excess of lawmaking, and to keep things in the same state in which they happen to be at any given period as much more likely to do good than harm; because it is favorable to greater stability in the system of legislation. The injury which may possibly be done by defeating a few good laws will be amply compensated by the advantage of preventing a number of bad ones.

Nor is this all. The superior weight and influence of the legislative body in a free government and the hazard to the executive in a trial of strength with that body afford a satisfactory security that the negative would generally be employed with great caution; and that there would oftener be room for a charge of timidity than of rashness in the exercise of it. A king of Great Britain, with all his train of sovereign attributes, and with all the influence he draws from a thousand sources, would, at this day, hesitate to put a negative upon the joint resolutions of the two houses of Parliament. He would not fail to exert the utmost resources of that influence to strangle a measure disagreeable to him, in its progress to the throne, to avoid being reduced to the dilemma of permitting it to take effect, or of risking the displeasure of the nation by an opposition to the sense of the legislative body. Nor is it probable that he would ultimately venture to exert his prerogative, but in a case of manifest propriety, or extreme necessity. All well-informed men in that kingdom will accede to the justness of this remark. A very considerable period has elapsed since the negative of the crown has been exercised.

If a magistrate so powerful and so well fortified as a British monarch would have scruples about the exercise of the power under consideration, how much greater caution may be reasonably expected in a President of the United States, clothed for the short period of four years with the executive authority of a government wholly and purely republican?

It is evident that there would be greater danger of his not using his power when necessary, than of his using it too often, or too much. An argument, indeed, against its expediency, has been drawn from this very source. It has been represented, on this account, as a power odious in appearance, useless in practice. But it will not follow, that because it might be rarely exercised, it would never be exercised. In the case for which it is chiefly designed, that of an immediate attack upon the constitutional rights of the executive, or in a case in which the public good was evidently and palpably sacrificed, a man of tolerable firmness would avail himself of his constitutional means of defense, and would listen to the admonitions of duty and responsibility. In the former supposition, his fortitude would be stimulated by his immediate interest in the power of his office; in the latter, by the probability of the sanction of his constituents who, though they would naturally incline to the legislative body in a doubtful case, would hardly suffer their partiality to delude them in a very plain case. I speak now with an eye to a magistrate possessing only a common share of firmness. There are men who, under any circumstances, will have the courage to do their duty at every hazard.

But the convention have pursued a mean in this business, which will both facilitate the exercise of the power vested in this respect in the executive magistrate, and make its efficacy to depend on the sense of a considerable part of the legislative body. Instead of an absolute negative, it is proposed to give the executive the qualified negative already described. This is a power which would be much more readily exercised than the other. A man who might be afraid to defeat a law by his single VETO might not scruple to return it for reconsideration, subject to being finally rejected only in the event of more than one third of each house concurring in the sufficiency of his objections. He would be encouraged by the reflection that if his opposition should prevail, it would embark in it a very respectable proportion of the legislative body whose influence would be united with his in supporting the propriety of his conduct in the public opinion. A direct and categorical negative has something in the appearance of it more harsh, and more apt to irritate, than the mere suggestion of argumentative objections to be approved or disapproved by those to whom they are addressed. In proportion as it would be less apt to offend, it would be more apt to be exercised; and for this very reason it may in practice be found more effectual. It is to be hoped that it will not often happen that improper views will govern so large a proportion as two thirds of both branches of the legislature at the same time; and this, too, in defiance of the counterpoising weight of the executive. It is at any rate far less probable that this should be the case than that such views should taint the resolutions and conduct of a bare majority. A power of this nature in the executive will often have a silent and unperceived, though forcible, operation. When men, engaged in unjustifiable pursuits, are aware that obstructions may come from a quarter which they cannot control, they will often be restrained by the bare apprehension of opposition from doing what they would with eagerness rush into if no such external impediments were to be feared.

This qualified negative, as has been elsewhere remarked, is in this State vested in a council, consisting of the governor, with the chancellor and judges of the Supreme Court, or any two of them. It has been freely employed upon a variety of occasions, and frequently with success. And its utility has become so apparent, that persons who, in compiling the Constitution, were violent opposers of it, have from experience become its declared admirers.[*]

I have in another place remarked that the convention, in the formation of this part of their plan, had departed from the model of the constitution of this State in favor of that of Massachusetts.

---

[*]Mr. Abraham Yates, a warm opponent of the plan of the convention, is of this number.

Two strong reasons may be imagined for this preference. One is that the judges, who are to be the interpreters of the law, might receive an improper bias from having given a previous opinion in their revisionary capacities; the other is that by being often associated with the executive, they might be induced to embark too far in the political views of that magistrate, and thus a dangerous combination might by degrees be cemented between the executive and judiciary departments. It is impossible to keep the judges too distinct from every other avocation than that of expounding the laws. It is peculiarly dangerous to place them in a situation to be either corrupted or influenced by the executive.

PUBLIUS

No. 78: The Judiciary Department

We proceed now to an examination of the judiciary department of the proposed government.

In unfolding the defects of the existing Confederation, the utility and necessity of a federal judicature have been clearly pointed out. It is the less necessary to recapitulate the considerations there urged as the propriety of the institution in the abstract is not disputed; the only questions which have been raised being relative to the manner of constituting it, and to its extent. To these points, therefore, our observations shall be confined.

The manner of constituting it seems to embrace these several objects: 1st. The mode of appointing the judges. 2nd. The tenure by which they are to hold their places. 3rd. The partition of the judiciary authority between different courts and their relations to each other.

First. As to the mode of appointing the judges: this is the same with that of appointing the officers of the Union in general and has been so fully discussed in the two last numbers that nothing can be said here which would not be useless repetition.

Second. As to the tenure by which the judges are to hold their places: this chiefly concerns their duration in office, the provisions for their support, the precautions for their responsibility.

According to the plan of the convention, all judges who may be appointed by the United States are to hold their offices *during good behavior;* which is conformable to the most approved of the State constitutions, and among the rest, to that of this State. Its propriety having been drawn into question by the adversaries of that plan is no light symptom of the rage for objection which disorders their imaginations and judgments. The standard of good behavior for the continuance in office of the judicial magistracy is certainly one of the most valuable of the modern improvements in the practice of government. In a monarchy it is an excellent barrier to the despotism of the prince; in a republic it is a no less excellent barrier to the encroachments and oppressions of the representative body. And it is the best expedient which can be devised in any government to secure a steady, upright, and impartial administration of the laws.

Whoever attentively considers the different departments of power must perceive that, in a government in which they are separated from each other, the judiciary, from the nature of its functions, will always be the least dangerous to the political rights of the Constitution;

because it will be least in a capacity to annoy or injure them. The executive not only dispenses the honors but holds the sword of the community. The legislature not only commands the purse but prescribes the rules by which the duties and rights of every citizen are to be regulated. The judiciary, on the contrary, has no influence over either the sword or the purse; no direction either of the strength or of the wealth of the society, and can take no active resolution whatever. It may truly be said to have neither FORCE nor WILL but merely judgment; and must ultimately depend upon the aid of the executive arm even for the efficacy of its judgments.

This simple view of the matter suggests several important consequences. It proves incontestably that the judiciary is beyond comparison the weakest of the three departments of power;* that it can never attack with success either of the other two; and that all possible care is requisite to enable it to defend itself against their attacks. It equally proves that though individual oppression may now and then proceed from the courts of justice, the general liberty of the people can never be endangered from that quarter; I mean so long as the judiciary remains truly distinct from both the legislature and the executive. For I agree that "there is no liberty if the power of judging be not separated from the legislative and executive powers."† And it proves, in the last place, that as liberty can have nothing to fear from the judiciary alone, but would have everything to fear from its union with either of the other departments; that as all the effects of such a union must ensue from a dependence of the former on the latter, notwithstanding a nominal and apparent separation; that as, from the natural feebleness of the judiciary, it is in continual jeopardy of being overpowered, awed, or influenced by its co-ordinate branches; and that as nothing can contribute so much to its firmness and independence as permanency in office, this quality may therefore be justly regarded as an indispensable ingredient in its constitution, and, in a great measure, as the citadel of the public justice and the public security.

The complete independence of the courts of justice is peculiarly essential in a limited Constitution. By a limited Constitution, I understand one which contains certain specified exceptions to the legislative authority; such, for instance, as that it shall pass no bills

---

*The celebrated Montesquieu, speaking of them, says: "Of the three powers above mentioned, the JUDICIARY is next to nothing." —*Spirit of Laws,* Vol. I, page 186.
†*Idem,* page 181.

of attainder, no *ex post facto* laws, and the like. Limitations of this kind can be preserved in practice no other way than through the medium of courts of justice, whose duty it must be to declare all acts contrary to the manifest tenor of the Constitution void. Without this, all the reservations of particular rights or privileges would amount to nothing.

Some perplexity respecting the rights of the courts to pronounce legislative acts void, because contrary to the Constitution, has arisen from an imagination that the doctrine would imply a superiority of the judiciary to the legislative power. It is urged that the authority which can declare the acts of another void must necessarily be superior to the one whose acts may be declared void. As this doctrine is of great importance in all the American constitutions, a brief discussion of the grounds on which it rests cannot be unacceptable.

There is no position which depends on clearer principles than that every act of a delegated authority, contrary to the tenor of the commission under which it is exercised, is void. No legislative act, therefore, contrary to the Constitution, can be valid. To deny this would be to affirm that the deputy is greater than his principal; that the servant is above his master; that the representatives of the people are superior to the people themselves; that men acting by virtue of powers may do not only what their powers do not authorize, but what they forbid.

If it be said that the legislative body are themselves the constitutional judges of their own powers, and that the construction they put upon them is conclusive upon the other departments, it may be answered that this cannot be the natural presumption where it is not to be collected from any particular provisions in the Constitution. It is not otherwise to be supposed that the Constitution could intend to enable the representatives of the people to substitute their *will* to that of their constituents. It is far more rational to suppose that the courts were designed to be an intermediate body between the people and the legislature in order, among other things, to keep the latter within the limits assigned to their authority. The interpretation of the laws is the proper and peculiar province of the courts. A constitution is, in fact, and must be regarded by the judges as, a fundamental law. It therefore belongs to them to ascertain its meaning as well as the meaning of any particular act proceeding from the legislative body. If there should happen to be an irreconcilable variance between the two, that which has the superior obligation and validity ought, of course, to be preferred; or, in other words, the Constitution ought to be preferred to the statute, the intention of the people to the intention of their agents.

Nor does this conclusion by any means suppose a superiority of the judicial to the legislative power. It only supposes that the power of the people is superior to both, and that where the will of the legislature, declared in its statutes, stands in opposition to that of the people, declared in the Constitution, the judges ought to be governed by the latter rather than the former. They ought to regulate their decisions by the fundamental laws rather than by those which are not fundamental.

This exercise of judicial discretion in determining between two contradictory laws is exemplified in a familiar instance. It not uncommonly happens that there are two statutes existing at one time, clashing in whole or in part with each other and neither of them containing any repealing clause or expression. In such a case, it is the province of the courts to liquidate and fix their meaning and operation. So far as they can, by any fair construction, be reconciled to each other, reason and law conspire to dictate that this should be done; where this is impracticable, it becomes a matter of necessity to give effect to one in exclusion of the other. The rule which has obtained in the courts for determining their relative validity is that the last in order of time shall be preferred to the first. But this is a mere rule of construction, not derived from any positive law but from the nature and reason of the thing. It is a rule not enjoined upon the courts by legislative provision but adopted by themselves, as consonant to truth and propriety, for the direction of their conduct as interpreters of the law. They thought it reasonable that between the interfering acts of an *equal* authority that which was the last indication of its will should have the preference.

But in regard to the interfering acts of a superior and subordinate authority of an original and derivative power, the nature and reason of the thing indicate the converse of that rule as proper to be followed. They teach us that the prior act of a superior ought to be preferred to the subsequent act of an inferior and subordinate authority; and that accordingly, whenever a particular statute contravenes the Constitution, it will be the duty of the judicial tribunals to adhere to the latter and disregard the former.

It can be of no weight to say that the courts, on the pretense of a repugnancy, may substitute their own pleasure to the constitutional intentions of the legislature. This might as well happen in the case of two contradictory statutes; or it might as well happen in every adjudication upon any single statute. The courts must declare the sense of the law; and if they should be disposed to exercise WILL instead of JUDGMENT, the consequence would equally be the substitution of their pleasure to that of the legislative body. The observation, if it proved anything, would prove that there ought to be no judges distinct from that body.

If, then, the courts of justice are to be considered as the bulwarks of a limited Constitution against legislative encroachments, this consideration will afford a strong argument for the permanent tenure of judicial offices, since nothing will contribute so much as this to that independent spirit in the judges which must be essential to the faithful performance of so arduous a duty.

This independence of the judges is equally requisite to guard the Constitution and the rights of individuals from the effects of those ill humors which the arts of designing men, or the influence of particular conjunctures, sometimes disseminate among the people themselves, and which, though they speedily give place to better information, and more deliberate reflection, have a tendency, in the meantime, to occasion dangerous innovations in the government, and serious oppressions of the minor party in the community. Though I trust the friends of the proposed Constitution will never concur with its enemies[*] in questioning that fundamental principle of republican government which admits the right of the people to alter or abolish the established Constitution whenever they find it inconsistent with their happiness; yet it is not to be inferred from this principle that the representatives of the people, whenever a momentary inclination happens to lay hold of a majority of their constituents incompatible with the provisions in the existing Constitution would, on that account, be justifiable in a violation of those provisions; or that the courts would be under a greater obligation to connive at infractions in this shape than when they had proceeded wholly from the cabals of the representative body. Until the people have, by some solemn and authoritative act, annulled or changed the established form, it is binding upon themselves collectively, as well as individually; and no presumption, or even knowledge of their sentiments, can warrant their representatives in a departure from it prior to such an act. But it is easy to see that it would require an uncommon portion of fortitude in the judges to do their duty as faithful guardians of the

---

[*] *Vide Protest of the Minority of the Convention of Pennsylvania,* Martin's speech, etc.

Constitution, where legislative invasions of it had been instigated by the major voice of the community.

But it is not with a view to infractions of the Constitution only that the independence of the judges may be an essential safeguard against the effects of occasional ill humors in the society. These sometimes extend no farther than to the injury of the private rights of particular classes of citizens, by unjust and partial laws. Here also the firmness of the judicial magistracy is of vast importance in mitigating the severity and confining the operation of such laws. It not only serves to moderate the immediate mischiefs of those which may have been passed, but it operates as a check upon the legislative body in passing them; who, perceiving that obstacles to the success of an iniquitous intention are to be expected from the scruples of the courts, are in a manner compelled, by the very motives of the injustice they meditate, to qualify their attempts. This is a circumstance calculated to have more influence upon the character of our governments than but few may be aware of. The benefits of the integrity and moderation of the judiciary have already been felt in more States than one; and though they may have displeased those whose sinister expectations they may have disappointed, they must have commanded the esteem and applause of all the virtuous and disinterested. Considerate men of every description ought to prize whatever will tend to beget or fortify that temper in the courts; as no man can be sure that he may not be tomorrow the victim of a spirit of injustice, by which he may be a gainer today. And every man must now feel that the inevitable tendency of such a spirit is to sap the foundations of public and private confidence and to introduce in its stead universal distrust and distress.

That inflexible and uniform adherence to the rights of the Constitution, and of individuals, which we perceive to be indispensable in the courts of justice, can certainly not be expected from judges who hold their offices by a temporary commission. Periodical appointments, however regulated, or by whomsoever made, would, in some way or other, be fatal to their necessary independence. If the power of making them was committed either to the executive or legislature there would be danger of an improper complaisance to the branch which possessed it; if to both, there would be an unwillingness to hazard the displeasure of either; if to the people, or to persons chosen by them for the special purpose, there would be too great a disposition to consult popularity to justify a reliance that nothing would be consulted but the Constitution and the laws.

There is yet a further and a weighty reason for the permanency of the judicial offices which is deducible from the nature of the qualifications they require. It has been frequently remarked with great propriety that a voluminous code of laws is one of the inconveniences necessarily connected with the advantages of a free government. To avoid an arbitrary discretion in the courts, it is indispensable that they should be bound down by strict rules and precedents which serve to define and point out their duty in every particular case that comes before them; and it will readily be conceived from the variety of controversies which grow out of the folly and wickedness of mankind that the records of those precedents must unavoidably swell to a very considerable bulk and must demand long and laborious study to acquire a competent knowledge of them. Hence it is that there can be but few men in the society who will have sufficient skill in the laws to qualify them for the stations of judges. And making the proper deductions for the ordinary depravity of human nature, the number must be still smaller of those who unite the requisite integrity with the requisite knowledge. These considerations apprise us that the government can have no great option between fit characters; and that a temporary duration in office which would naturally discourage such characters from quitting a lucrative line of practice to accept a seat on the bench would have a tendency to throw the administration of justice into hands less able and less well qualified to conduct it with utility and dignity. In the present circumstances of this country and in those in which it is likely to be for a long time to come, the disadvantages on this score would be greater than they may at first sight appear; but it must be confessed that they are far inferior to those which present themselves under the other aspects of the subject.

Upon the whole, there can be no room to doubt that the convention acted wisely in copying from the models of those constitutions which have established *good behavior* as the tenure of their judicial offices, in point of duration; and that so far from being blamable on this account, their plan would have been inexcusably defective if it had wanted this important feature of good government. The experience of Great Britain affords an illustrious comment on the excellence of the institution.

PUBLIUS

No. 79: The Judiciary Continued

Next to permanency in office, nothing can contribute more to the independence of the judges than a fixed provision for their support. The remark made in relation to the President is equally applicable here. In the general course of human nature, *a power over a man's subsistence amounts to a power over his will*. And we can never hope to see realized in practice the complete separation of the judicial from the legislative power, in any system which leaves the former dependent for pecuniary resources on the occasional grants of the latter. The enlightened friends to good government in every State have seen cause to lament the want of precise and explicit precautions in the State constitutions on this head. Some of these indeed have declared that *permanent** salaries should be established for the judges; but the experiment has in some instances shown that such expressions are not sufficiently definite to preclude legislative evasions. Something still more positive and unequivocal has been evinced to be requisite. The plan of the convention accordingly has provided that the judges of the United States "shall at *stated times* receive for their services a compensation which shall not be *diminished* during their continuance in office."

This, all circumstances considered, is the most eligible provision that could have been devised. It will readily be understood that the fluctuations in the value of money and in the state of society rendered a fixed rate of compensation in the Constitution inadmissible. What might be extravagant today might in half a century become penurious and inadequate. It was therefore necessary to leave it to the discretion of the legislature to vary its provisions in conformity to the variations in circumstances, yet under such restrictions as to put it out of the power of that body to change the condition of the individual for the worse. A man may then be sure of the ground upon which he stands, and can never be deterred from his duty by the apprehension of being placed in a less eligible situation. The clause which has been quoted combines both advantages. The salaries of judicial offices may from time to time be altered, as occasion shall require, yet so as never to lessen the allowance with which any particular judge comes into office, in respect to him. It will be observed that a difference has been made by the convention between the compensation of the President

---

Vide Constitution of Massachusetts, Chapter 2, Section 1, Article 13.

and of the judges. That of the former can neither be increased nor diminished; that of the latter can only not be diminished. This probably arose from the difference in the duration of the respective offices. As the President is to be elected for no more than four years, it can rarely happen that an adequate salary, fixed at the commencement of that period, will not continue to be such to the end of it. But with regard to the judges who, if they behave properly, will be secured in the places for life, it may well happen, especially in the early stages of the government, that a stipend which would be very sufficient at their first appointment would become too small in the progress of their service.

This provision for the support of the judges bears every mark of prudence and efficacy; and it may be safely affirmed that, together with the permanent tenure of their offices, it affords a better prospect of their independence than is discoverable in the constitutions of any of the States in regard to their own judges.

The precautions for their responsibility are comprised in the article respecting impeachments. They are liable to be impeached for malconduct by the House of Representatives and tried by the Senate; and, if convicted, may be dismissed from office and disqualified for holding any other. This is the only provision on the point which is consistent with the necessary independence of the judicial character, and is the only one which we find in our own Constitution in respect to our own judges.

The want of a provision for removing the judges on account of inability has been a subject of complaint. But all considerate men will be sensible that such a provision would either not be practiced upon or would be more liable to abuse than calculated to answer any good purpose. The mensuration of the faculties of the mind has, I believe, no place in the catalogue of known arts. An attempt to fix the boundary between the regions of ability and inability would much oftener give scope to personal and party attachments and enmities, than advance the interests of justice or the public good. The result, except in the case of insanity, must for the most part be arbitrary; and insanity, without any formal or express provision, may be safely pronounced to be a virtual disqualification.

The constitution of New York, to avoid investigations that must forever be vague and dangerous, has taken a particular age as the criterion of inability. No man can be a judge beyond sixty. I believe there are few at present who do not disapprove of this provision. There is no station in relation to which it is less proper than to that of a judge. The deliberating and comparing faculties generally preserve their strength much beyond that period in men who survive it; and when, in addition to this circumstance, we consider how few there are who outlive the season of intellectual vigor and how improbable it is that any considerable portion of the bench, whether more or less numerous, should be in such a situation at the same time, we shall be ready to conclude that limitations of this sort have little to recommend them. In a republic where fortunes are not affluent and pensions not expedient, the dismission of men from stations in which they have served their country long and usefully, on which they depend for subsistence, and from which it will be too late to resort to any other occupation for a livelihood, ought to have some better apology to humanity than is to be found in the imaginary danger of a superannuated bench.

PUBLIUS

No. 84: Certain General and Miscellaneous Objections to the Constitution Considered and Answered

In the course of the foregoing review of the Constitution, I have taken notice of, and endeavored to answer most of the objections which have appeared against it. There however remain a few which either did not fall naturally under any particular head or were forgotten in their proper places. These shall now be discussed; but as the subject has been drawn into great length, I shall so far consult brevity as to comprise all my observations on these miscellaneous points in a single paper.

The most considerable of these remaining objections is that the plan of the convention contains no bill of rights. Among other answers given to this, it has been upon different occasions remarked that the constitutions of several of the States are in a similar predicament. I add that New York is of this number. And yet the opposers of the new system, in this State, who profess an unlimited admiration for its constitution, are among the most intemperate partisans of a bill of rights. To justify their zeal in this matter they allege two things: one is that, though the constitution of New York has no bill of rights prefixed to it, yet it contains, in the body of it, various provisions in favor of particular privileges and rights which, in substance, amount to the same thing; the other is that the Constitution adopts, in their full extent, the common and statute law of Great Britain, by which many other rights not expressed in it are equally secured.

To the first I answer that the Constitution proposed by the convention contains, as well as the constitution of this State, a number of such provisions.

Independent of those which relate to the structure of the government, we find the following: Article 1, section 3, clause 7—"Judgment in cases of impeachment shall not extend further than to removal from office and disqualification to hold and enjoy any office of honor, trust, or profit under the United States; but the party convicted shall nevertheless be liable and subject to indictment, trial, judgment, and punishment according to law." Section 9, of the same article, clause 2—"The privilege of the writ of *habeas corpus* shall not be suspended, unless when in cases of rebellion or invasion the public safety may require it." Clause 3—"No bill of attainder or *ex post facto* law shall be passed." Clause 7—"No title of nobility shall be granted by the United States; and no person holding any office of profit or trust under them shall, without the consent of the Congress, accept of any present, emolument, office, or title of any kind whatever, from any king, prince, or foreign state." Article 3, section 2, clause 3—"The trial of all crimes, except in cases of impeachment, shall be by jury; and such trial shall be held in the State where the said crimes shall have been committed; but when not committed within any State, the trial shall be at such place or places as the Congress may by law have directed." Section 3, of the same article—"Treason against the United States shall consist only in levying war against them, or in adhering to their enemies, giving them aid and comfort. No person shall be convicted of treason, unless on the testimony of two witnesses to the same overt act, or on confession in open court." And clause 3, of the same section—"The Congress shall have power to declare the punishment of treason; but no attainder of treason shall work corruption of blood, or forfeiture, except during the life of the person attainted."

It may well be a question whether these are not, upon the whole, of equal importance with any which are to be found in the constitution of this State. The establishment of the writ of *habeas corpus,* the prohibition of *ex post facto* laws, and of TITLES OF NOBILITY, *to which we have no corresponding provision in our Constitution,* are perhaps greater securities to liberty and republicanism than any it contains. The creation of crimes after the commission of the fact, or, in other words, the subjecting of men to punishment for things which, when they were done, were breaches of no law, and the practice of arbitrary imprisonments, have been, in all ages, the favorite and most formidable instruments of tyranny. The observations of the judicious Blackstone,[*] in reference to the latter, are well worthy of recital: "To bereave a man of life [says he] or by violence to confiscate his estate, without accusation or trial, would be so gross and notorious an act of despotism as must at once convey the alarm of tyranny throughout the whole nation; but confinement of the person, by secretly hurrying him to jail, where his sufferings are unknown or forgotten, is a less public, a less striking, and therefore a *more dangerous engine* of arbitrary government." And as a remedy for this fatal evil he is everywhere peculiarly emphatical

---

[*]*Vide* Blackstone's *Commentaries,* Vol. 1, Page 136.

in his encomiums on the *habeas corpus* act, which in one place he calls "the BULWARK of the British Constitution."*

Nothing need be said to illustrate the importance of the prohibition of titles of nobility. This may truly be denominated the cornerstone of republican government; for so long as they are excluded there can never be serious danger that the government will be any other than that of the people.

To the second, that is, to the pretended establishment of the common and statute law by the Constitution, I answer that they are expressly made subject "to such alterations and provisions as the legislature shall from time to time make concerning the same." They are therefore at any moment liable to repeal by the ordinary legislative power, and of course have no constitutional sanction. The only use of the declaration was to recognize the ancient law and to remove doubts which might have been occasioned by the Revolution. This consequently can be considered as no part of a declaration of rights, which under our constitutions must be intended as limitations of the power of the government itself.

It has been several times truly remarked that bills of rights are, in their origin, stipulations between kings and their subjects, abridgments of prerogative in favor of privilege, reservations of rights not surrendered to the prince. Such was MAGNA CHARTA, obtained by the barons, sword in hand, from King John. Such were the subsequent confirmations of that charter by subsequent princes. Such was the *Petition of Right* assented to by Charles the First in the beginning of his reign. Such, also, was the Declaration of Right presented by the Lords and Commons to the Prince of Orange in 1688, and afterwards thrown into the form of an act of Parliament called the Bill of Rights. It is evident, therefore, that, according to their primitive signification, they have no application to constitutions, professedly founded upon the power of the people and executed by their immediate representatives and servants. Here, in strictness, the people surrender nothing; and as they retain everything they have no need of particular reservations, "WE, THE PEOPLE of the United States, to secure the blessings of liberty to ourselves and our posterity, do *ordain* and *establish* this Constitution for the United States of America." Here is a better recognition of popular rights than volumes of those aphorisms which make the principal figure in several of our State bills of rights and

---

*Idem, Vol. 4, Page 438.

which would sound much better in a treatise of ethics than in a constitution of government.

But a minute detail of particular rights is certainly far less applicable to a Constitution like that under consideration, which is merely intended to regulate the general political interests of the nation, than to a constitution which has the regulation of every species of personal and private concerns. If, therefore, the loud clamors against the plan of the convention, on this score, are well founded, no epithets of reprobation will be too strong for the constitution of this State. But the truth is that both of them contain all which, in relation to their objects, is reasonably to be desired.

I go further and affirm that bills of rights, in the sense and to the extent in which they are contended for, are not only unnecessary in the proposed Constitution but would even be dangerous. They would contain various exceptions to powers which are not granted; and, on this very account, would afford a colorable pretext to claim more than were granted. For why declare that things shall not be done which there is no power to do? Why, for instance, should it be said that the liberty of the press shall not be restrained, when no power is given by which restrictions may be imposed? I will not contend that such a provision would confer a regulating power; but it is evident that it would furnish, to men disposed to usurp, a plausible pretense for claiming that power. They might urge with a semblance of reason that the Constitution ought not to be charged with the absurdity of providing against the abuse of an authority which was not given, and that the provision against restraining the liberty of the press afforded a clear implication that a power to prescribe proper regulations concerning it was intended to be vested in the national government. This may serve as a specimen of the numerous handles which would be given to the doctrine of constructive powers, by the indulgence of an injudicious zeal for bills of rights.

On the subject of the liberty of the press, as much as has been said, I cannot forbear adding a remark or two: in the first place, I observe, that there is not a syllable concerning it in the constitution of this State; in the next, I contend that whatever has been said about it in that or any other State amounts to nothing. What signifies a declaration that "the liberty of the press shall be inviolably preserved"? What is the liberty of the press? Who can give it any definition which would not leave the utmost latitude for evasion? I hold it to be impracticable; and from this I infer that its security, whatever fine declarations may be inserted in any constitution respecting it, must altogether depend on public opinion, and on the general spirit of the people and of the government.* And here, after all, as is intimated upon another occasion, must we seek for the only solid basis of all our rights.

There remains but one other view of this matter to conclude the point. The truth is, after all the declamations we have heard, that the Constitution is itself, in every rational sense, and to every useful purpose, A BILL OF RIGHTS. The several bills of rights in Great Britain form its Constitution, and conversely the constitution of each State is its bill of rights. And the proposed Constitution, if adopted, will be the bill of rights of the Union. Is it one object of a bill of rights to declare and specify the political privileges of the citizens in the structure and administration of the government? This is done in the most ample and precise manner in the plan of the convention; comprehending various precautions for the public security which are not to be found in any of the State constitutions. Is another object of a bill of rights to define certain immunities and modes of proceeding, which are relative to personal and private concerns? This we have seen has also been attended to in a variety of cases in the same plan. Adverting therefore to the substantial meaning of a bill of rights, it is absurd to allege that it is not to be found in the work of the convention. It may be said that it does not go far enough though it will not be easy to make this appear; but it can with no propriety be contended that there is no such thing. It certainly must be immaterial what mode is observed as to the order of declaring the rights of the citizens if they are to be

---

*To show that there is a power in the Constitution by which the liberty of the press may be affected, recourse has been had to the power of taxation. It is said that duties may be laid upon the publications so high as to amount to a prohibition. I know not by what logic it could be maintained that the declarations in the State constitutions, in favor of the freedom of the press, would be a constitutional impediment to the imposition of duties upon publications by the State legislatures. It cannot certainly be pretended that any degree of duties, however low, would be an abridgment of the liberty of the press. We know that newspapers are taxed in Great Britain, and yet it is notorious that the press nowhere enjoys greater liberty than in that country. And if duties of any kind may be laid without a violation of that liberty, it is evident that the extent must depend on legislative discretion, regulated by public opinion; so that, after all, general declarations respecting the liberty of the press will give it no greater security than it will have without them. The same invasions of it may be effected under the State constitutions which contain those declarations through the means of taxation, as under the proposed Constitution, which has nothing of the kind. It would be quite as significant to declare that government ought to be free, that taxes ought not to be excessive, etc., as that the liberty of the press ought not to be restrained.

found in any part of the instrument which establishes the government. And hence it must be apparent that much of what has been said on this subject rests merely on verbal and nominal distinctions, entirely foreign from the substance of the thing.

Another objection which has been made, and which, from the frequency of its repetition, it is to be presumed is relied on, is of this nature: "It is improper [say the objectors] to confer such large powers as are proposed upon the national government, because the seat of that government must of necessity be too remote from many of the States to admit of a proper knowledge on the part of the constituent of the conduct of the representative body." This argument, if it proves anything, proves that there ought to be no general government whatever. For the powers which, it seems to be agreed on all hands, ought to be vested in the Union, cannot be safely intrusted to a body which is not under every requisite control. But there are satisfactory reasons to show that the objection is in reality not well founded. There is in most of the arguments which relate to distance a palpable illusion of the imagination. What are the sources of information by which the people in Montgomery County must regulate their judgment of the conduct of their representatives in the State legislature? Of personal observation they can have no benefit. This is confined to the citizens on the spot. They must therefore depend on the information of intelligent men, in whom they confide; and how must these men obtain their information? Evidently from the complexion of public measures, from the public prints, from correspondences with their representatives, and with other persons who reside at the place of their deliberations. This does not apply to Montgomery County only, but to all the counties at any considerable distance from the seat of government.

It is equally evident that the same sources of information would be open to the people in relation to the conduct of their representatives in the general government, and the impediments to a prompt communication which distance may be supposed to create will be overbalanced by the effects of the vigilance of the State governments. The executive and legislative bodies of each State will be so many sentinels over the persons employed in every department of the national administration; and as it will be in their power to adopt and pursue a regular and effectual system of intelligence, they can never be at a loss to know the behavior of those who represent their constituents in the national councils, and can readily communicate the same knowledge to the people. Their disposition to apprise the community of whatever may prejudice its interests from another quarter may be relied upon, if it were only from the rivalship of power. And we may conclude with the fullest assurance that the people, through that channel, will be better informed of the conduct of their national representatives than they can be by any means they now possess, of that of their State representatives.

It ought also to be remembered that the citizens who inhabit the country at and near the seat of government will, in all questions that affect the general liberty and prosperity, have the same interest with those who are at a distance, and that they will stand ready to sound the alarm when necessary, and to point out the actors in any pernicious project. The public papers will be expeditious messengers of intelligence to the most remote inhabitants of the Union.

Among the many extraordinary objections which have appeared against the proposed Constitution, the most extraordinary and the least colorable one is derived from the want of some provision respecting the debts due *to* the United States. This has been represented as a tacit relinquishment of those debts, and as a wicked contrivance to screen public defaulters. The newspapers have teemed with the most inflammatory railings on this head; and yet there is nothing clearer than that the suggestion is entirely void of foundation, and is the offspring of extreme ignorance or extreme dishonesty. In addition to the remarks I have made upon the subject in another place, I shall only observe that as it is a plain dictate of common sense, so it is also an established doctrine of political law, that *"States neither lose any of their rights, nor are discharged from any of their obligations, by a change in the form of their civil government."**

The last objection of any consequence, which I at present recollect, turns upon the article of expense. If it were even true that the adoption of the proposed government would occasion a considerable increase of expense, it would be an objection that ought to have no weight against the plan.

The great bulk of the citizens of America are with reason convinced that Union is the basis of their political happiness. Men of sense of all parties now with few exceptions agree that it cannot be preserved under the present system, nor without radical alterations; that new and extensive powers ought to be granted to the national head, and that these require a different organization of the federal government—a

---

Vide Rutherforth's Institutes, Vol. 2, book II, Chapter X, Sections XIV and XV.
    Vide also Grotius, Book II, Chapter IX, Sections VIII and IX.

single body being an unsafe depositary of such ample authorities. In conceding all this, the question of expense must be given up; for it is impossible, with any degree of safety, to narrow the foundation upon which the system is to stand. The two branches of the legislature are, in the first instance, to consist of only sixty-five persons, which is the same number of which Congress, under the existing Confederation, may be composed. It is true that this number is intended to be increased; but this is to keep pace with the increase of the population and resources of the country. It is evident that a less number would, even in the first instance, have been unsafe, and that a continuance of the present number would, in a more advanced stage of population, be a very inadequate representation of the people.

Whence is the dreaded augmentation of expense to spring? One source pointed out is the multiplication of offices under the new government. Let us examine this a little.

It is evident that the principal departments of the administration under the present government are the same which will be required under the new. There are now a Secretary of War, a Secretary for Foreign Affairs, a Secretary for Domestic Affairs, a Board of Treasury, consisting of three persons, a treasurer, assistants, clerks, etc. These offices are indispensable under any system and will suffice under the new as well as under the old. As to ambassadors and other ministers and agents in foreign countries, the proposed Constitution can make no other difference than to render their characters, where they reside, more respectable, and their services more useful. As to persons to be employed in the collection of the revenues, it is unquestionably true that these will form a very considerable addition to the number of federal officers; but it will not follow that this will occasion an increase of public expense. It will be in most cases nothing more than an exchange of State officers for national officers. In the collection of all duties, for instance, the persons employed will be wholly of the latter description. The States individually will stand in no need of any for this purpose. What difference can it make in point of expense to pay officers of the customs appointed by the State or those appointed by the United States? There is no good reason to suppose that either the number or the salaries of the latter will be greater than those of the former.

Where then are we to seek for those additional articles of expense which are to swell the account to the enormous size that has been represented to us? The chief item which occurs to me respects the support of the judges of the United States. I do not add the President, because there is now a president of Congress, whose expenses may not be far, if anything, short of those which will be incurred on account of the President of the United States. The support of the judges will clearly be an extra expense, but to what extent will depend on the particular plan which may be adopted in practice in regard to this matter. But it can upon no reasonable plan amount to a sum which will be an object of material consequence.

Let us now see what there is to counterbalance any extra expense that may attend the establishment of the proposed government. The first thing that presents itself is that a great part of the business which now keeps Congress sitting through the year will be transacted by the President. Even the management of foreign negotiations will naturally devolve upon him, according to general principles concerted with the Senate, and subject to their final concurrence. Hence it is evident that a portion of the year will suffice for the session of both the Senate and the House of Representatives; we may suppose about a fourth for the latter and a third, or perhaps a half, for the former. The extra business of treaties and appointments may give this extra occupation to the Senate. From this circumstance we may infer that, until the House of Representatives shall be increased greatly beyond its present number, there will be a considerable saving of expense from the difference between the constant session of the present and the temporary session of the future Congress.

But there is another circumstance of great importance in the view of economy. The business of the United States has hitherto occupied the State legislatures, as well as Congress. The latter has made requisitions which the former have had to provide for. Hence it has happened that the sessions of the State legislatures have been protracted greatly beyond what was necessary for the execution of the mere local business of the States. More than half their time has been frequently employed in matters which related to the United States. Now the members who compose the legislatures of the several States amount to two thousand and upwards, which number has hitherto performed what under the new system will be done in the first instance by sixty-five persons, and probably at no future period by above a fourth or a fifth of that number. The Congress under the proposed government will do all the business of the United States themselves, without the intervention of the State legislatures, who thenceforth will have only to attend to the affairs of their particular States, and will not have to sit in any proportion as long as they have heretofore done. This difference in the time of the sessions of the State legislatures will be all clear gain, and will alone form an article of saving, which may be regarded as an equivalent for any additional objects of expense that may be occasioned by the adoption of the new system.

The result from these observations is that the sources of additional expense from the establishment of the proposed Constitution are much fewer than may have been imagined; that they are counterbalanced by considerable objects of saving; and that while it is questionable on which side the scale will preponderate, it is certain that a government less expensive would be incompetent to the purposes of the Union.

PUBLIUS

No. 85: Concluding Remarks

According to the formal division of the subject of these papers announced in my first number, there would appear still to remain for discussion two points: "the analogy of the proposed government to your own State constitution," and "the additional security which its adoption will afford to republican government, to liberty, and to property." But these heads have been so fully anticipated and exhausted in the progress of the work that it would now scarcely be possible to do anything more than repeat, in a more dilated form, what has been heretofore said, which the advanced stage of the question and the time already spent upon it conspire to forbid.

It is remarkable that the resemblance of the plan of the convention to the act which organizes the government of this State holds, not less with regard to many of the supposed defects than to the real excellences of the former. Among the pretended defects are the re-eligibility of the executive, the want of a council, the omission of a formal bill of rights, the omission of a provision respecting the liberty of the press. These and several others which have been noted in the course of our inquiries are as much chargeable on the existing constitution of this State as on the one proposed for the Union; and a man must have slender pretensions to consistency who can rail at the latter for imperfections which he finds no difficulty in excusing in the former. Nor indeed can there be a better proof of the insincerity and affectation of some of the zealous adversaries of the plan of the convention among us who profess to be the devoted admirers of the government under which they live, than the fury with which they have attacked that plan, for matters in regard to which our own constitution is equally or perhaps more vulnerable.

The additional securities to republican government, to liberty, and to property to be derived from the adoption of the plan under consideration, consist chiefly in the restraints which the preservation of the Union will impose on local factions and insurrections, and on the ambition of powerful individuals in single States who might acquire credit and influence enough from leaders and favorites to become the despots of the people; in the diminution of the opportunities to foreign intrigue, which the dissolution of the Confederacy would invite and facilitate; in the prevention of extensive military establishments, which could not fail to grow out of wars between the States in a disunited situation; in the express guaranty of a republican form of government to each; in the absolute and universal exclusion of titles of nobility; and in the precautions against the repetition of those practices on the part of the State governments which have undermined the foundations of property and credit, have planted mutual distrust in the breasts of all classes of citizens, and have occasioned an almost universal prostration of morals.

Thus have I, fellow-citizens, executed the task I had assigned to myself; with what success your conduct must determine. I trust at least you will admit that I have not failed in the assurance I gave you respecting the spirit with which my endeavors should be conducted. I have addressed myself purely to your judgments, and have studiously avoided those asperities which are too apt to disgrace political disputants of all parties and which have been not a little provoked by the language and conduct of the opponents of the Constitution. The charge of a conspiracy against the liberties of the people which has been indiscriminately brought against the advocates of the plan has something in it too wanton and too malignant not to excite the indignation of every man who feels in his own bosom a refutation of the calumny. The perpetual changes which have been rung upon the wealthy, the well-born, and the great have been such as to inspire the disgust of all sensible men. And the unwarrantable concealments and misrepresentations which have been in various ways practiced to keep the truth from the public eye have been of a nature to demand the reprobation of all honest men. It is not impossible that these circumstances may have occasionally betrayed me into intemperances of expression which I did not intend; it is certain that I have frequently felt a struggle between sensibility and moderation; and if the former has in some instances prevailed, it must be my excuse that it has been neither often nor much.

Let us now pause and ask ourselves whether, in the course of these papers, the proposed Constitution has not been satisfactorily vindicated from the aspersions thrown upon it; and whether it has not been shown to be worthy of the public approbation and necessary to the public safety and prosperity. Every man is bound to answer these questions to himself, according to the best of his conscience and understanding, and to act agreeably to the genuine and sober dictates of his judgment. This is a duty from which nothing can give him a dispensation. 'Tis one that he is called upon, nay, constrained by all the obligations that form the bands of society, to discharge sincerely and honestly. No partial motive, no particular interest, no pride of opinion, no temporary passion or prejudice, will justify to himself, to his country, or to his posterity, an improper election of the part he is to act. Let him beware of an obstinate adherence to party; let him reflect that the object upon which he is to decide is not a particular interest of the community, but the very existence of the nation; and let him remember that a majority of America has already given its sanction to the plan which he is to approve or reject.

I shall not dissemble that I feel an entire confidence in the arguments which recommend the proposed system to your adoption, and that I am unable to discern any real force in those by which it has been opposed. I am persuaded that it is the best which our political situation, habits, and opinions will admit, and superior to any the revolution has produced.

Concessions on the part of the friends of the plan that it has not a claim to absolute perfection have afforded matter of no small triumph to its enemies. "Why," say they, "should we adopt an imperfect thing? Why not amend it and make it perfect before it is irrevocably established?" This may be plausible enough, but it is only plausible. In the first place I remark that the extent of these concessions has been greatly exaggerated. They have been stated as amounting to an admission that the plan is radically defective and that without material alterations the rights and the interests of the community cannot be safely confided to it. This, as far as I have understood the meaning of those who make the concessions, is an entire perversion of their sense. No advocate of the measure can be found who will not declare as his sentiment that the system, though it may not be perfect in every part, is, upon the whole, a good one; is the best that the present views and circumstances of the country will permit; and is such a one as promises every species of security which a reasonable people can desire.

I answer in the next place that I should esteem it the extreme of imprudence to prolong the precarious state of our national affairs and to expose the Union to the jeopardy of successive experiments in the chimerical pursuit of a perfect plan. I never expect to see a perfect work from imperfect man. The result of the deliberations of all collective bodies must necessarily be a compound; as well of the errors and prejudices as of the good sense and wisdom of the individuals of whom they are composed. The compacts which are to embrace thirteen distinct States in a common bond of amity and union must as necessarily be a compromise of as many dissimilar interests and inclinations. How can perfection spring from such materials?

The reasons assigned in an excellent little pamphlet lately published in this city* are unanswerable to show the utter improbability of assembling a new convention under circumstances in any degree so favorable to a happy issue as those in which the late convention met, deliberated, and concluded. I will not repeat the arguments there used, as I presume the production itself has had an extensive circulation. It is certainly well worth the perusal of every friend to his country. There is, however, one point of light in which the subject of amendments still remains to be considered, and in which it has not yet been exhibited to public view. I cannot resolve to conclude without first taking a survey of it in this aspect.

It appears to me susceptible of absolute demonstration that it will be far more easy to obtain subsequent than previous amendments to the Constitution. The moment an alteration is made in the present plan it becomes, to the purpose of adoption a new one, and must undergo a new decision of each State. To its complete establishment throughout the Union it will therefore require the concurrence of thirteen States. If, on the contrary, the Constitution proposed should once be ratified by all the States as it stands, alterations in it may at any time be effected by nine States. Here, then, the chances are as thirteen to nine† in favor of subsequent amendment, rather than of the original adoption of an entire system.

This is not all. Every Constitution for the United States must inevitably consist of a great variety of particulars in which thirteen independent States are to be accommodated in their interests or opinions of interest. We may of course expect to see, in any body of men charged with its original formation, very different combinations of the parts upon different points. Many of those who form a majority on one question may become the minority on a second, and an association dissimilar to either may constitute the majority on a third. Hence the necessity of moulding and arranging all the particulars which are to compose the whole in such a manner as to satisfy all the parties to the compact; and hence, also, an immense multiplication of difficulties and casualties in obtaining the collective assent to a final act. The degree of that multiplication must evidently be in a ratio to the number of particulars and the number of parties.

---

*Entitled "An Address to the People of the State of New York."
†It may rather be said TEN, for though two thirds may set on foot the measure, three fourths must ratify.

But every amendment to the Constitution, if once established, would be a single proposition, and might be brought forward singly. There would then be no necessity for management or compromise in relation to any other point—no giving nor taking. The will of the requisite number would at once bring the matter to a decisive issue. And consequently, whenever nine, or rather ten States, were united in the desire of a particular amendment, that amendment must infallibly take place. There can, therefore, be no comparison between the facility of affecting an amendment and that of establishing, in the first instance, a complete Constitution.

In opposition to the probability of subsequent amendments, it has been urged that the persons delegated to the administration of the national government will always be disinclined to yield up any portion of the authority of which they were once possessed. For my own part, I acknowledge a thorough conviction that any amendments which may, upon mature consideration, be thought useful, will be applicable to the organization of the government, not to the mass of its powers; and on this account alone I think there is no weight in the observation just stated. I also think there is little weight in it on another account. The intrinsic difficulty of governing THIRTEEN STATES at any rate, independent of calculations upon an ordinary degree of public spirit and integrity will, in my opinion, constantly *impose* on the national rulers the *necessity* of a spirit of accommodation to the reasonable expectations of their constituents. But there is yet a further consideration, which proves beyond the possibility of doubt that the observation is futile. It is this: that the national rulers, whenever nine States concur, will have no option upon the subject. By the fifth article of the plan, the Congress will be *obliged* "on the application of the legislatures of two thirds of the States [which at present amount to nine], to call a convention for proposing amendments which *shall be valid,* to all intents and purposes, as part of the Constitution, when ratified by the legislatures of three fourths of the states, or by conventions in three fourths thereof." The words of this article are peremptory. The Congress *"shall* call a convention." Nothing in this particular is left to the discretion of that body. And of consequence all the declamation about the disinclination to a change vanishes in air. Nor however difficult it may be supposed to unite two thirds or three fourths of the State legislatures in amendments which may affect local interests can there be any room to apprehend any such difficulty in a union on points which are merely relative to the general liberty or security of the people. We may safely rely on the disposition of the State legislatures to erect barriers against the encroachments of the national authority.

If the foregoing argument is a fallacy, certain it is that I am myself deceived by it for it is, in my conception, one of those rare instances in which a political truth can be brought to the test of mathematical demonstration. Those who see the matter in the same light with me, however zealous they may be for amendments, must agree in the propriety of a previous adoption as the most direct road to their own object.

The zeal for attempts to amend, prior to the establishment of the Constitution, must abate in every man who is ready to accede to the truth of the following observations of a writer equally solid and ingenious: "To balance a large state or society [says he], whether monarchical or republican, on general laws, is a work of so great difficulty that no human genius, however comprehensive, is able, by the mere dint of reason and reflection, to effect it. The judgments of many must unite in the work; EXPERIENCE must guide their labor; TIME must bring it to perfection, and the FEELING of inconveniences must correct the mistakes which they *inevitably* fall into in their first trials and experiments."* These judicious reflections contain a lesson of moderation to all the sincere lovers of the Union, and ought to put them upon their guard against hazarding anarchy, civil war, a perpetual alienation of the States from each other, and perhaps the military despotism of a victorious demagogue, in the pursuit of what they are not likely to obtain, but from TIME and EXPERIENCE. It may be in me a defect of political fortitude but I acknowledge that I cannot entertain an equal tranquillity with those who affect to treat the dangers of a longer continuance in our present situation as imaginary. A NATION, without a NATIONAL GOVERNMENT, is, in my view, an awful spectacle. The establishment of a Constitution, in time of profound peace, by the voluntary consent of a whole people, is a PRODIGY, to the completion of which I look forward with trembling anxiety. I can reconcile it to no rules of prudence to let go the hold we now have, in so arduous an enterprise, upon seven out of the thirteen States, and after having passed over so considerable a part of the ground, to recommence the course. I dread the more the consequences of new attempts because I know that POWERFUL INDIVIDUALS, in this and in other States, are enemies to a general national government in every possible shape.

PUBLIUS

---

*Hume's *Essays,* Vol. I, page 128: "The Rise of Arts and Sciences."

6

Speech at the New York Ratifying Convention, June 20, 1788

In mid-June 1788, Alexander Hamilton delivered the following speech to the convention assembled in Poughkeepsie, New York, to debate and vote on ratification of the Constitution, which had been drafted in Philadelphia the previous year. When the New York convention met, eight states had already ratified the Constitution and only one more was needed to approve it, but the sides were deadlocked in the remaining five states: New York, Virginia, New Hampshire, North Carolina, and Rhode Island. Debate mostly centered around the question of how powerful the government should be as well as the existence of a Bill of Rights outlining basic political rights, such as freedom of religion, speech, and the press.

As the Constitution was debated throughout the states, the Bill of Rights did not exist. The Federalists, including Hamilton, argued that it wasn't necessary because the Constitution did not grant the federal government the power to limit the rights of individual citizens. This did not reassure Anti-Federalists, who feared what the power of the federal government might become without a Bill of Rights. A week into the New York convention, while debate over the Bill of Rights and other issues was going on, news came that the question had been rendered somewhat moot because New Hampshire had ratified the Constitution on June 21. With nine states on board, the Constitution was the law of the land for all the states.

Ratification by New York and Virginia was essential because it was widely felt that the new government could fail without their support. Both states ratified after hearing the news from New Hampshire, with Virginia on June 25 and New York on July 26. Although it took some time, the Federalist Party wisely recognized the strong feelings throughout the country for a Bill of Rights. Many of the states that voted for ratification sent their demands concerning what should be in the Bill of Rights, with New York's list being the longest, with twenty-five items. After much debate concerning exactly what should be included, the first ten amendments were added to the Constitution by votes in Congress, not long after its official ratification.

Hamilton's speech presents the case for the Constitution forcefully. He was speaking in June 1788, with the experience of writing fifty-one essays in *The Federalist Papers* just completed, so he knew what he wanted to say. His speech is credited as a major factor in leading to the formal vote to ratify by a thin three-vote majority at the New York convention. It was widely believed that sentiment at the convention before the debates was strongly anti-ratification. Several members who opposed the Constitution abstained from voting. If the final vote had been taken on the day when the convention was convened, the Constitution could have easily been voted down, so this was a significant victory.

In this speech, Hamilton refers—as he often did in his writings—to events in ancient Greek political history involving the Amphyctionic and Achaean leagues of city-states. These events figured prominently in accounts by the ancient authors whose works Hamilton grew up reading. Much of his political thinking was based on the efforts of these ancient city-states to find a way to be allied without giving up their individual freedoms and without leaving themselves open to attack from more powerful outside forces. In Hamilton's mind, their difficulties mirrored what the thirteen American states encountered under the Articles of Confederation. He saw a better future when Americans would be citizens of America in areas such as taxation and national defense, while the individual states would continue to dominate on local issues.

Hamilton touched on many subjects in this speech, including the question of how slaves would be counted in terms of representation under the Constitution. Like most of the Founding Fathers, Hamilton didn't seem to contemplate, or argue for, the end of slavery. (He was, however, involved in New York with an organization whose goal was the manumission of slaves, the freeing of slaves by their owners.) This speech represented the end of Hamilton's long battle for ratification of the Constitution. This seems to come through in his closing remark: "Many other observations might be made on this subject [the Constitution], but I cannot now pursue them; for I feel myself not a little exhausted: I beg leave therefore to wave for the present the further discussion of this question." When the delegates left Poughkeepsie, the battle was over and the Constitution was ratified.

[Poughkeepsie, New York, June 20, 1788]

Mr. Chairman the honorable Member, who spoke yesterday, went into an explanation of a variety of circumstances to prove the expediency of a change in our national government, and the necessity of a firm union: At the same time he described the great advantages which this State, in particular, receives from the confederacy, and its peculiar weaknesses when abstracted from the Union. In doing this, he advanced a variety of arguments, which deserve serious consideration. Gentlemen have this day come forward, to answer him. He has been treated as having wandered in the flowery fields of fancy; and attempts have been made, to take off from the minds of the committee, that sober impression, which might be expected from his arguments. I trust, sir, that observations of this kind are not thrown out to cast a light air on this important subject; or to give any personal bias, on the great question before us. I will not agree with gentlemen, who trifle with the weaknesses of our country; and suppose, that they are enumerated to answer a party purpose, and to terrify with ideal dangers. No; I believe these weaknesses to be real, and pregnant with destruction. Yet, however weak our country may be, I hope we shall never sacrifice our liberties. If, therefore, on a full and candid discussion, the proposed system shall appear to have that tendency, for God's sake, let us reject it! But, let us not mistake words for things, nor accept doubtful surmises as the evidence of truth. Let us consider the Constitution calmly and dispassionately, and attend to those things only which merit consideration.

No arguments drawn from embarrassment or inconvenience, ought to prevail upon us to adopt a system of government radically bad; yet it is proper that these arguments, among others, should be brought into view. In doing this, yesterday, it was necessary to reflect upon our situation; to dwell upon the imbecility of our Union; and to consider whether we, as a State, could stand alone. Although I am persuaded this Convention will be resolved to adopt nothing that is bad; yet I think every prudent man will consider the merits of the plan in connection with the circumstances of our country; and that a rejection of the Constitution may involve most fatal consequences. I make these remarks to shew, that tho' we ought not to be actuated by unreasonable fear, yet we ought to be prudent.

This day, sir, one gentleman has attempted to answer the arguments advanced by my honorable friend; another has treated him as having wandered from the subject: This being the case, I trust I shall be equally indulged in reviewing the remarks which have been made.

Sir, it appears to me extraordinary, that while gentlemen in one breath acknowledge, that the old confederation requires many material amendments, they should in the next deny, that its defects have been the cause of our political weakness, and the consequent calamities of our country. I cannot but infer from this, that there is still some lurking favorite imagination, that this system, with corrections, might become a safe and permanent one. It is proper that we should examine this matter. We contend that the radical vice in the old confederation is, that the laws of the Union apply only to States in their corporate capacity. Has not every man, who has been in our legislature, experienced the truth of this position? It is inseparable from the disposition of bodies, who have a constitutional power of resistance, to examine the merits of a law. This has ever been the case with the federal requisitions. In this examination, not being furnished with those lights, which directed the deliberations of the general government; and incapable of embracing the general interests of the Union, the States have almost uniformly weighed the requisitions by their own local interests; and have only executed them so far as answered their particular conveniency or advantage. Hence there have ever been thirteen different bodies to judge of the measures of Congress—and the operations of government have been distracted by their taking different courses: Those, which were to be benefited have complied with the requisitions; others have totally disregarded them. Have not all of us been witnesses to the unhappy embarrassments which resulted from these proceedings? Even during the late war, while the pressure of common danger connected strongly the bond of our union, and incited to vigorous exertions, we have felt many distressing effects of the impotent system. How have we seen this State, though most exposed to the calamities of the war, complying, in an unexampled manner, with the federal requisitions, and compelled by the delinquency of others, to bear most unusual burthens! Of this truth we have the most solemn proof on our records. In 1779 and 1780, when the State, from the ravages of war, and from her great exertions to resist them, became weak, distressed and forlorn, every man avowed the principle which we now contend for; that our misfortunes, in a great degree, proceeded from the want of vigor in the continental government. These were our sentiments when we did not speculate, but feel. We saw our weakness, and found ourselves its victims. Let us reflect that this may again in all probability be our situation. This is a weak State; and its relative station is dangerous. Your capital is accessible by land, and by sea is exposed to every daring invader; and on the North West, you are open to the inroads of a powerful foreign nation. Indeed this State, from its situation, will, in time of war, probably be the theatre of its operations.

Gentlemen have said that the non-compliance of the States has been occasioned by their sufferings. This may in part be true. But has this State been delinquent? Amidst all our distresses, *we* have fully complied. If New-York could comply wholly with the requisitions, is it not to be supposed, that the other States, could in part comply? Certainly every State in the Union might have executed them in some degree. But New Hampshire, who has not suffered at all, is totally delinquent: North-Carolina is totally delinquent: Many others have contributed in a very small proportion; and Pennsylvania and New-York are the only states, which have perfectly discharged their Federal duty.

From the delinquency of those States who have suffered little by the war, we naturally conclude, that they have made no efforts; and a knowledge of human nature will teach us, that their ease and security have been a principal cause of their want of exertion. While danger is distant, its impression is weak, and while it affects only our neighbours we have few motives to provide against it. Sir, if we have national objects to pursue, we must have national revenues. If you make requisitions and they are not complied with, what is to be done? It has been well observed, that to coerce the States is one of the maddest projects that was ever devised. A failure of compliance will never be confined to a single State: This being the case, can we suppose it wise to hazard a civil war? Suppose Massachusetts or any large State should refuse; and Congress should attempt to compel them; would they not have influence to procure assistance, especially from those states who are in the same situation as themselves? What picture does this idea present to our view? A complying state at war with a non-complying state: Congress marching the troops of one state into the bosom of another: This state collecting auxiliaries and forming perhaps a majority against its Federal head. Here is a nation at war with itself. Can any reasonable man be well disposed towards a government which makes war and carnage the only means of supporting itself? a government that can exist only by the sword? Every such war must involve the innocent with the guilty. This single consideration should be sufficient to dispose every peaceable citizen against such a government.

But can we believe that one state will ever suffer itself to be used as an instrument of coercion? The thing is a dream. It is impossible. Then we are brought to this dilemma: Either a federal standing army is to enforce the requisitions, or the Federal Treasury is left without supplies, and the government without support. What, Sir, is the cure for this great evil? Nothing, but to enable the national laws to operate on individuals, in the same manner as those of the states do. This is the true reasoning upon the subject, Sir. The gentlemen appear to acknowledge its force; and yet while they yield to the principle, they seem to fear its application to the government.

What then shall we do? Shall we take the Old Confederation, as the basis of a new system? Can this be the object of the gentlemen? certainly not. Will any man who entertains a wish for the safety of his country, trust the sword and the purse with a single Assembly organized on principles so defective—so rotten? Though we might give to such a government certain powers with safety, yet to give them the full and unlimited powers of taxation and the national forces would be to establish a despotism; the definition of which is, a government, in which all power is concentred in a single body. To take the Old Confederation, and fashion it upon these principles, would be establishing a power which would destroy the liberties of the people. These considerations show clearly, that a government totally different must be instituted. They had weight in the convention who formed the new system. It was seen, that the necessary powers were too great to be trusted to a single body: They therefore formed two branches; and divided the powers, that each might be a check upon the other. This was the result of their wisdom; and I presume that every reasonable man will agree to it. The more this subject is explained, the more clear and convincing it will appear to every member of this body. The fundamental principle of the Old Confederation is defective. We must totally eradicate and discard this principle before we can expect an efficient government. The gentlemen who have spoken to day have taken up the subject of the antient Confederacies: But their view of them has been extremely partial and erroneous: The fact is, the same false and impracticable principle ran through most of the antient governments. The first of these governments that we read of, was the Amphyctionic confederacy. The council which managed the affairs of this league possessed powers of a similar complexion to those of our present Congress. The same feeble mode of legislation in the head, and the same power of resistance in the members, prevailed. When a requisition was made, it rarely met a compliance; and a civil war was the consequence. Those which were attacked called in foreign aid to protect them; and the ambitious Philip under the mask of an ally to one, invaded the liberties of each, and finally subverted the whole.

The operation of this principle appears in the same light in the Dutch Republics. They have been obliged to levy taxes by an armed force. In this confederacy, one large province, by its superior wealth and influence, is commonly a match for all the rest; and when they do not comply, the province of Holland is obliged to compel them. It is observed, that the United Provinces have existed a long time; but they have been constantly the sport of their neighbors; and have been supported only by the external pressure of the surrounding powers. The policy of Europe, not the policy of their government, has saved them from dissolution. Besides, the powers of the Stadholder have served to give an energy to the operations of this government, which is not to be found in ours. This prince has a vast personal influence: He has independent revenues: He commands an army of forty thousand men.

The German confederacy has also been a perpetual source of wars: They have a diet, like our Congress, who have authority to call for supplies: These calls are never obeyed; and in time of war, the Imperial army never takes the field, till the enemy are returning from it. The Emperor's Austrian dominions, in which he is an absolute prince, alone enable him to make head against the common foe. The members of this confederacy are ever divided and opposed to each other. The king of Prussia is a member; yet he has been constantly in opposition to the Emperor. Is this a desirable government?

I might go more particularly into the discussion of examples, and shew, that wherever this fatal principle has prevailed, even as far back as the Lycian and Achæan leagues, as well as the Amphyctionic confederacy; it has proved the destruction of the government. But I think observations of this kind might have been spared. Had they not been entered into by others, I should not have taken up so much of the time of the committee. No inference can be drawn from these examples, that republics cannot exist: We only contend that they have hitherto been founded on false principles. We have shewn how they have been conducted, and how they have been destroyed. Weakness in the head has produced resistence in the members: This has been the immediate parent of civil war: Auxiliary force has been invited, and a foreign power has annihilated their liberties and their name. Thus Philip subverted the Amphyctionic, and Rome the Achæan Republic.

We shall do well, sir, not to deceive ourselves with the favorable events of the late war. Common danger prevented the operation of the ruinous principle, in its full extent: But since the peace, we have experienced the evils; we have felt the poison of the system in its unmingled purity.

Without dwelling any longer on this subject, I shall proceed to the question immediately before the committee.

In order that the committee may understand clearly the principles on which the general convention acted, I think it necessary to explain some preliminary circumstances.

Sir, the natural situation of this country seems to divide its interests into different classes. There are navigating and non-navigating States. The Northern are properly the navigating States: The Southern appear to possess neither the means nor the spirit of navigation. This difference of situation naturally produces a dissimilarity of interests and views respecting foreign commerce. It was the interest of the Northern States, that there should be no restraints on their navigation, and that they should have full power, by a majority in Congress, to make commercial regulations in favour of their own, and in restraint of the navigation of foreigners. The Southern States wished to impose a restraint on the Northern, by requiring that two thirds in Congress, should be requisite to pass an act in regulation of commerce: They were apprehensive that the restraints of a navigation law, would discourage foreigners, and by obliging them to employ the shipping of the Northern States would probably enhance their freight. This being the case, they insisted strenuously on having this provision engrafted in the constitution; and the Northern States were as anxious in opposing it. On the other hand, the small states seeing themselves embraced by the confederation upon equal terms, wished to retain the advantages which they already possessed: The large states, on the contrary, thought it improper that Rhode Island and Delaware should enjoy an equal suffrage with themselves: From these sources a delicate and difficult contest arose. It became necessary, therefore, to compromise; or the Convention must have dissolved without affecting any thing. Would it have been wise and prudent in that body, in this critical situation, to have deserted their country? No. Every man who hears me—every wise man in the United States, would have condemned them. The Convention were obliged to appoint a Committee for accommodation: In this Committee, the arrangement was formed, as it now stands; and their report was accepted. It was a delicate point; and it was necessary that all parties should be indulged. Gentlemen will see, that if there had not been a unanimity, nothing could have been done: For the Convention had no power to establish, but only to recommend a government. Any other system would have been impracticable. Let a Convention be called to-morrow. Let them meet twenty times; nay, twenty thousand times; they will have the same difficulties to encounter; the same clashing interests to reconcile.

But dismissing these reflections, let us consider how far the arrangement is in itself entitled to the approbation of this body. We will examine it upon its own merits.

The first thing objected to, is that clause which allows a representation for three fifths of the negroes. Much has been said of the impropriety of representing men, who have no will of their own. Whether this be reasoning or declamation, I will not presume to say. It is the unfortunate situation of the Southern States, to have a great part of their population, as well as property in blacks. The regulation complained of was one result of the spirit of accommodation, which governed the Convention; and without this indulgence, no union could possibly have been formed. But, Sir, considering some peculiar advantages which we derive from them, it is entirely just that they should be gratified. The Southern States possess certain staples, tobacco, rice, indigo, &c. which must be capital objects in treaties of commerce with foreign nations; and the advantage which they necessarily procure in these treaties, will be felt throughout all the States. But the justice of this plan will appear in another view. The best writers on government have held that representation should be compounded of persons and property. This rule has been adopted, as far as it could be, in the Constitution of New York. It will however by no means be admitted, that the slaves are considered altogether as property. They are men, though degraded to the condition of slavery. They are persons known to the municipal laws of the states which they inhabit, as well as to the laws of nature. But representation and taxation go together—and one uniform rule ought to apply to both. Would it be just to compute these slaves in the assessment of taxes; and discard them from the estimate in the apportionment of representatives? Would it be just to impose a singular burthen, without conferring some adequate advantage?

Another circumstance ought to be considered. The rule we have been speaking of is a general rule, and applies to all the States. Now, you have a great number of people in your State, which are not represented at all; and have no voice in your government: These will be included in the enumeration—not two fifths—nor three fifths, but the whole. This proves that the advantages of the plan are not confined to the southern States, but extend to other parts of the Union.

I now proceed to consider the objection with regard to the number of representatives, as it now stands: I am persuaded the system, in this respect, stands on a better footing than the gentlemen imagine.

It has been asserted that it will be in the power of Congress to reduce the number. I acknowledge, that there are no direct words of prohibition. But, I contend, that the true and genuine construction of the clause gives Congress no power whatever to reduce the representation below the number, as it now stands. Although they may limit, they can never diminish the number. One representative for every thirty thousand inhabitants is fixed as the standard of increase; till, by the natural course of population, it shall become necessary to limit the ratio. Probably at present, were this standard to be immediately applied, the representation would considerably exceed sixty-five: In three years it would exceed a hundred. If I understand the gentlemen, they contend that the number may be enlarged or may not. I admit that this is in the discretion of Congress; and I submit to the committee whether it be not necessary and proper. Still, I insist, that an immediate limitation is not probable; nor was it in the contemplation of the Convention. But, Sir, who will presume to say to what precise point the representation ought to be increased? This is a matter of opinion; and opinions are vastly different upon the subject. A proof of this is drawn from the representations in the state legislatures. In Massachusetts, the Assembly consists of about three hundred, In South-Carolina, of nearly one hundred, In New-York there are sixty five. It is observed generally that the number ought to be large. Let the gentlemen produce their criterion. I confess it is difficult for me to say what number may be said to be sufficiently large. On one hand, it ought to be considered, that a small number will act with more facility, system, and decision: On the other, that a large one may enhance the difficulty of corruption. The Congress is to consist at first of ninety-one members. This, to a reasonable man, may appear to be as near the proper medium as any number whatever; at least for the present. There is one source of increase, also, which does not depend upon any constructions of the Constitution; it is the creation of new states. Vermont, Kentuckey, and Franklin, will probably soon become independent: New members of the Union will also be formed from the unsettled tracts of Western Territory. These must be represented; and will all contribute to swell the federal legislature. If the whole number in the United States be, at present, three millions, as is commonly supposed, according to the ratio of one for thirty thousand, we shall have, on the first census, a hundred representatives: In ten years, thirty more will be added; and in twenty-five years, the number will double: Then, Sir, we shall have two hundred; if the increase goes on in the same proportion. The Convention of Massachusetts who made the same objection, have fixed upon this number as the point at which they chose to limit the representation. But can we pronounce with certainty, that it will not be expedient to go beyond this number? We cannot. Experience alone must determine. This matter may, with more safety, be left to the discretion of the legislature, as it will be the interest of the larger and increasing states, of Massachusetts, New-York, Pennsylvania, &c. to augment the representation. Only Connecticut, Rhode-Island, Delaware, and Maryland, can be interested in limiting it. We may therefore safely calculate upon a growing representation, according to the advance of population, and the circumstances of the country.

The State governments possess inherent advantages, which will ever give them an influence and ascendency over the national government; and will forever preclude the possibility of federal encroachments. That their liberties indeed can be subverted by the federal head, is repugnant to every rule of political calculation. Is not this arrangement then, Sir, a most wise and prudent one? Is not the present representation fully adequate to our present exigencies; and sufficient to answer all the purposes of the Union? I am persuaded that an examination of the objects of the federal government will afford a conclusive answer.

Many other observations might be made on this subject, but I cannot now pursue them; for I feel myself not a little exhausted: I beg leave therefore to wave for the present the further discussion of this question.

7

Report on Public Credit, January 9, 1790

When the American Revolution came to an end in 1781, Alexander Hamilton looked at America and saw a small, agrarian republic on the fringe of the civilized world, which had just completed the remarkable feat of securing its independence from the Old World. He wanted to lose as little time as possible turning it into a self-sufficient modern nation that would be able to provide what it needed for its own defense and everything else. He wanted America to rank in economic power—and be able to trade on equal terms—with the nations of Europe. He didn't want to abandon America's agrarian history but rather develop and enlarge it. He never doubted that farming would be central to the nation's economy, but he wanted to support the growth of a modern manufacturing and industrial economy as well. The major reports he wrote as the first secretary of the Treasury were both an analysis of the nation's situation and problems as he understood them and a blueprint for the future that reflected his vision.

George Washington was inaugurated as the first president of the United States on April 30, 1789, and signed the law creating the Department of the Treasury on the following September 2. Washington offered the position of secretary of the Treasury to New York banker Robert Morris, who had great credibility in this area from his tireless work as the de facto "financier of the American Revolution." Morris declined and recommended Hamilton for the position, knowing that they shared similar views on the new nation's direction and what the Treasury should hope to accomplish. Morris was aware of Washington's long relationship with Hamilton and how much Washington valued Hamilton's opinions and advice.

Hamilton became secretary of the Treasury on September 11, 1789. The question of how the government would deal with the nation's accumulated war debts was so pressing to the members of Congress that on September 21, 1789—just ten days after Hamilton took office—the House of Representatives directed him to prepare a report on the subject proposing his solutions. On January 14, 1790, Hamilton sent Congress his "Report Relative to a Provision for the Support of Public Credit." A substantial excerpt from that report is reprinted in this volume.

Calculating the national government's debt as $54 million, with individual states owing an additional $25 million, the approximately $80 million debt seemed very daunting. The government's income from federal tariffs and excise taxes was about $4.4 million per year, just enough to cover current expenses.

Hamilton understood that the economic progress he envisioned depended on having a strong financial program that provided public credit where there had been none. This meant moving on from the financial world under the Articles of Confederation, where chaotic debts had been routinely repudiated and bankruptcy seemed to be the major economic activity. Hamilton's program also involved establishing a widely accepted circulating medium as well as modern financial and banking services.

Hamilton's report divided the subject of the debts to be paid into three parts. First, he proposed payment of the foreign debts of the national government with full interest. Second, he proposed paying the domestic debts of the government in full but with interest rates lowered from their original levels. There was little debate on these two aspects, but the final proposal brought forth intense controversy. Hamilton proposed that the national government assume the unpaid debts of the individual states, with a delay on paying interest for a few years because of the government's limited resources.

The question of "assumption" of the states' debts provoked argument on several levels. Some states, such as Georgia, North Carolina, and Maryland, had small debts and were against a program that gave large amounts of relief to other states. Other states, such as South Carolina, New York, New Jersey, and Massachusetts, had substantial debts and supported a program that would help them get their financial houses in order. Virginia had already paid a substantial part of its large war debt and felt that the state wouldn't benefit much from the program. It was a further stumbling block that many individuals had loaned money to their states via the purchase of bonds and other obligations, but in the years since, the lenders had lost hope of being paid back and many had sold their bonds at large and varying discounts to speculators, who would benefit from the proposed government actions. In general, the more rural, agrarian states, especially in the South, looked unfavorably on the program, which they saw as benefiting northern financiers and businessmen more than their own states. This was the essential political divide that emerged in the decade after the Revolution and defined American politics for some time to come.

One of the major early compromises in American political history solved the debt problem. Known as the "dinner table agreement," Thomas Jefferson—the dinner table in question was in his house—and James Madison agreed to support Hamilton's debt plans. In return, Hamilton supported the plan to build the new national capital at the site that had been selected at Georgetown on the Potomac River. As a nod to Morris, who had hoped that the federal government would be permanently based in Philadelphia, all agreed that the government would move from New York to Philadelphia in 1790 for ten years during the building of the new capital in Washington. On July 12, 1790, the bill to establish the new site of the federal government—where it remains today—became law. Later that month, the debt funding and assumption measures were passed by Congress, by margins of two votes in the Senate and three in the House.

Although the timely compromise settled the debt issue, the North/South, city/country, business/agrarian, Federalist/Anti-Federalist divides that surfaced in the debt debates would be with the nation indefinitely. They formed the basis for the nation's first conflict involving its political parties. The Washington administration's work in these areas established the nation on the path that led to modern capitalism. It also intensified the disconnect between Federalists, who endorsed this program, and the Republican proponents of states' rights, who looked back to the traditional, agrarian society they knew and feared putting power in the hands of a new central authority. The politics of these decades was dominated by this conflict.

The Secretary of the Treasury, in obedience to the resolution of the House of Representatives, of the twenty-first day of September last, has, during the recess of Congress, applied himself to the consideration of a proper plan for the support of the public Credit, with all the attention which was due to the authority of the House, and to the magnitude of the object.

In the discharge of this duty, he has felt, in no small degree, the anxieties which naturally flow from a just estimate of the difficulty of the task, from a well-founded diffidence of his own qualifications for executing it with success, and from a deep and solemn conviction of the momentous nature of the truth contained in the resolution under which his investigations have been conducted, "That an *adequate* provision for the support of the Public Credit, is a matter of high importance to the honor and prosperity of the United States."

With an ardent desire that his well-meant endeavors may be conducive to the real advantage of the nation, and with the utmost deference to the superior judgment of the House, he now respectfully submits the result of his enquiries and reflections, to their indulgent construction.

In the opinion of the Secretary, the wisdom of the House, in giving their explicit sanction to the propostion which has been stated, cannot but be applauded by all, who will seriously consider, and trace through their obvious consequences, these plain and undeniable truths

That exigencies are to be expected to occur, in the affairs of nations, in which there will be a necessity for borrowing.

That loans in times of public danger, especially from foreign war, are found an indispensable resource, even to the wealthiest of them.

And that in a country, which, like this, is possessed of little active wealth, or in other words, little monied capital, the necessity for that resource, must, in such emergencies, be proportionably urgent.

And as on the one hand, the necessity for borrowing in particular emergencies cannot be doubted, so on the other, it is equally evident, that to be able to borrow upon *good terms,* it is essential that the credit of a nation should be well established.

For when the credit of a country is in any degree questionable, it never fails to give an extravagant premium, in one shape or another, upon all the loans it has occasion to make. Nor does the evil end here; the same disadvantage must be sustained upon whatever is to be bought on terms of future payment.

From this constant necessity of *borrowing* and *buying dear,* it is easy to conceive how immensely the expences of a nation, in a course of time, will be augmented by an unsound state of the public credit.

To attempt to enumerate the complicated variety of mischiefs in the whole system of the social œconomy, which proceed from a neglect of the maxims that uphold public credit, and justify the solicitude manifested by the House on this point, would be an improper intrusion on their time and patience.

In so strong a light nevertheless do they appear to the Secretary, that on their due observance at the present critical juncture, materially depends, in his judgment, the individual and aggregate prosperity of the citizens of the United States; their relief from the embarrassments they now experience; their character as a People; the cause of good government.

If the maintenance of public credit, then, be truly so important, the next enquiry which suggests itself is, by what means it is to be effected? The ready answer to which question is, by good faith, by a punctual performance of contracts. States, like individuals, who observe their engagements, are respected and trusted: while the reverse is the fate of those, who pursue an opposite conduct.

Every breach of the public engagements, whether from choice or necessity, is in different degrees hurtful to public credit. When such a necessity does truly exist, the evils of it are only to be palliated by a scrupulous attention, on the part of the government, to carry the violation no farther than the necessity absolutely requires, and to manifest, if the nature of the case admits of it, a sincere disposition to make reparation, whenever circumstances shall permit. But with every possible mitigation, credit must suffer, and numerous mischiefs ensue. It is therefore highly important, when an appearance of necessity seems to press upon the public councils, that they should examine well its reality, and be perfectly assured, that there is no method of escaping from it, before they yield to its suggestions. For though it cannot safely be affirmed, that occasions have never existed, or may not exist, in which violations of the public faith, in this respect, are inevitable; yet there is great reason to believe, that they exist far less frequently than precedents indicate; and are oftenest either pretended through levity, or want of firmness, or supposed through want of knowledge. Expedients might often have been devised to effect, consistently with good faith, what has been done in contravention of it. Those who are most commonly creditors of a nation, are, generally speaking, enlightened men; and there are signal examples to warrant a conclusion, that when a candid and fair appeal is made to them, they will understand their true interest too well to refuse their concurrence in such modifications of their claims, as any real necessity may demand.

While the observance of that good faith, which is the basis of public credit, is recommended by the strongest inducements of political expediency, it is enforced by considerations of still greater authority. There are arguments for it, which rest on the immutable principles of moral obligation. And in proportion as the mind is disposed to contemplate, in the order of Providence, as intimate connection between public virtue and public happiness, will be its repugnancy to a violation of those principles.

This reflection derives additional strength from the nature of the debt of the Unites States. It was the price of liberty. The faith of America has been repeatedly pledged for it, and with solemnities, that give peculiar force to the obligation. There is indeed reason to regret that it has not hitherto been kept; that the necessities of the war, conspiring with inexperience in the subjects of finance, produced direct infractions; and that the subsequent period has been a continued scene of negative violation, or non-compliance. But a diminution of this regret arises from the reflection, that the last seven years have exhibited an earnest and uniform effort, on the part of the government of the union, to retrieve the national credit, by doing justice to the creditors of the nation; and that the embarrassments of a defective constitution, which defeated this laudable effort, have ceased.

From this evidence of a favorable disposition, given by the former government, the institution of a new one, cloathed with powers competent to calling forth the resources of the community, has excited correspondent expectations. A general belief, accordingly, prevails, that the credit of the United States will quickly be established on the firm foundation of an effectual provision for the existing debt. The influence, which this has had at home, is witnessed by the rapid increase, that has taken place in the market value of the public securities. From January to November, they rose thirty-three and a third per cent, and from that period to this time, they have risen fifty per cent more. And the intelligence from abroad announces effects proportionably favourable to our national credit and consequence.

It cannot but merit particular attention, that among ourselves the most enlightened friends of good government are those, whose expectations are the highest.

To justify and preserve their confidence; to promote the encreasing respectability of the American name; to answer the calls of justice; to restore landed property to its due value; to furnish new resources both to agriculture and commerce; to cement more closely the union of the states; to add to their security against foreign attack; to establish public order on the basis of an upright and liberal policy. These are the great and invaluable ends to be secured, by a proper and adequate provision, at the present period, for the support of public credit.

To this provision we are invited, not only by the general considerations, which have been noticed, but by others of a more particular nature. It will procure to every class of the community some important advantages, and remove some no less important disadvantages.

The advantage to the public creditors from the increased value of that part of their property which constitutes the public debt, needs no explanation.

But there is a consequence of this, less obvious, though not less true, in which every other citizen is interested. It is a well known fact, that in countries in which the national debt is properly funded, and an object of established confidence, it answers most of the purposes of money. Transfers of stock or public debt are there equivalent to payments in specie; or in other words, stock, in the principal transactions of business, passes current as specie. The same thing would, in all probability happen here, under the like circumstances.

The benefits of this are various and obvious.

First. Trade is extended by it; because there is a larger capital to carry it on, and the merchant can at the same time, afford to trade for smaller profits; as his stock, which, when unemployed, brings him in an interest from the government, serves him also as money, when he has a call for it in his commercial operations.

Secondly. Agriculture and manufactures are also promoted by it: For the like reason, that more capital can be commanded to be employed in both; and because the merchant, whose enterprize in foreign trade, gives to them activity and extension, has greater means for enterprize.

Thirdly. The interest of money will be lowered by it; for this is always in a ratio, to the quantity of money, and to the quickness of circulation. This circumstances will enable both the public and individuals to borrow on easier and cheaper terms.

And from the combination of these effects, addition aids will be furnished to labour, to industry, and to arts of every kind.

But these good effects of a public debt are only to be looked for, when, by being well funded, it has acquired an *adequate* and *stable* value. Till then, it has rather a contrary tendency. The fluctuation and insecurity incident to it in an unfunded state, render it a mere commodity, and a precarious one. As such, being only an object of occasional and particular speculation, all the money applied to it is so much diverted from the more useful channels of circulation, for which the thing itself affords no substitute: So that, in fact, one serious inconvenience of an unfunded debt is, that it contributes to the scarcity of money.

This distinction which has been little if at all attended to, is of the greatest moment. It involves a question immediately interesting to every part of the community; which is no other than this—Whether the public debt, by a provision for it on true principles, shall be rendered a *substitute* for money; or whether, by being left as it is, or by being provided for in such a manner as will wound those principles, and destroy confidence, it shall be suffered to continue, as it is, a pernicious drain of our cash from the channels of productive industry.

The effect, which the funding of the public debt, on right principles, would have upon landed property, is one of the circumstances attending such an arrangement, which has been least adverted to, though it deserves the most particular attention. The present depreciated state of that species of property is a serious calamity. The value of cultivated lands, in most of the states, has fallen since the revolution from 25 to 50 per cent. In those farthest south, the decrease is still more considerable. Indeed, if the representations, continually received from that quarter, may be credited, lands there will command no price, which may not be deemed an almost total sacrifice.

This decrease, in the value of lands, ought, in a great measure, to be attributed to the scarcity of money. Consequently whatever produces an augmentation of the monied capital of the country, must have a proportional effect in raising that value. The beneficial tendency of a funded debt, in this respect, has been manifested by the most decisive experience in Great-Britain.

The proprietors of lands would not only feel the benefit of this increase in the value of their property, and of a more prompt and better sale, when they had occasion to sell; but the necessity of selling would be, itself, greatly diminished. As the same cause would contribute to the facility of loans, there is reason to believe, that such of them as are indebted, would be able through that resource, to satisfy their more urgent creditors.

It ought not however to be expected, that the advantages, described as likely to result from funding the public debt, would be instantaneous. It might require some time to bring the value of stock to its natural level, and to attach to it that fixed confidence, which is necessary to its quality as money. Yet the late rapid rise of the public securities encourages an expectation, that the progress of stock to the desirable point, will be much more expeditious than could have been foreseen. And as in the mean time it will be increasing in value, there is room to conclude, that it will, from the outset, answer many of the purposes in contemplation. Particularly it seems to be probable, that from creditors, who are not themselves necessitous, it will early meet with a ready reception in payment of debts, at its current price.

Having now taken a concise view of the inducements to a proper provision for the public debt, the next enquiry which presents itself is, what ought to be the nature of such a provision? This requires some preliminary discussions.

It is agreed on all hands, that that part of the debt which has been contracted abroad, and is denominated the foreign debt, ought to be provided for, according to the precise terms of the contracts relating to it. The discussions, which can arise, therefore, will have reference essentially to the domestic part of it, or to that which has been contracted at home. It is to be regretted, that there is not the same unanimity of sentiment on this part, as on the other.

The Secretary has too much deference for the opinions of every part of the community, not to have observed one, which has, more than once, made its appearance in the public prints, and which is occasionally to be met with in conversation. It involves this question, whether a discrimination ought not be made between original holders of the public securities, and present possessors, by purchase. Those who advocate a discrimination are for making a full provision for the securities of the former, at their nominal value; but contend, that the latter ought to receive no more than the cost to them, and the interest: And the idea is sometimes suggested of making good the difference to the primitive possessor.

In favor of this scheme, it is alledged, that it would be unreasonable to pay twenty shillings in the pound, to one who had not given more for it than three or four. And it is added, that it would be hard to aggravate the misfortune of the first owner, who, probably through necessity, parted with his property at so great a loss, by obliging him to contribute to the profit of the person, who had speculated on his distresses.

The Secretary, after the most mature reflection on the force of this argument, is induced to reject the doctrine it contains, as equally unjust and impolitic, as highly injurious, even to the original holders of public securities; as ruinous to public credit.

It is inconsistent with justice, because in the first place, it is a breach of contract; in violation of the rights of a fair purchaser.

The nature of the contract in its origin, is, that the public will pay the sum expressed in the security, to the first holder, or his *assignee.* The *intent*, in making the security assignable, is, that the proprietor may be able to make use of his property, by selling it for as much as it *may be worth in the market*, and that the buyer may be *safe* in the purchase.

Every buyer therefore stands exactly in the place of the seller, has the same right with him to the identical sum expressed in the security, and having acquired that right, by fair purchase, and in conformity to the original *agreement* and *intention* of the government, his claim cannot be disputed, without manifest injustice.

That he is to be considered as a fair purchaser, results from this: Whatever necessity the seller may have been under, was occasioned by the government, in not making a proper provision for its debts. The buyer had no agency in it, and therefore ought not to suffer. He is not even chargeable with having taken an undue advantage. He paid what the commodity was worth in the market, and took the risks of reimbursement upon himself. He of course gave a fair equivalent, and ought to reap the benefit of his hazard; a hazard which was far from inconsiderable, and which, perhaps, turned on little less than a revolution in government.

That the case of those, who parted with their securities from necessity, is a hard one, cannot be denied. But whatever complaint of injury, or claim of redress, they may have, respects the government solely. They have not only nothing to object to the persons who relieved their necessities, by giving them the current price of their property, but they are even under an implied condition to contribute to the reimbursement of those persons. They knew, that by the terms of the contract with themselves, the public were bound to pay to those, to whom they should convey their title, the sums stipulated to be paid to them; and, that as citizens of the United States, they were to bear their proportion of the contribution for that purpose. This, by the act of assignment, they tacitly engage to do; and if they had an option, they could not, with integrity or good faith, refuse to do it, without the consent of those to whom they sold.

But though many of the original holders sold from necessity, it does not follow, that this was the case with all of them. It may well be supposed, that some of them did it either through want of confidence in an eventual provision, or from the allurements of some profitable speculation. How shall these different classes be discriminated from each other? How shall it be ascertained, in any case, that the money, which the original holder obtained for his security, was not more beneficial to him, than if he had held it to the pressent time, to avail himself of the provision which shall be made? How shall it be known, whether if the purchaser had employed his money in some other way, he would not be in a better situation, than by having applied it in the purchase of securities, though he should now receive their full amount? And if neither of these things can be known, how shall it be determined whether a discrimination, independent of the breach of contract, would not do a real injury to purchasers; and if it included a compensation to the primitive proprietors, would not give them an advantage, to which they had no equitable pretension.

It may well be imagined, also, that there are not wanting instances, in which individuals, urged by a present necessity, parted with the securities received by them from the public, and shortly after replaced them with others, as an indemnity for their first loss. Shall they be deprived of the indemnity which they have endeavoured to secure by so provident an arrangement?

Questions of this sort, on a close inspection, multiply themselves without end, and demonstrate the injustice of a discrimination, even on the most subtile calculations of equity, abstracted from the obligation of contract.

The difficulties too of regulating the details of a plan for that purpose, which would have even the semblance of equity, would be found immense. It may well be doubted whether they would not be insurmountable, and replete with such absurd, as well as inequitable consequences, as to disgust even the proposers of the measure.

As a specimen of its capricious operation, it will be sufficient to notice the effect it would have upon two persons, who may be supposed two years ago to have purchased, each, securities at three shillings in the pound, and one of them to retain those bought by him, till the discrimination should take place; the other to have parted with those bought by him, within a month past, at nine shillings. The former, who had had most confidence in the government, would in this case only receive at the rate of three shillings and the interest; while the latter, who had had less confidence would receive *for what cost him the same money* at the rate of nine shillings, and his representative, *standing in his place,* would be entitled to a like rate.

The impolicy of a discrimination results from two considerations; one, that it proceeds upon a principle destructive of that *quality* of the public debt, or the stock of the nation, which is essential to its capacity for answering the purposes of money—that is the *security* of *transfer;* the other, that as well on this account, as because it includes a breach of faith, it renders property in the funds less valuable; consequently induces lenders to demand a higher premium for what they lend, and produces every other inconvenience of a bad state of public credit.

It will be perceived at first sight, that the transferable quality of stock is essential to its operation as money, and that this depends on the idea of complete security to the transferree, and a firm persuasion, that no distinction can in any circumstances be made between him and the original proprietor.

The precedent of an invasion of this fundamental principle, would of course tend to deprive the community of an advantage, with which no temporary savings could bear the least comparison.

And it will as readily be perceived, that the same cause would operate a diminution of the value of stock in the hands of the first, as well as of every other holder. The price, which any man, who should incline to purchase, would be willing to give for it, would be in a compound ratio to the immediate profit it afforded, and to the chance of the continuance of his profit. If there was supposed to be any hazard of the latter, the risk would be taken into the calculation, and either there would be no purchase at all, or it would be at a proportionably less price.

For this diminution of the value of stock, every person, who should be about to lend to the government, would demand a compensation; and would add to the actual difference, between the nominal and the market value, an equivalent for the chance of greater decrease; which, in a precarious state of public credit, is always to be taken into the account.

Every compensation of this sort, it is evident, would be an absolute loss to the government.

In the preceding discussion of the impolicy of a discrimination, the injurious tendency of it to those, who continue to be the holders of the securities, they received from the government, has been explained. Nothing need be added, on this head, except that this is an additional and interesting light, in which the injustice of the measure may be seen. It would not only divest present proprietors by purchase, of the rights they had acquired under the sanction of public faith, but it would depreciate the property of the remaining original holders.

It is equally unnecessary to add any thing to what has been already said to demonstrate the fatal influence, which the principle of discrimination would have on the public credit.

But there is still a point in view in which it will appear perhaps even more exceptionable, than in either of the former. It would be repugnant to an express provision of the Constitution of the United States. This provision is, that "all debts contracted and engagements entered into before the adoption of that Constitution shall be as valid against the United States under it, as under the confederation." which amounts to a constitutional ratification of the contracts respecting the debt, in the state in which they existed under the confederation. And resorting to that standard, there can be no doubt, that the rights of assignees and original holders, must be considered as equal.

In exploding thus fully the principle of discrimination, the Secretary is happy in reflecting, that he is only the advocate of what has been already sanctioned by the formal and express authority of the government of the Union, in these emphatic terms—"The remaining class of creditors (say Congress in their circular address to the states, of the 26th of April 1783) is composed, partly of such of our fellow-citizens as originally lent to the public the use of their funds, or have since manifested *most confidence* in their country, by receiving transfers from the lenders; and partly of those, whose property has been either advanced or assumed for the public service. To *discriminate* the merits of these several descriptions of creditors, would be a task equally unnecessary and invidious. If the voice of humanity plead more loudly in favor of some than of others, the voice of policy, no less than of justice, pleads in favor of all, A WISE NATION will never permit those who relieve the wants of their country, or who *rely most* on its *faith,* its *firmness,* and its *resources,* when either of them is distrusted to suffer by the event."

The Secretary concluding, that a discrimination, between the different classes of creditors of the United States, cannot with propriety be *made,* proceeds to examine whether a difference ought to be permitted to *remain* between them, and another description of public creditors—Those of the states individually.

The Secretary, after mature reflection on this point, entertains a full conviction, that an assumption of the debts of the particular states by the union, and a like provision for them, as for those of the union, will be a measure of sound policy and substantial justice.

It would, in the opinion of the Secretary, contribute, in an eminent degree, to an orderly, stable and satisfactory arrangement of the national finances.

Admitting, as ought to be the case, that a provision must be made in some way or other, for the entire debt; it will follow, that no greater revenues will be required, whether that provision be made wholly by the United States, or partly by them, and partly by the states separately.

The principal question then must be, whether such a provision cannot be more conveniently and effectually made, by one general plan issuing from one authority, than by different plans or originating in different authorities.

In the first case there can be no competition for resources; in the last, there must be such a competition. The consequences of this, without the greatest caution on both sides, might be interfering regulations, and thence collision and confusion. Particular branches of industry might also be oppressed by it. The most productive objects of revenue are not numerous. Either these must be wholly engrossed by one side, which might lessen the efficacy of the provisions by the other; or both must have recourse to the same objects in different modes, which might occasion an accumulation upon them, beyond what they could properly bear. If this should not happen, the caution requisite to avoiding it, would prevent the revenue's deriving the full benefit of each object. The danger of interference and of excess would be apt to impose restraints very unfriendly to the complete command of those resources, which are the most convenient; and to compel the having recourse to others, less eligible in themselves, and less agreeable to the community.

The difficulty of an effectual command of the public resources, in case of separate provisions for the debt, may be seen in another, and perhaps more striking light. It would naturally happen that different states, from local considerations, would in some instances have recourse to different objects, in others, to the same objects, in different degrees, for procuring the funds of which they stood in need. It is easy to conceive how this diversity would affect the aggregate revenue of the country. By the supposition, articles which yielded a full supply in some states, would yield nothing, or an insufficient product, in others. And hence the public revenue would not derive the full benefit of those articles, from state regulations. Neither could the deficiencies be made good by those of the union. If is a provision of the national constitution, that "all duties, imposts and excises, shall be uniform throughout the United States." And as the general government would be under a necessity from motives of policy, of paying regard to the duty, which may have been previously imposed upon any article, though but in a single state, it would be constrained, either to refrain wholly from any further imposition, upon such article, where it had been already rated as high as was proper, or to confine itself to the difference between the existing rate, and what the article would reasonably bear. Thus the preoccupancy of an article by a single state, would tend to arrest or abridge the impositions of the union on that article. And as it is supposeable, that a great variety of articles might be placed in this situation, by dissimiliar arrangments of the particular states, it is evident, that the aggregate revenue of the country would be likely to be very materially contracted by the plan of separate provisions.

If all the public creditors receive their dues from one source, distributed with an equal hand, their interest will be the same. And having the same interests, they will unite in the support of the fiscal arrangements of the government: As these, too, can be made with more convenience, where there is no competition: These circumstances combined will insure to the revenue laws a more ready and more satisfactory execution.

If on the contrary there are distinct provisions, there will be distinct interests, drawing different ways. That union and concert of views, among the creditors, which in every government is of great importance to their security, and to that of public credit, will not only not exist, but will be likely to give place to mutual jealousy and opposition. And from this cause, the operation of the systems which may be adopted, both by the particular states, and by the union, with relation to their respective debts, will be in danger of being counteracted.

There are several reasons, which render it probable, that the situation of the state creditors would be worse, than that of the creditors of the union, if there be not a national assumption of the state debts. Of these it will be sufficient to mention two; one, that a principal branch of revenue is exclusively vested in the union; the other, that a state must always be checked in the imposition of taxes on articles of consumption, from the want of power to extend the same regulation to the other states, and from the tendency of partial duties to injure its industry and commerce. Should the state creditors stand upon a less eligible footing than the others, it is unnatural to expect they would see with pleasure a provision for them. The influence which their dissatisfaction might have, could not but operate injuriously, both for the creditors, and the credit, of the United States.

Hence it is even the interest of the creditors of the union, that those of the individual states should be comprehended in a general provision. Any attempt to secure to the former either exclusive or peculiar advantages, would materially hazard their interests.

Neither would it be just, that one class of the public creditors should be more favoured than the other. The objects for which both descriptions of the debt were contracted, are in the main the same. Indeed a great part of the particular debts of the States has arisen from assumptions by them on account of the union. And it is most equitable, that there should be the same measure of retribution for all.

There is an objection, however, to an assumption of the state debts, which deserves particular notice. It may be supposed, that it would increase the difficulty of an equitable settlement between them and the United States.

The principles of that settlement, whenever they shall be discussed, will require all the moderation and wisdom of the government. In the opinion of the Secretary, that discussion, till further lights are obtained, would be premature.

All therefore which he would now think adviseable on the point in question, would be, that the amount of the debts assumed and provided for, should be charged to the respective states, to abide an eventual arrangement. This, the United States, as assignees to the creditors, would have an indisputable right to do.

8

Opinion on the Constitutionality of the Bank, February 23, 1791

The corollary to Alexander Hamilton's debt and public credit plans was a national bank, which he felt would be of immense value in strengthening the national government. The bank would issue currency, organize the nation's financial transactions, put the receipt of taxes and tariffs on a solid foundation, deal with foreign countries that already had comparable financial infrastructure on an equal basis, and facilitate commerce and industry in manifold ways. Hamilton thought that without such a bank, the country would forever be stuck in the fog of the Articles of Confederation as far as business, trade, and industry were concerned. "The tendency of a national bank is to increase public and private credit," he had written to Robert Morris in 1781. "The former gives power to the state for the protection of its rights and interests, and the latter facilitates and extends the operations of commerce among individuals. Industry is increased, commodities are multiplied, agriculture and manufactures flourish, and herein consist the true wealth and prosperity of a state."

Hamilton submitted his plan for the national bank to Congress on December 13, 1790. By mid-February 1791, the bill establishing the bank had passed both houses of Congress and was submitted to President George Washington for his signature. The southern, agrarian states that opposed the bank didn't have the votes to block it in Congress. Representatives from those states argued not so much against the desirability or practicality of Hamilton's plan but rather that the establishment of a national bank was unconstitutional. Washington found these arguments troubling and asked his attorney general, Virginia's Edmund Randolph, for his opinion.

Randolph was against the bank, but his opinion was not convincing enough to persuade Washington to veto the bill. Washington next turned to Secretary of State Thomas Jefferson. Jefferson set forth a "strict constructionist" view against the bank, arguing that because the Constitution had not expressly granted Congress the right to charter a national bank, it must be unconstitutional, as his southern colleagues had argued.

Washington had requested two opinions by senior members of his administration, and both had come down against the bank on constitutional grounds. Washington sent Randolph's and Jefferson's opinions to Hamilton and asked for his comments. This was an argument that Hamilton had trained himself to win, and he replied with an opinion that historian Jacob E. Cooke has described as "the most brilliant argument for a broad interpretation of the Constitution in American political literature." Writing with forcefulness and clarity, Hamilton turned the tables on Jefferson. Where Jefferson had argued that any action by the federal government not explicitly allowed in the Constitution was unconstitutional, Hamilton argued that any action that would help the government achieve its goals and was not specifically prohibited by the Constitution must be constitutional.

Washington signed the bank bill into law on February 25, 1791. The bank functioned very well for the duration of its twenty-year charter, but all the issues that its creation had raised flared up again with renewed vigor when the charter expired. By that time, all the players in the initial national bank drama were gone. Hamilton's complete opinion on the constitutionality of the national bank is reprinted here.

The Secretary of the Treasury having perused with attention the papers containing the opinions of the Secretary of State and Attorney General concerning the constitutionality of the bill for establishing a National Bank proceeds according to the order of the President to submit the reasons which have induced him to entertain a different opinion.

It will naturally have been anticipated that, in performing this task he would feel uncommon solicitude. Personal considerations alone arising from the reflection that the measure originated with him would be sufficient to produce it. The sense which he has manifested of the great importance of such an institution to the successful administration of the department under his particular care, and an expectation of serious ill consequences to result from a failure of the measure, do not permit him to be without anxiety on public accounts. But the chief solicitude arises from a firm persuasion, that principles of construction like those espoused by the Secretary of State and the Attorney General would be fatal to the just and indispensable authority of the United States.

In entering upon the argument it ought to be premised, that the objections of the Secretary of State and Attorney General are founded on a general denial of the authority of the United States to erect corporations. The latter indeed expressly admits, that if there be anything in the bill which is not warranted by the constitution, it is the clause of incorporation.

Now it appears to the Secretary of the Treasury, that this *general principle* is *inherent* in the very *definition* of *Government* and *essential* to every step of the progress to be made by that of the United States, namely—that every power vested in a Government is in its nature *sovereign,* and includes by *force* of the *term,* a right to employ all the *means* requisite, and fairly *applicable* to the attainment of the *ends* of such power; and which are not precluded by restrictions and exceptions specified in the constitution, or not immoral, or not contrary to the essential ends of political society.

This principle in its application to Government in general would be admited as an axiom. And it will be incumbent upon those, who may incline to deny it, to *prove* a distinction and to shew that a rule which in the general system of things is essential to the preservation of the social order, is inapplicable to the United States.

The circumstances that the powers of sovereignty are in this country divided between the National and State Governments, does not afford the distinction required. It does not follow from this, that each of the *portions* of powers delegated to the one or to the other is not sovereign *with regard to its proper objects*. It will only *follow* from it, that each has sovereign power as to *certain things,* and not as to *other things*. To deny that the Goverment of the United States has sovereign power as to its declared purposes and trusts, because its power does not extend to all cases, would be equally to deny, that the State Governments have sovereign power in any case; because their power does not extend to every case. The tenth section of the first article of the constitution exhibits a long list of very important things which they may not do. And thus the United States would furnish the singular spectacle of a *political society* without *sovereignty,* or of a people *governed* without *government*.

If it would be necessary to bring proof to a proposition so clear as that which affirms that the powers of the federal Government, *as to its objects,* are sovereign, there is a clause of its constitution which would be decisive. It is that which declares, that the constitution and the laws of the United States made in pursuance of it, and all treaties made or which shall be made under their authority shall be the supreme law of the land. The power which can create the *Supreme law* of the land, in any case, is doubtless sovereign *as to such case*.

This general and indisputable principle puts at once an end to the *abstract* question. Whether the United States have power to *erect a corporation?* that is to say, to give a *legal* or *artificial capacity* to one or more persons, distinct from the natural. For it is unquestionably incident to *sovereign power* to erect corporations, and consequently to *that* of the United States, in *relation to the objects* intrusted to the management of the government. The difference is this—where the authority of the government is general, it can create corporations in *all cases;* where it is confined to certain branches of legislation, it can create corporations only in those cases.

Here then as far as concerns the reasonings of the Secretary of State and the Attorney General, the affirmative of the constitutionality of the bill might be permitted to rest. It will occur to the President that the principle here advanced has been untouched by either of them.

For a more complete elucidation of the point nevertheless, the arguments which they had used against the power of the government to erect corporations, however foreign they are to the great and fundamental rule which has been stated, shall be particularly examined. And after shewing that they do not tend to impair its force, it shall also be shewn that the power of incorporation incident to the government in certain cases, does fairly extend to the particular case which is the object of the bill.

The first of these arguments is, that the foundation of the constitution is laid on this ground "that all powers not delegated to the United States by the Constitution, nor prohibited by it to the States are reserved to the States or to the people," whence it is meant to be inferred, that congress can in no case exercise any power not included in those enumerated in the constitution. And it is affirmed that the power of erecting a corporation is not included in any of the enumerated powers.

The main proposition here laid down, in its true signification is not to be questioned. It is nothing more than a consequence of this republican maxim, that all government is a delegation of power. But how much is delegated in each case, is a question of fact to be made out by fair reasoning and construction, upon the particular provisions of the constitution—taking as guides the general principles and general ends of government.

It is not denied, that there are *implied,* as well as *express powers,* and that the *former* are as effectually delegated as the latter. And for the sake of accuracy it shall be mentioned, that there is another class of powers, which may be properly denominated *resulting* powers. It will not be doubted that if the United States should make a conquest of any of the territories of its neighbours, they would possess sovereign jurisdiction over the conquered territory. This would rather be a result from the whole mass of the powers of the government and from the nature of political society, than a consequence of either of the powers specially enumerated.

But be this as it may, it furnishes a striking illustration of the general doctrine contended for. It shows an extensive case, in which a power of erecting corporations is either implied in, or would result from some or all of the powers, vested in the National Government. The jurisdiction acquired over such conquered territory would certainly be competent to every species of legislation.

To return—It is conceded, that implied powers are to be considered as delegated equally with express ones.

Then it follows, that as a power of erecting a corporation may as well be *implied* as any other thing; it may as well be employed as an *instrument* or *means* of carrying into execution any of the specified powers, as any other instrument or mean whatever. The only question must be, in this as in every other case, whether the mean to be employed, or in this instance the corporation to be erected, has a natural, relation to any of the acknowledged objects or lawful ends of the government. Thus a corporation may not be erected by congress, for superintending the police of the city of Philadelphia because they are not authorized to *regulate* the *police* of that city; but one may be erected in relation to the collection of taxes, or to the trade with foreign countries, or to the trade between the States, or with the Indian Tribes, because it is the province of the federal government to *regulate those objects* and because it is incident to a general *sovereign* or *legislative power* to *regulate* a thing, to employ all the means which relate to its regulation to the *best* and *greatest advantage*.

A strange fallacy seems to have crept into the manner of thinking and reasoning upon this subject. Imagination appears to have been unusually busy concerning it. An incorporation seems to have been regarded as some great, independent, substantive thing—as a political end of peculiar magnitude and moment; whereas it is truly to be considered as a *quality, capacity, or means* to an end. Thus a mercantile company is formed with a certain capital for the purpose of carrying on a particular branch of business. Here the business to be prosecuted is the *end;* the association in order to form the requisite capital is the primary mean. Suppose than an incorporation were added to this; it would only be to add a new *quality* to that association; to give it an artificial capacity by which it would be enabled to prosecute the business with more safety and convenience.

That the importance of the power of incorporation has been exaggerated, leading to erroneous conclusions, will further appear from tracing it to its origin. The roman law is the source of it, according to which a *voluntary* association of individuals at *any time* or *for any purpose* was capable of producing it. In England, whence our notions of it are immediately borrowed, it forms a part of the executive authority, and the exercise of it has been often *delegated* by that authority. Whence therefore the ground of the supposition, that it lies beyond the reach of all those very important portions of sovereign power, legislative as well as executive, which belong to the government of the United States?

To this mode of reasoning respecting the right of employing all the means requisite to the execution of the specified powers of the Government, it is objected that none but *necessary* and proper means are to be employed, and the Secretary of State maintains, that no means are to be considered as *necessary*, but those without which the grant of the power would be *nugatory*. Nay so far does he go in his restrictive interpretation of the word, as even to make the case of *necessity* which shall warrant the constitutional exercise of the power to depend on *casual* and *temporary* circumstances; an idea which alone refutes the construction. The *expediency* of exercising a particular power, at a particular time, must indeed depend on *circumstances;* but the constitutional right of exercising it must be uniform and invariable—the same to day as to morrow.

All the arguments therefore against the constitutionality of the bill derived from the accidental existence of certain State banks— institutions which *happen* to exist today, and, for ought that concerns the government of the United States, may disappear tomorrow, must not only be rejected as falacious, but must be viewed as demonstrative, that there is a *radical* source of error in the reasoning.

It is essential to the being of the National government, that so erroneous a conception of the meaning of the word *necessary,* should be exploded.

It is certain, that neither the grammatical nor popular sense of the term requires that construction. According to both, *necessary* often means no more than *needful, requisite, incidental, useful,* or *conductive to.* It is a common mode of expression to say, that it is *necessary* for a government or a person to do this or that thing, when nothing more is intended or understood, than that the interests of the government or person require, or will be promoted, by the doing of this or that thing. The imagination can be at no loss for exemplifications of the use of the word in this sense.

And it is the true one in which it is to be understood as used in the constitution. The whole turn of the clause containing it indicates, that it was the intent of the convention, by that clause to give a liberal latitude to the exercise of the specified powers. The expressions have peculiar comprehensiveness. They are, "to make *all laws,* necessary and proper for *carrying into execution* the foregoing powers and *all other powers* vested by the constitution in the *government* of the United States, or in any *department* or *officer* thereof." To understand the word as the Secretary of State does, would be to depart from its obvious and popular sense, and to give it a *restrictive* operation; an idea never before entertained. It would be to give it the same force as if the word *absolutely* or *indispensably* had been prefixed to it.

Such a construction would beget endless uncertainty and embar- rassment. The cases must be palpable and extreme in which it could be pronounced with certainty that a measure was absolutely necessary, or one without which the exercise of a given power would be nugatory. There are few measures of any government, which would stand so severe a test. To insist upon it, would be to make the criterion of the exercise of any implied power *a case of extreme necessity;* which is rather a rule to justify the overleaping of the bounds of constitutional authority, than to govern the ordinary exercise of it.

It may be truly said of every government, as well as of that of the United States, that it has only a right, to pass such laws as are necessary and proper to accomplish the objects intrusted to it. For no government has a right to do *merely what it pleases.* Hence by a process of reasoning similar to that of the Secretary of State, it might be proved, that neither of the State governments has the right to incorporate a bank. It might be shown, that all the public business of the State, could be performed without a bank, and inferring thence that it was unnecessary it might be argued that it could not be done, because it is against the rule which has been just mentioned. A like mode of reasoning would prove, that there was no power to incorporate the Inhabitants of a town, with a view to a more perfect police. For it is certain, that an incorporation may be dispensed with, though it is better to have one. It is to be remembered that there is no *express* power in any State constitution to erect corporations.

The *degree* in which a measure is necessary, can never be a test of the *legal* right to adopt it. That must be a matter of opinion; and can only be a test of expendiency. The *relation* between the *measure* and the *end,* between the *nature* of *the mean* employed towards the execution of a power and the object of that power, must be the criterion of constitutionality not the more or less of *necessity* or *utility.*

The practice of the government is against the rule of construction advocated by the Secretary of State. Of this the act concerning light houses, beacons, buoys and public piers, is a decisive example. This doubtless must be referred to the power of regulating trade, and is fairly relative to it. But it cannot be affirmed, that the exercise of that power, in this instance, was strictly necessary, or that the power itself would be *nugatory* without that of regulating establishments of this nature.

This restrictive interpretation of the word *necessary* is also contrary to this sound maxim of construction; namely, that the powers contained in a constitution of government, especially those which concern the general administration of the affairs of a country, its finances, trade, defence etc. ought to be construed liberally, in advancement of the public good. This rule does not depend on the particular form of a government or on the particular demarkation of the boundaries of its powers, but on the nature and objects of government itself. The means by which national exigencies are to be provided for, national inconveniences obviated, national prosperity promoted, are of such infinite variety, extent and complexity that there must, of necessity be great latitude of discretion in the selection and application of those means. Hence consequently, the necessity and propriety of exercising the authorities intrusted to a government on principles of liberal construction.

The Attorney General admits the *rule,* but takes a distinction between a State, and the federal constitution. The latter, he thinks, ought to be construed with great strictness, because there is more danger of error in defining partial than general powers.

But the reason of the *rule* forbids such a distinction. This reason is—the variety and extent of public exigencies, a far greater proportion of which and of a far more critical kind are objects of national than of State administration. The greater danger of error, as far as it is supposable, may be a prudential reason for caution in practice, but it cannot be a rule of restrictive interpretation.

In regard to the clause of the constitution immediately under consideration, it is admitted by the Attorney General, that no *restrictive* effect can be ascribed to it. He defines the word necessary thus: "To be necessary is to be *incidental,* and may be denominated the natural means of executing a power."

But while on the one hand, the construction of the Secretary of State is deemed inadmissable, it will not be contended on the other, that the clause in question gives any *new* or *independent* power. But it gives an explicit sanction to the doctrine of *implied* powers, and is equivalent to an admission of the proposition, that the government, *as to its specified powers and objects,* has plenary and sovereign authority, in some cases paramount to that of the States in others co-ordinate with it. For such is the plain import of the declaration, that it may pass all *laws* necessary and proper to carry into execution those powers.

It is no valid objection to the doctrine to say, that it is calculated to extend the powers of the general government throughout the entire sphere of State legislation. The same thing has been said, and may be said with regard to every exercise of power by *implication* or *construction.* The moment the literal meaning is departed from there is a chance of error and abuse. And yet an adherence to the letter of its powers would at once arrest the motions of the government. It is not only agreed, on all hands, that the exercise of constructive powers is indispensable, but every act which has been passed is more or less an exemplification of it. One has been already mentioned, that relating to light houses etc. That which declares the power of the President to remove officers at pleasure, acknowledges the same truth in another, and a signal instance.

The truth is, that difficulties on this point are inherent in the nature of the federal constitution. They result inevitably from a division of the legislative power. The consequence of this division is, that there will be cases clearly within the power of the National Government; others clearly without its powers; and a third class, which will leave room for controversy and difference of opinion, and concerning which a reasonable latitude of judgment must be allowed.

But the doctrine which is contended for is not chargeable with the consequence imputed to it. It does not affirm that the National government is sovereign in all respects, but that it is sovereign to a certain extent: that is, to the *extent* of the objects of its specified powers.

It leaves therefore a criterion of what is constitutional, and of what is not so. This criterion is the *end,* to which the measure relates as a *mean.* If the end be clearly comprehended within any of the specified powers, and if the measure have an obvious relation to that end, and is not forbidden by any particular provision of the constitution—it may safely be deemed to come within the compass of the national authority. There is also this further criterion which may materially assist the decision: Does the proposed measure abridge a pre-existing right of any State, or of any individual? If it does not, there is a strong presumption in favour of its constitutionality; and slighter relations to any declared object of the constitution may be permitted to turn the scale.

The general objections which are to be inferred from the reasonings of the Secretary of State and of the Attorney General to the doctrine which has been advanced, have been stated and it is hoped satisfactorily answered. Those of a more particular nature shall now be examined.

The Secretary of State introduces his opinion with an observation, that the proposed incorporation undertakes to create certain capacities properties or attributes which are *against* the laws of *alienage, descents, escheat* and *forfeiture, distribution* and *monopoly,* and to confer a power to make laws paramount to those of the States. And nothing says he, in another place, but a *necessity, invincible* by *other means* can justify such a *prostration* of *laws* which constitute the pillars of our whole system of jurisprudence, and are the foundation laws of the State Governments.

If these are truly the foundation laws of the several states, then have most of them subverted their own foundations. For there is scarcely one of them which has not, since the establishment of its particular constitution made material alterations in some of those branches of its jurisprudence especially the law of descents. But it is not conceived how any thing can be called the fundamental law of a State Government which is not established in its constitution unalterable by the ordinary legislature. And with regard to the question of necessity it has been shewn, that this can only constitute a question of expediency, not of right.

To erect a corporation is to substitute a *legal* or *artificial* to a *natural* person, and where a number are concerned to give them *individuality*. To that legal or artificial person once created, the common law of every state of itself *annexes* all those incidents and attributes, which are represented as a prostration of the main pillars of their jurisprudence. It is certainly not accurate to say, that the erection of a corporation is *against* those different *heads* of the State laws: because it is rather to create a kind of person or entity, to which *they* are inapplicable, and to which the general rule of those laws assign a different regimen. The laws of alienage cannot apply to an artificial person, because it can have no country. Those of descent cannot apply to it, because it can have no heirs. Those of escheat are foreign from it for the same reason. Those of forfeiture, because it cannot commit a crime. Those of distribution, because, though it may be dissolved, it cannot die. As truly might it be said, that the exercise of the power of prescribing the rule by which foreigners shall be naturalized, is against the law of alienage; while it is in fact only to put them in a situation to cease to be the subject of that law. To do a thing which is *against* a law, is to do something which it forbids or which is a violation of it.

But if it were even to be admitted that the erection of corporation is a direct alteration of the State laws in the enumerated particulars; it would do nothing toward proving, that the measure was unconstitutional. If the government of the United States can do no act, which amounts to an alteration of a State law, all its powers are nugatory. For almost every new law is an alteration, is some way or other of an old *law*, either *common*, or *statute*.

There are laws concerning bankruptcy in some states—some states have laws regulating the values of foreign coins. Congress are empowered to establish uniform laws concerning bankruptcy throughout the United States, and to regulate the values of foreign coins. The exercise of either of these powers by Congress necessarily involves an alteration of the laws of those states.

Again: Every person by the common law of each state may export his property to foreign countries, at pleasure. But Congress, in pursuance of the power of regulating trade, may prohibit the exportation of commodities: in doing which, they would alter the common law of each state in abridgement of individual rights.

It can therefore never be good reasoning to say this or that act is unconstitutional, because it alters this or that law of a State. It must be shewn that the act which makes the alteration is unconstitutional on other accounts, not *because* it makes the alteration

There are two points in the suggestions of the Secretary of State which have been noted that are peculiarly incorrect. One is, that the proposed incorporation is against the laws of monopoly, because it stipulates an exclusive right of banking under the national authority. The other that it gives power to the institution to make laws paramount to those of the states.

But with regard to the first point, the bill neither prohibits any State from erecting as many banks as they please, nor any number of Individuals from associating to carry on the business: and consequently is free from the charge of establishing a monopoly: for monopoly implies a *legal impediment* to the carrying on of the trade by others than those to whom it is granted.

And with regard to the second point, there is still less foundation. The bye-laws of such an institution as a bank can operate only upon its own members; can only concern the disposition of its own property and must essentially resemble the rules of a private mercantile partnership. They are expressly not to be contrary to law; and law must here mean the law of a State as well as of the United States. There never can be a doubt, that a law of the corporation, if contrary to the law of a state, must be overruled as void; unless the law of the State is contrary to that of the United States; and then the question will not be between the law of the State and that of the corporation, but between the law of the state and that of the United States.

Another argument made use of by the Secretary of State is, the rejection of a proposition by the convention to empower Congress to make corporations, either generally, or for some special purpose.

What was the precise nature or extent of this proposition, or what the reasons for refusing it, is not ascertained by any authentic document, or even by accurate recollection. As far as any such document exists, it specifies only canals. If this was the amount of it, it would at most only prove, that it was thought inexpedient to give a power to incorporate for the purpose of opening canals, for which purpose a special power would have been necessary; except with regard to the western Territory, there being nothing in any part of the constitution respecting the regulation of canals. It must be confessed however, that very different accounts are given of the import of the propostion and of the motives for rejecting it. Some affirm that it was confined to the opening of canals and obstructions in rivers; others, that it embraced banks; and others, that it extended to the power of incorporating generally. Some again alledge, that it was disagreed to, because it was thought improper to vest in Congress a power of erecting corporations—others, because it was thought unnecessary to specify the power, and inexpedient to furnish an additional topic of objection to the constitution. In this state of the matter, no inference whatever can be drawn from it.

But whatever may have been the nature of the proposition or the reasons for rejecting it concludes nothing in respect to the real merits of the question. The Secretary of State will not deny, that whatever may have been the intention of the framers of a constitution, or of a law, that intention is to be sought for in the instrument itself, according to the usual and established rules of construction. Nothing is more common than for laws to *express* and *effect,* more or less than was intended. If then a power to erect a corporation, in any case, be deducible by fair inference from the whole or any part of the numerous provisions of the constitution of the United States, arguments drawn from extrinsic circumstances, regarding the intention of the convention, must be rejected.

Most of the arguments of the Secretary of State which have not been considered in the foregoing remarks, are of a nature rather to apply to the expediency than to the constitutionality of the bill. They will however be noticed in the discussions which will be necessary in reference to the particular heads of the powers of the government which are involved in the question.

Those of the Attorney General will now properly come under review.

His first observation is, that the power of incorporation is not *expressly* given to Congress. This shall be conceded, but in *this sense* only, that it is not declared in *express terms* that congress may erect a *corporation.* But this cannot mean, that there are not certain *express* powers which *necessarily* include it.

For instance, Congress have express power "to exercise exclusive legislation in all cases whatsoever, over such *district* (not exceeding ten miles square) as may by cession of particular states, and the acceptance of Congress become the seat of the government of the United States; and to exercise *like authority* over all places purchased by consent of the legislature of the State in which the same shall be for the erection of forts, arsenals, dock yards and other needful buildings."

Here then is express power to exercise *exclusive legislation in all cases whatsoever over certain places;* that is to do in respect to those places, all that any governmen whatever may do: For language does not afford a more complete designation of sovereign power, than in those comprehensive terms. It is in other words a power to pass all laws whatsoever, and consequently to pass laws for erecting corporations, as well as for any other purpose which is the proper object of law in a free government. Surely it can never be believed, that Congress with *exclusive power of legislation in all cases whatsoever,* cannot erect a corporation within the district which shall become the seat of government, for the better regulation of its police. And yet there is an unqualified denial of the power to erect corporations in every case on the part both of the Secretary of State and of the Attorney General. The former indeed speaks of that power in those emphatical terms, that it is *a right remaining exclusively with the states.*

As far then as there is an express power to do any *particular act of legislation,* there is an express one to erect corporations in the case above described. But accurately speaking, no *particular power* is more than *implied* in a *general one.* Thus the power to lay a duty on a *gallon of rum,* is only a particular *implied* in the general power to lay and collect taxes, duties, imposts and excises. This serves to explain in what sense it may be said, that congress have not an express power to make corporations.

This may not be an improper place to take notice of an argument which was used in debate in the House of Representatives. It was there urged, that if the constitution intended to confer so important a power as that of erecting corporations, it would have been expressly mentioned. But the case which has been noticed is clearly one in which such a power exists, and yet without any specification or express grant of it, further than as every *particular implied* in a general power, can be said to be so granted.

But the argument itself is founded upon an exaggerated and erroneous conception of the nature of the power. It has been shewn that it *is* not of so transcendent a kind as the reasoning supposes; and that viewed in a just light it is a mean which ought to have been left to *implication,* rather than an *end* which ought to have been *expressly* granted.

Having observed, that the power of erecting corporations is not expressly granted to Congress, the Attorney General proceeds thus:

If it can be exercised by them, it must be

1. because the nature of the federal government implies it.

2. because it is involved in some of the specified powers of legislation. or

3. because it is necessary and proper to carry into execution some of the specified powers.

To be implied in the *nature of the federal government,* says he, would beget a doctrine so indefinite as to grasp every power.

This proposition it ought to be remarked is not precisely, or even substantially, that, which has been relied upon. The proposition relied upon is, that the *specified powers of Congress* are in their nature sovereign—that it is incident to sovereign power to erect corporations; and that therefore Congress have a right within the *sphere* and in *relation to the objects of their power, to erect corporations.*

It shall however be supposed, that the Attorney General would consider the two propositions in the same light, and that the objection made to the one, would be made to the other.

To this objection an answer has been already given. It is this; that the doctrine is stated with this express *qualification,* that the right to erect corporations does *only* extend to *cases* and *objects* within the *sphere* of the *specified* powers of the government. A general legislative authority implies a power to erect corporations *in all cases*—a particular legislative power implies authority to erect corporations, in relation to cases arising under that power only. Hence the affirming, that as an *incident* to sovereign power, congress may erect a corporation in relation to the *collection* of their taxes, is no more than to affirm that they may do whatever else they please; than the saying that they have a power to regulate trade would be to affirm that they have a power to regulate religion: or than the maintaining that they have sovereign power as to taxation, would be to maintain that they have sovereign power as to every thing else.

The Attorney General undertakes, in the next place, to shew, that the power of erecting corporations is not involved in any of the specified powers of legislation confided to the national government.

In order to do this he has attempted an enumeration of the particulars which he supposes to be comprehended under the several heads of the *powers* to lay and collect taxes etc.—to borrow money on the credit of the United States—to regulate commerce with foreign nations—between the states, and with the Indian Tribes—to dispose of and make all needful rules and regulations respecting the territory or other property belonging to the United States; the design of which enumeration is to shew *what* is included under those different heads of power, and *negatively,* that the power of erecting corporations is not included.

The truth of this inference or conclusion must depend on the accuracy of the enumeration. If it can be shewn that the enumeration is *defective,* the inference is destroyed. To do this will be attended with no difficulty.

The heads of the power to lay and collect taxes he states to be:

1. To ascertain the subject of taxation, etc.
2. to declare the quantum of taxation, etc.
3. to prescribe the *mode* of *collection*.
4. to ordain the manner of accounting for the taxes, etc.

The defectiveness of this enumeration consists in the generality of the third division "to *prescribe the mode* of collection," which is in itself an immense chapter. It will be shewn hereafter, that, among a vast variety of particulars, it comprises the very power in question; namely, to *erect corporations*.

The heads of the power to borrow money, are stated to be

1. to stipulate the sum to be lent.
2. an interest or no interest to be paid.
3. the time and manner of repaying, unless the loan be placed on an irredeemable fund.

This enumeration is liable to a variety of objections. It omits, in the first place, the *pledging* or *mortgaging* of a fund for the security of the money lent, an usual and in most cases an essential ingredient.

The idea of a stipulation of an *interest or no interest* is too confined. It should rather have been said, to stipulate *the consideration* of the loan. Individuals often borrow upon considerations other than the payment of interest. So may governments; and so they often find it necessary to do. Every one recollects the lottery tickets and other douceurs often given in Great Britian, as collateral inducements to the lending of money to the Government.

There are also frequently collateral conditions, which the enumeration does not contemplate. Every contract which has been made for moneys borrowed in Holland, includes stipulations that the sum due shall be *free from taxes,* and from sequestration in time of war, and mortgages all the land and property of the United States for the reimbursement.

It is also known, that a lottery is a common expedient for borrowing money, which certainly does not fall under either of the enumerated heads.

The heads of the power to regulate commerce with foreign nations are stated to be

1. to prohibit them or their commodities from our ports.

2. to impose duties on *them* where none existed before, or to increase existing duties on them.

3. to subject *them* to any species of customhouse regulation.

4. to grant *them* any exemptions or privileges which policy may suggest.

This enumeration is far more exceptionable than either of the former. It omits *every thing* that relates to the *citizens, vessels* or *commodities* of the United States. The following palpable omissions occur at once.

1. of the power to prohibit the exportation of commodities which not only exists at all times, but which in time of war it would be necessary to exercise, particularly with relation to naval and warlike stores.

2. of the power to prescribe rules concerning the *characteristics* and *privileges* of an american bottom—how she shall be navigated, as whether by citizens or foreigners, or by a proportion of each.

3. of the power of regulating the manner of contracting with seamen, the police of ships on their voyages etc. of which the act for the government and regulation of seamen in the merchants service is a specimen.

That the three preceding articles are omissions, will not be doubted. There is a long list of items in addition, which admit of little, if any question, of which a few samples shall be given.

1. The granting of bounties to certain kinds of vessels, and certain species of merchandise. Of this nature is the allowance on dried and pickled fish and salted provisions.

2. The prescribing of rules concerning the *inspection* of commodities to be exported. Though the states individually are competent to this regulation, yet there is no reason, in point of authority at least, why a general system might not be adopted by the United States.

3. The regulation of policies of insurance; of salvage upon goods found at sea, and the disposition of such goods.

4. The regulation of pilots.

5. The regulation of bills of exchange drawn by a merchant of *one state* upon a merchant of *another state*. This last rather belongs to the regulation of trade between the states, but is equally omitted in the specification under that head.

The last enumeration relates to the power "to dispose of and make *all needful rules and regulations* respecting the territory or *other property* belonging to the United States."

The heads of this power are said to be

1. to exert an ownership over the territory of the United States, which may be properly called the property of the United States, as in the Western Territory, and to *institute a government therein;* or

2. to exert an ownership over the other property of the United States.

This idea of exerting an ownership over the Territory or other property of the United States, is particularly indefinite and vague. It does not at all satisfy the conception of what must have been intended by a power to make all needful *rules* and *regulations;* nor would there have been any use for a special clause which authorized nothing more. For the right of exerting an ownership is implied in the very definition of property.

It is admitted that in regard to the western territory something more is intended—even the institution of a government; that is the creation of a body politic, or corporation of the highest nature; one, which in its maturity, will be able itself to create other corporations. Why then does not the same clause authorize the erection of a corporation in respect to the regulation or disposal of any other of the property of the United States? This idea will be enlarged upon in another place.

Hence it appears, that the enumerations which have been attempted by the Attorney General are so imperfect, as to authorize no conclusion whatever. They therefore have no tendency to disprove that each and every of the powers to which they relate, includes that of erecting corporations, which they certainly do, as the subsequent illustrations will more and more evince.

It is presumed to have been satisfactorily shewn in the course of the preceding observations

1. That the power of the government, *as to* the objects intrusted to its management, is in its nature sovereign.

2. That the right of erecting corporations is one, inherent in and inseparable from the idea of sovereign power.

3. That the position, that the government of the United States can exercise no power but such as is delegated to it by its constitution does not militate against this principle.

4. That the word *necessary* in the general clause can have no *restrictive* operation, derogating from the force of this principle; indeed, that

the degree in which a measure is, or is not necessary, cannot be a *test of constitutional right,* but of expediency only.

5. That the power to erect corporations is not to be considered as an *independent* or *substantive* power but as an *incidental* and *auxiliary* one; and was therefore more properly left to implication, than expressly granted.

6. that the principle in question does not extend the power of the government beyond the prescribed limits, because it only affirms a power to *incorporate* for *purposes within the sphere* of *the specified powers.*

And lastly that the right to exercise such a power, in certain cases, is unequivocally granted in the most *positive* and *comprehensive* terms.

To all which it only remains to be added that such a power has actually been exercised in two very eminent instances: namely in the erection of two governments, one, northwest of the river Ohio, and the other south west—the *last, independent* of *any antecedent compact.* And there results a full and complete demonstration, that the Secretary of State and Attorney General are mistaken, when they deny generally the power of the National government to erect corporations.

It shall now be endeavoured to be shewn that there is a power to erect one of the kind proposed by the bill. This will be done, by tracing a natural and obvious relation between the institution of a bank, and the objects of several of the enumerated powers of the government; and by shewing that, *politically* speaking, it is necessary to the effectual execution of one or more of those powers. In the course of this investigation, various instances will be stated, by way of illustration of a right to erect corporations under those powers.

Some preliminary observations may be proper.

The proposed bank is to consist of an association of persons for the purpose of creating a joint capital to be employed, chiefly and essentially, in loans. So far the object is not only lawful, but it is the mere exercise of a right, which the law allows to every individual. The bank of New York which is not incorporated, is an example of such an association. The bill proposes in addition, that the government shall become a joint proprietor in this undertaking, and that it shall permit the bills of the company payable on demand to be receivable in its revenues and stipulates that it shall not grant privileges similar to those which are to be allowed to this company, to any others. All this is incontrovertibly within the compass of the discretion of the government. The only question is, whether it has a right to incorporate this company, in order to enable it the more effectually to accomplish *ends,* which are in themselves lawful.

To establish such a right, it remains to shew the relation of such an institution to one or more of the specified powers of the government.

Accordingly it is affirmed, that it has a relation more or less direct, to the power of collecting taxes; to that of borrowing money; to that of regulating trade between the states; and to those of raising, supporting and maintaining fleets and armies. To the two former, the relation may be said to be *immediate*.

And, in the last place, it will be argued, that it is *clearly* within the provision which authorizes the making of all *needful* rules and *regulations* concerning the *property* of the United States, as the same has been practised upon by the government.

A Bank relates to the collection of taxes in two ways; *indirectly,* by increasing the quantity of circulating medium and quickening circulation, which facilitates the means of paying—*directly,* by creating a *convenient species* of *medium* in which they are to be paid.

To designate or appoint the money or *thing* in which taxes are to be paid, is not only a proper, but a necessary *exercise* of the power of collecting them. Accordingly congress in the law concerning the collection of the duties on imports and tonnage, have provided that they shall be payable in gold and silver. But while it was an indispensable part of the work to say in what they should be paid, the choice of the specific thing was mere matter of discretion. The payment might have been required in the commodities themselves. Taxes in kind, however ill judged, are not without precedents, even in the United States. Or it might have been in the paper money of the several states; or in the bills of the banks of North America, New York and Massachusetts, all or either of them: or it might have been in bills issued under the authority of the United States.

No part of this can, it is presumed, be disputed. The appointment, then, of the *money* or *thing,* in which the taxes are to be paid, is an incident to the power of collection. And among the expedients which may be adopted, is that of bills issued under the authority of the United States.

Now the manner of issuing these bills is again matter of discretion. The government might, doubtless, proceed in the following manner. It might provide, that they should be issued under the direction of certain officers, payable on demand; and in order to support their credit and give them a ready circulation, it might, besides giving them a currency in its taxes, set apart out of any monies in its Treasury, a given sum and appropriate it under the direction of those officers as a fund for answering the bills as presented for payment.

The constitutionality of all this would not admit of a question. And yet it would amount to the institution of a bank, with a view to the more convenient collection of taxes. For the simplest and most precise idea of a bank, is, a deposit of coin or other property, as a fund for *circulating* a *credit* upon it, which is to answer the purpose of money. That such an arrangement would be equivalent to the establishment of a bank would become obvious, if the place where the fund to be set apart was kept should be made a receptacle of the monies of all other persons who should incline to deposit them there for safe keeping; and would become still more so, if the officers charged with the direction of the fund were authorized to make discounts at the usual rate of interest, upon good security. To deny the power of the government to add these ingredients to the plan, would be to refine away all government.

This process serves to exemplify the natural and direct relation which may subsist between the institution of a bank and the collection of taxes. It is true that the species of bank which has been designated, does not include the idea of incorporation. But the argument intended to be founded upon it is this: that the institution comprehended in the idea of a bank being one immediately relative to the collection of taxes *in regard to the appointment of the money or thing* in which they are to be paid; the sovereign power of providing for the collection of taxes necessarily includes the right of granting a corporate capacity to such an institution, as a requisite to its greater security, utility and more convenient management.

A further process will still more clearly illustrate the point. Suppose, when the species of bank which has been described was about to be instituted, it were to be urged, that in order to secure to it a due degree of confidence the fund ought not only to be set apart and appropriated generally, but ought to be specifically vested in the officers who were to have the direction of it, and in their *successors* in office, to the end that it might acquire the character of *private property* incapable of being resumed without a violation of the sanctions by which the rights of property are protected and occasioning more serious and general alarm, the apprehension of which might operate as a check upon the government. Such a proposition might be opposed by arguments against the expediency of it or the solidity of the reason assigned for it, but it is not conceivable what could be urged against its constitutionality.

And yet such a disposition of the thing would amount to the erection of a corporation. For the true definition of a corporation seems to be this. It is a *legal* person, or a person created by act of law, consisting of one or more natural persons authorized to hold property or a franchise in succession in a legal as contradistinguished from natural capacity.

Let the illustration proceed a step further. Suppose a bank of the nature which has been described with or without incorporation, had been instituted, and that experience had evinced as it probably would, that being wholly under public direction it possessed not the confidence requisite to the credit of its bills. Suppose also that, by some of those adverse conjunctures which occasionally attend nations, there had been a very great drain of the specie of the country, so as not only to cause general distress for want of an adequate medium of circulation, but to produce, in consequence of that circumstance, considerable defalcations in the public revenues. Suppose also, that there was no bank instituted in any state—in such a posture of things, would it not be most manifest that the incorporation of a bank, like that proposed by the bill, would be a measure immediately relative to the *effectual collection* of the taxes and completely within the province of the sovereign power of providing by all laws necessary and proper for that collection?

If it be said, that such a state of things would render that necessary and therefore constitutional, which is not so now—the answer to this, and a solid one it doubtless is, must still be, that which has been already stated—circumstances may affect the expendiency of the measure, but they can neither add to, nor diminish its constitutionality.

A Bank has a direct relation to the power of borrowing money, because it is an usual and in sudden emergencies an essential instrument in the obtaining of loans to government.

A nation is threatened with war. Large sums are wanted, on a sudden, to make the requisite preparations. Taxes are laid for the purpose, but it requires time to obtain the benefit of them. Anticipation is indispensable. If there be a bank, the supply can, at once be had; if there be none loans from Individuals must be sought. The progress of these is often too slow for the exigency: in some situations they are not practicable at all. Frequently when they are, it is of great consequence to be able to anticipate the product of them by advances from a bank.

The essentiality of such an institution as an instrument of loans is exemplified at this very moment. An Indian expedition is to be prosecuted. The only fund out of which the money can arise consistently with the public engagements, is a tax which will only begin to be collected in July next. The preparations, however, are instantly to be made. The money must therefore be borrowed. And of whom could it be borrowed, if there were no public banks?

It happens, that there are institutions of this kind, but if there were none, it would be indispensable to create one.

Let it then be supposed, that the necessity existed, (as but for a casualty would be the case) that proposals were made for obtaining a loan; that a number of individuals came forward and said, we are willing to accommodate the government with this money; with what we have in hand and the credit we can raise upon it we doubt not of being able to furnish the sum required: but in order to do this, it is indispensible, *that we* should be incorporated as a bank. This is essential towards putting it in our power to do what is desired and we are obliged on that account to make it that *consideration* or condition of the loan.

Can it be believed, that a compliance with this proposition would be unconstitutional? Does not this alone evince the contrary? It is a necessary part of a power to borrow to be able to stipulate the consideration or conditions of a loan. It is evident, as has been remarked elsewhere, that this is not confined to the mere stipulation of a sum of money by way of interest—why may it not be deemed to extend where a government is the contracting party, to the stipulation of a *franchise?* If it may, and it is not perceived why it may not, then the grant of a corporate capacity may be stipulated as a consideration of the loan? There seems to be nothing unfit, or foreign from the nature of the thing in giving individuality or a corporate capacity to a number of persons who are willing to lend a sum of money to the government, the better to enable them to do it, and make them an ordinary instrument of loans in future emergencies of the state.

But the more general view of the subject is still more satisfactory. The legislative power of borrowing money, and of making all laws necessary and proper for carrying into execution that power, seems obviously competent to the appointment of the *organ* through which the abilities and wills of individuals may be most efficaciously exerted, for the accommodation of the government by loans.

The Attorney General opposes to this reasoning the following observation. "To borrow money presupposes the accumulation of a fund to be lent, and is secondary to the creation of an ability to lend." This is plausible in theory, but is not true in fact. In a great number of cases, a previous accumulation of a fund equal to the whole sum required does not exist. And nothing more can be actually presupposed, than that there exist resources, which put into activity to the greatest advantage by the nature of the operation with the government, will be equal to the effect desired to be produced. All the provisions and operations of government must be presumed to contemplate things as they *really* are.

The institution of a bank has also a natural relation to the regulation of trade between the States: in so far as it is conducive to the creation of a convenient medium of *exchange* between them, and to the keeping up a full circulation by preventing the frequent displacement of the metals in reciprocal remittances. Money is the very hinge on which commerce turns. And this does not mean merely gold and silver, many other things have served the purpose with different degrees of utility. Paper has been extensively employed.

It cannot therefore be admitted, with the Attorney General, that the regulation of trade between the States, as it concerns the medium of circulation and exchange ought to be considered as confined to coin. It is even supposable in argument, that the whole, or the greatest part of the coin of the country, might be carried out of it.

The Secretary of State objects to the relation here insisted upon, by the following mode of reasoning—To erect a bank, says he, and to regulate commerce, are very different acts. He who creates a bank, creates a subject of commerce, so does he, who makes a bushel of wheat, or digs a dollar out of the mines. Yet neither of these persons regulates commerce thereby. To make a thing which may be bought and sold is not to *prescribe* regulations for *buying* and *selling*. Thus making the regulation of commerce to consist in prescribing rules for *buying* and *selling*.

This indeed is a species of regulation of trade; but is one which falls more aptly within the province of the local jurisdictions than within that of the general government, whose care must be presumed to have been intended to be directed to those general political arrangements concerning trade on which its aggregate interests depend, rather than to the details of buying and selling.

Accordingly such only are the regulations to be found in the laws of the United States; whose objects are to give encouragement to the enterprise of our own merchants, and to advance our navigation and manufactures.

And it is in reference to these general relations of commerce, that an establishment which furnishes facilities to circulation and a convenient medium of exchange and alienation, is to be regarded as a regulation of trade.

The Secretary of State further argues, that if this was a regulation of commerce, it would be void, as *extending as much to the internal commerce of every state as to its external.* But what regulation of commerce does not extend to the internal commerce of every state? what are all the duties upon imported articles amounting to prohibitions, but so many bounties upon domestic manufactures affecting the interest of different classes of citizens in different ways? what are all the provisions in the coasting act, which relate to the trade between district and district of the same State? In short what regulation of trade between the States, but must affect the internal trade of each State? What can operate upon the whole but must extend to every part!

The relation of a bank to the execution of the powers, that concern the common defence has been anticipated. It has been noted, that at this very moment the aid of such an institution is essential to the measures to be pursued for the protection of our frontier.

It now remains to shew, that the incorporation of a bank is within the operation of the provision which authorizes Congress to make all needful rules and regulations concerning the property of the United States. But it is previously necessary to advert to a distinction which has been taken by the Attorney General.

He admits, that the word *property* may signify personal property however acquired. And yet asserts, that it cannot signify money arising from the sources of revenue pointed out in the constitution, because, says he, "the disposal and regulation of money is the final cause for raising it by taxes."

But it would be more accurate to say, that the *object* to which money is intended to be aplied is the *final cause* for raising it, than that the disposal and regulation of it is *such.* The support of Government; the support of troops for the common defence; the payment of the public debt, are the true *final causes* for raising money. The disposition and regulation of it when raised, are the steps by which it is applied to the *ends* for which it was raised, not the ends themselves. Hence therefore the money to be raised by taxes as well as any other personal property, must be supposed to come within the meaning as they certainly do within the letter of authority, to make all needful rules and regulations concerning the property of the United States.

A case will make this plainer: suppose the public debt discharged, and the funds now pledged for it liberated. In some instances it would be found expedient to repeal the taxes; in others, the repeal might injure our own industry, our agriculture and manufactures. In these cases they would of course be retained. Here then would be monies arising from the authorized sources of revenue which would not fall within the rule by which the Attorney General endeavours to except them from other personal property, and from the operation of the clause in question.

The monies being in the coffers of the government, what is to hinder such a disposition to be made of them as is contemplated in the bill or what an incorporation of the parties concerned under the clause which has been cited.

It is admitted that with regard to the Western territory they give a power to erect a corporation—that is to institute a government. And by what rule of construction can it be maintained, that the same words in a constitution of government will not have the same effect when applied to one species of property, as to another, as far as the subject is capable of it? or that a legislative power to make all needful rules and regulations, or to pass all laws necessary and proper concerning the public property which is admitted to authorize an incorporation in one case will not authorize it in another? will justify the institution of a government over the western territory and will not justify the incorporation of a bank, for the more useful management of the money of the nation? If it will do the last, as well as the first, then under this provision alone the bill is constitutional, because it contemplates that the United States shall be joint proprietors of the stock of the bank.

There is an observation of the Secretary of State to this effect, which may require notice in this place. Congress, says he, are not to lay taxes *ad libitum for any purpose they please,* but only to pay the debts, or provide for the *welfare* of the Union. Certainly no inference can be drawn from this against the power of applying their money for the institution of a bank. It is true, that they cannot without breach of trust, lay taxes for any other purpose than the general welfare but so neither can any other government. The welfare of the community is the only legitimate end for which money can be raised on the community. Congress can be considered as under only one restriction, which does not apply to other governments. They cannot rightfully apply the money they raise to any purpose *merely* or purely local. But with this exception they have as large a discretion in relation to the *application* of money as any legislature whatever. The constitutional *test* of a right application must always be, whether it be for a purpose of *general* or *local* nature. If the former, there can be no want of constitutional power. The quality of the object, as how far it will really promote or not the welfare of the union, must be matter of conscientious discretion. And the arguments for or against a measure in this light, must be arguments concerning expediency or inexpediency, not constitutional right. Whatever relates to the general order of the finances, to the general interests of trade etc. being general objects are constitutional ones for *the application* of *money*.

A Bank then whose bills are to circulate in all the revenues of the country, is *evidently* a general object, and for that very reason a constitutional one as far as regards the appropriation of money to it. Whether it will really be a beneficial one, or not, is worthy of careful examination, but is no more a constitutional point, in the particular referred to; than the question whether the western lands shall be sold for twenty or thirty cents per acre.

A hope is entertained, that it has by this time been made to appear, to the satisfaction of the President, that a bank has a natural relation to the power of collecting taxes; to that of borrowing money; to that of regulating trade; to that of providing for the common defence: and that as the bill under consideration contemplates the government in the light of a joint proprietor of the stock of the bank, it brings the case within the provision of the clause of the constitution which immediately respects the property of the United States.

Under a conviction that such a relation subsists, the Secretary of the Treasury, with all deference conceives, that it will result as a necessary consequence from the position, that all specified powers of government are sovereign as to the proper objects, that the incorporation of a bank is a constitutional measure, and that the objections taken to the bill, in this respect, are ill founded.

But from an earnest desire to give the utmost possible satisfaction to the mind of the President, on so delicate and important a subject, the Secretary of the Treasury will ask his indulgence while he gives some additional illustrations of cases in which a power of erecting corporations may be exercised, under some of those heads of the specified powers of the Government, which are alledged to include the right of incorporating a bank.

1. It does not appear susceptible of a doubt, that if Congress had thought proper to provide in the collection law, that the bonds to be given for the duties should be given to the collector of each district in the name of the collector of the district A or B as the case might require, to enure to him and his successors in office, in trust for the United States, that it would have been consistent with the constitution to make such an arrangment. And yet this it is conceived would amount to an incorporation.

2. It is not an unusual expedient of taxation to farm particular branches of revenue, that is to mortgage or sell the product of them for certain definite sums, leaving the collection to the parties to whom they are mortgaged or sold. There are even examples of this in the United States. Suppose that there was any particular branch of revenue which it was manifestly expedient to place on this footing, and there were a number of persons willing to engage with the Government, upon condition that they should be incorporated and the funds vested in them, as well for their greater safety as for the more convenient recovery and management of the taxes. Is it supposable that there could be any constitutional obstacle to the measure? It is presumed that there could be none. It is certainly a mode of collection which it would be in the discretion of the Government to adopt; though the circumstances must be very extraordinary, that would induce the Secretary to think it expedient.

3. Suppose a new and unexplored branch of trade should present itself with some foreign country. Suppose it was manifest, that, to undertake it with advantage, required an union of the capitals of a number of individuals, and that those individuals would not be disposed to embark without an incorporation, as well to obviate that consequence of a private partnership, which makes every individual liable in his whole estate for the debts of the company to their utmost extent, as for the more convenient management of the business—what reason can there be to doubt, that the national government would have a constitutional right to institute and incorporate such a company? None.

They possess a general authority to regulate trade with foreign countries. This is a mean which has been practiced to that end by all the principal commercial nations; who have trading companies to this day which have subsisted for centuries. Why may not the United States *constitutionally* employ the means *usual* in other countries for attaining the ends intrusted to them?

A power to make all needful rules and regulations concerning territory has been construed to mean a power to erect a government. A power to *regulate* trade is a power to make all needful rules and regulations concerning trade. Why may it not then include that of erecting a trading company as well as in the other case to erect a Government?

It is remarkable, that the State Conventions who had proposed amendments in relation to this point, have most, if not all of them, expressed themselves nearly thus: "Congress shall not grant monopolies, nor *erect any company* with exclusive advantages of commerce," thus at the same time expressing their sense, that the power to erect trading companies or corporations was inherent in Congress, and objecting to it no further, than as to the grant of *exclusive* privileges.

The Secretary entertains all the doubts which prevail concerning the utility of such companies, but he cannot fashion to his own mind a reason to induce a doubt, that there is a constitutional authority in the United States to establish them. If such a reason were demanded, none could be given unless it were this—that congress cannot erect a corporation; which would be no better than to say they cannot do it, because they cannot do it: first presuming an inability, without reason, and then assigning that *inability* as the cause of itself.

Illustrations of this kind might be multiplied without end. They shall however be pursued no further.

There is a sort of evidence on this point, arising from an aggregate view of the constitution, which is of no inconsiderable weight. The very general power of laying and collecting taxes and appropriating their proceeds—that of borrowing money indefinitely—that of coining money and regulating foreign coins—that of making all needful rules and regulations respecting the property of the United States—these powers combined, as well as the reason and nature of the thing speak strongly this language: That it is the manifest design and scope of the constitution to vest in congress all the powers requisite to the effectual administration of the finances of the United States. As far as concerns this object, there appears to be no parsimony of power.

To suppose then, that the government is precluded from the employment of so usual as well as so important an instrument for the administration of its finances as that of a bank, is to suppose, what does not coincide with the general tenor and complexion of the constitution, and what is not agreeable to impressions that any mere spectator would entertain concerning it—little less than a prohibitory clause can destroy the strong presumptions which result from the general aspect of the government. Nothing but demonstration should exclude the idea, that the power exists

In all questions of this nature the practice of mankind ought to have great weight against the theories of Individuals.

The fact, for instance, that all the principal commercial nations have made use of trading corporations or companies for the purpose of *external commerce,* is a satisfactory proof, that the establishment of them is an incident to the regulation of that commerce.

This other fact, that banks are a usual engine in the administration of national finances, and an ordinary and the most effectual instrument of loans and one which in this country has been found essential, pleads strongly against the supposition, that a government clothed with most of the most important prerogatives of sovereignty in relation to its revenues, its debts, its credits, its defence, its trade, its intercourse with foreign nations—is forbidden to make use of that instrument as an appendage to its own authority.

It has been stated as an auxiliary test of constitutional authority, to try, whether it abridges any preexisting right of any state, or any individual. The proposed incorporation will stand the most severe examination on this point. Each state may still erect as many banks as it pleases; every individual may still carry on the banking business to any extent he pleases.

Another criterion may be this, whether the institution or thing has a more direct relation as to its uses, to the objects of the reserved powers of the State Governments, than to those of the powers delegated by the United States. This rule indeed is less precise than the former, but it may still serve as some guide. Surely a bank has more reference to the objects intrusted to the national government, than to those, left to the care of the State Governments. The common defence is decisive in this comparison.

It is presumed, that nothing of consequence in the observations of the Secretary of State and Attorney General has been left unnoticed.

There are indeed a variety of observations of the Secretary of State designed to shew that the utilities ascribed to a bank in relation to the collection of taxes and to trade, could be obtained without it, to analyze which would prolong the discussion beyond all bounds. It shall be forborne for two reasons—first because the report concerning the Bank may speak for itself in this respect; and secondly, because all those observations are grounded on the erroneous idea, that the *quantum* of necessity or utility is the test of a constitutional exercise of power.

One or two remarks only shall be made: one is, that he has taken no notice of a very essential advantage to trade in general which is mentioned in the report, as peculiar to the existence of a bank circulation equal, in the public estimation to Gold and silver. It is this, that renders it unnecessary to *lock* up the money of the country to accumulate for months successively in order to the periodical payment of interest. The other is this, that his arguments to shew that treasury orders and bills of exchange from the course of trade will prevent any considerable displacement of the metals, are founded on a partial view of the subject. A case will prove this: The sums collected in a state may be small in comparison with the debt due to it. The balance of its trade, direct and circuitous, with the seat of government may be even or nearly so. Here then without bank bills, which in that state answer the purpose of coin, there must be a displacement of the coin, in proportion to the difference between the sum collected in the State and that to be paid in it. With bank bills no such displacement would take place, or as far as it did, it would be gradual and insensible. In many other ways also, would there be at least a temporary and inconvenient displacement of the coin, even where the course of trade would eventually return it to its proper channels.

The difference of the two situations in point of convenience to the Treasury can only be appreciated by one, who experiences the embarrassments of making provision for the payment of the interest on a stock continually changing place in thirteen different places.

One thing which has been omitted just occurs, although it is not very material to the main argument. The Secretary of State affirms, that the bill only contemplates a repayment, not a loan to the government. But here he is, certainly, mistaken. It is true, the government invests in the stock of the bank a sum equal to that which it receives on loan. But let it be remembered, that it does not therefor, cease to be a proprietor of the stock; which would be the case, if the money received back were in the nature of a repayment. It remains a proprietor still, and will share in the profit, or loss, of the institution, according as the dividend is more or less than the interest it is to pay on the sum borrowed. Hence that sum is manifestly, and, in the strictest sense, a loan.

Philadelphia, February 23d 1791.

9

Report on Manufactures, December 5, 1791

Alexander Hamilton's final major report as secretary of the Treasury was the Report on the Subject of Manufactures—generally referred to as the Report on Manufactures—which was presented to Congress on December 5, 1791. Hamilton argued forcefully that while the new nation was largely agrarian, its future depended on using protectionist tariffs and subsidies to encourage manufacturing. This would stimulate the use of America's abundant natural resources, provide jobs for a growing population, promote economic activity of all kinds, and lessen dependence on imports from England and Europe. Hamilton called for protective tariffs to help young American industries and encourage new inventions, especially in the realm of machinery. He wanted America to be able to produce the weaponry that would be used to defend itself, and although he admired England's industry and political and banking systems, he wanted to depend on English imports as little as possible. The divide has often been defined as between the Jeffersonian vision of a nation of farmers working their own land, which was seen as the foundation of their freedom and independence, and the Hamiltonian vision of a modern, growing nation, which valued farmers but stressed a modern economy based on investment, manufacturing, and commerce.

A substantial excerpt of this classic document of economic history is reprinted here to give an idea of the scope of Hamilton's thinking. It demonstrates his detailed grasp of the nature and potential of the American economy. Congress didn't take any action to implement this report in any major way, and no part of it was the subject of any vote. However, the tariff proposals were generally implemented, although not at such a high level as to discourage imports. It was a crucial part of Hamilton's financial plan to fund the bonds that would pay off the nation's accumulated war debt by collecting tariffs on imports. His view of the long-term future was not to depend on those imports and tariffs but rather develop America's own manufacturing base. This would provide jobs and capital for the development of population centers and stimulate economic activity, which would grow the domestic market for agricultural and industrial products.

The Secretary of the Treasury, in obedience to the order of ye House of Representatives, of the 15th day of January, 1790, has applied his attention, at as early a period as his other duties would permit, to the subject of Manufactures; and particularly to the means of promoting such as will tend to render the United States, independent on foreign nations for military and other essential supplies. And he thereupon respectfully submits the following Report.

The expediency of encouraging manufactures in the United States, which was not long since deemed very questionable, appears at this time to be pretty generally admitted. The embarrassments, which have obstructed the progress of our external trade, have led to serious reflections on the necessity of enlarging the sphere of our domestic commerce: the restrictive regulations, which in foreign markets abridge the vent of the increasing surplus of our Agricultural produce, serve to beget an earnest desire, that a more extensive demand for that surplus may be created at home: And the complete success, which has rewarded manufacturing enterprise, in some valuable branches, conspiring with the promising symptoms, which attend some less mature essays, in others, justify a hope, that the obstacles to the growth of this species of industry are less formidable than they were apprehended to be, and that it is not difficult to find, in its further extension, a full indemnification for any external disadvantages, which are or may be experienced, as well as an accession of resources, favorable to national independence and safety.

There still are, nevertheless, respectable patrons of opinions, unfriendly to the encouragement of manufactures. The following are, substantially, the arguments by, which these opinions are defended.

"In every country (say those who entertain them) Agriculture is the most beneficial and *productive* object of human industry. This position, generally, if not universally true, applies with peculiar emphasis to the United States, on account of their immense tracts of fertile territory, uninhabited and unimproved. Nothing can afford so advantageous an employment for capital and labour, as the conversion of this extensive wilderness into cultivated farms. Nothing equally with this, can contribute to the population, strength and real riches of the country.

"To endeavor, by the extraordinary patronage of Government, to accelerate the growth of manufactures, is, in fact, to endeavor, by force and art, to transfer the natural current of industry from a more, to a less beneficial channel. Whatever has such a tendency must necessarily be unwise. Indeed it can hardly ever be wise in a government, to attempt to give a direction to the industry of its citizens. This under the quicksighted guidance of private interest, will, if left to itself, infallibly find its own way to the most profitable employment: and 'tis by such employment, that the public prosperity will be most effectually promoted. To leave industry to itself, therefore, is, in almost every case, the soundest as well as the simplest policy.

"This policy is, not only recommended to the United States, by considerations which affect all nations it is, in a manner, dictated to them by the imperious force of a very peculiar situation. The smallness of their population compared with their territory—the constant allurements to emigration from the settled to the unsettled parts of the country—the facility, with which the less independent condition of an artisan can be exchanged for the more independent condition of a farmer—these, and similar causes conspire to produce, and, for a length of time must continue to occasion, a scarcity of hands for manufacturing occupation, and dearness of labor generally. To these disadvantages for the prosecution of manufactures, a deficiency of pecuniary capital being added, the prospect of a successful competition with the manufactures of Europe must be regarded as little less than desperate. Extensive manufactures can only be the offspring of a redundant, at least of a full population. Till the latter shall characterize the situation of this country, 'tis vain to hope for the former."

"If contrary to the natural course of things, an unseasonable and premature spring can be given to certain fabrics, by heavy duties, prohibitions, bounties, or by other forced expedients; this will only be to sacrifice the interests of the community to those of particular classes. Besides the misdirection of labor, a virtual monopoly will be given to the persons employed on such fabrics; and an enhancement of price, the inevitable consequence of every monopoly, must be defrayed at the expense of the other parts of the society. It is far preferable, that those persons should be engaged in the cultivation of the earth, and that we should procure, in exchange for its productions, the commodities, with which foreigners are able to supply us in greater perfection, and upon better terms."

This mode of reasoning is founded upon facts and principles, which have certainly respectable pretensions. If it had governed the conduct of nations more generally, than it has done, there is room to suppose, that it might have carried them faster to prosperity and greatness, than they have attained, by the pursuit of maxims too widely opposite. Most general theories, however, admit of numerous exceptions, and there are few, if any, of the political kind, which do not blend a considerable portion of error, with the truths they inculcate.

In order to an accurate judgement how far that which has been just stated ought to be deemed liable to a similar imputation, it is necessary to advert carefully to the considerations, which plead in favour of manufactures, and which appear to recommend the special and positive encouragement of them; in certain cases, and under certain reasonable limitations.

It ought readily to be conceded that the cultivation of the earth—as the primary and most certain source of national supply—as the immediate and chief source of subsistence to man—as the principal source of those materials which constitute the nutriment of other kinds of labor—as including a state most favourable to the freedom and independence of the human mind—one, perhaps, most conducive to the multiplication of the human species—has *intrinsically a strong claim to pre-eminence over every other kind of industry*.

But, that it has a title to any thing like an exclusive predilection, in any country, ought to be admitted with great caution. That it is even more productive than every other branch of Industry requires more evidence than has yet been given in support of the position. That its real interests, precious and important as without the help of exaggeration, they truly are, will be advanced, rather than injured by the due encouragement of manufactures, may, it is believed, be satisfactorily demonstrated. And it is also believed that the expediency of such encouragement in a general view may be shown to be recommended by the most cogent and persuasive motives of national policy.

It has been maintained that Agriculture is, not only, the most productive, but the only productive, species of industry. The reality of this suggestion in either aspect, has, however, not been verified by any accurate detail of facts and calculations; and the general arguments, which are adduced to prove it, are rather subtile and paradoxical, than solid or convincing.

Those which maintain its exclusive productiveness are to this effect—

Labour bestowed upon the cultivation of land produces enough not only to replace all the necessary expenses incurred in the business, and to maintain the persons who are employed in it, but to afford, together with the *ordinary profit* on the stock or capital of the Farmer, a net surplus, or *rent* for the landlord or proprietor of the soil. But the labor of Artificers does nothing more, than to replace the Stock which employs them (or which furnishes materials tools and wages) and yield the *ordinary profit* upon that Stock. It yields nothing equivalent to the *rent* of land. Neither does it add any thing to the *total value* of the *whole annual produce* of the land and labor of the country. The additional value given to those parts of the produce of land, which are wrought into manufactures, is counterbalanced by the value of those other parts of that produce, which are consumed by the manufacturers. It can therefore only be by saving, or *parsimony* not by the positive *productiveness* of their labour, that the classes of Artificers can in any degree augment the revenue of the Society.

To this it has been answered,

I. "That, inasmuch as it is acknowledged, that manufacturing labor reproduces a value equal to that which is expended or consumed in carrying it on, and continues in existence the original Stock or capital employed—it ought, on that account alone, to escape being considered as wholly unproductive. That though it should be admitted, as alleged, that the consumption of the produce of the soil, by the classes of Artificers or Manufacturers, is exactly equal to the value added by their labour to the materials upon which it is exerted; yet it would not thence follow, that it added nothing to the Revenue of the Society, or to the aggregate value of the annual produce of its land and labour. If the consumption for any given period amounted to a *given sum* and the *increased value* of the produce manufactured, in the same period, to a *like sum,* the total amount of the consumption and production during that period, would be equal to the *two sums,* and consequently double the value of the agricultural produce consumed. And though the increment of value produced by the classes of Artificers should at no time exceed the value of the produce of the land consumed by them, yet there would be at every moment, in consequence of their labour, a greater value of goods in the market than would exist independent of it."

II. "That the position, that Artificers can augment the revenue of a society only by parsimony, is true in no other sense than in one which is equally applicable to Husbandmen or Cultivators. It may be alike affirmed of all these classes, that the fund acquired by their labor and destined for their support is not, in an ordinary way, more than equal to it. And hence it will follow that augmentations of the wealth or capital of the community (except in the instances of some extraordinary dexterity or skill) can only proceed, with respect to any of them, from the savings of the more thrifty and parsimonious."

III. "That the annual produce of the land and labour of a country can only be increased in two ways—by some improvement in the *productive powers* of the useful labour, which actually exists within it, or by some increase in the quantity of such labour: That with regard to the first, the labor of Artifiers being capable of greater subdivision and simplicity of operation than that of Cultivators, it is susceptible, in a proportionably greater degree, of improvement in its *productive powers,* whether to be derived from an accession of Skill, or from the application of ingenious machinery; in which particular, therefore, the labor employed in the culture of land can pretend to no advantage over that engaged in manufactures: That with regard to an augmentation of the quantity of useful labour, this, excluding adventitious circumstances, must depend essentially upon an increase of *capital,* which again must depend upon the savings made out of the revenues of those, who furnish or manage *that* which is at any time employed, whether in Agriculture, or in Manufactures, or in any other way."

But while the *exclusive* productiveness of Agricultural labour has been thus denied and refuted, the superiority of its productiveness has been conceded without hesitation. As this concession involves a point of considerable magnitude, in relation to maxims of public administration, the grounds on which it rests are worthy of a distinct and particular examination.

One of the arguments made use of in support of the idea may be pronounced both quaint and superficial—It amounts to this—That in the productions of the soil, nature co-operates with man; and that the effect of their joint labour must be greater than that of the labour of man alone.

This however, is far from being a necessary inference. It is very conceivable, that the labor of man alone, laid out upon a work requiring great skill and art to bring it to perfection, may be more productive, *in value,* than the labour of nature and man combined, when directed towards more simple operations and objects: And when it is recollected to what an extent the Agency of nature, in the application of the mechanical powers, is made auxiliary to the prosecution of manufactures, the suggestion, which has been noticed, loses even the appearance of plausibility.

It might also be observed, with a contrary view, that the labor employed in Agriculture is in a great measure periodical and occasional, depending on seasons, liable to various and long intermissions; while that occupied in many manufactures is constant and regular, extending through the year, embracing in some instances night as well as day. It is also probable, that there are among the cultivators of land, more examples of remissness, than among artificers. The farmer, from the peculiar fertility of his land, or some other favorable circumstance, may frequently obtain a livelihood, even with a considerable degree of carelessness in the mode of cultivation; but the artisan can with difficulty effect the same object, without exerting himself pretty equally with all those who are engaged in the same pursuit. And if it may likewise be assumed as a fact, that manufactures open a wider field to exertions of ingenuity than agriculture, it would not be a strained conjecture, that the labour employed in the former, being at once more *constant,* more uniform and more ingenious, than that which is employed in the latter, will be found, at the same time more productive.

But it is not meant to lay stress on observations of this nature—they ought only to serve as a counterbalance to those of a similar complexion. Circumstances so vague and general, as well as so abstract, can afford little instruction in a matter of this kind.

Another, and that which seems to be the principal argument offered for the superior productiveness of Agricultural labour, turns upon the allegation, that labour employed in manufactures yields nothing equivalent to the rent of land, or to that nett surplus, as it is called, which accrues to the proprietor of the soil.

But this distinction, important as it has been deemed, appears rather *verbal* than *substantial*.

It is easily discernible, that what in the first instance is divided into two parts under the denominations of the *ordinary profit* of the Stock of the farmer and *rent* to the landlord, is in the second instance united under the general appellation of the *ordinary profit* on the Stock of the Undertaker; and that this formal or verbal distinction constitutes the whole difference in the two cases. It seems to have been overlooked, that the land is itself a Stock or capital, advanced or lent by its owner to the occupier or tenant, and that the rent he receives is only the ordinary profit of a certain Stock in land, not managed by the proprietor himself, but by another, to whom he lends or lets it, and who on his part advances a second capital to stock and improve the land, upon which he also receives the usual profit. The rent of the landlord and the profit of the farmer are therefore nothing more than the *ordinary profits* of *two* capitals belonging to *two* different persons, and united in the cultivation of a farm: As in the other case, the surplus which arises upon any manufactory, after replacing the expenses of carrying it on, answers to the ordinary profits of *one* or *more* capitals engaged in the prosecution of such manufactory. It is said *one* or *more* capitals; because in fact, the same thing which is contemplated in the case of the farm, sometimes happens in that of a manufactory. There is one, who furnishes a part of the capital, or lends a part of the money, by which it is carried on, and another, who carries it on, with the addition of his own capital. Out of the surplus which remains, after defraying expenses, an interest is paid to the moneylender, for the portion of the capital furnished by him, which exactly agrees with the rent paid to the landlord; and the residue of that surplus constitutes the profit of the undertaker or manufacturer, and agrees with what is denominated the ordinary profits on the Stock of the farmer. Both together make the ordinary profits of two capitals employed in a manufactory; as in the other case the rent of the landlord and the revenue of the farmer compose the ordinary profits of two Capitals employed in the cultivation of a farm.

The rent therefore accruing to the proprietor of the land, far from being a criterion of *exclusive* productiveness, as has been argued, is no criterion even of superior productiveness. The question must still be, whether the surplus, after defraying expenses, of a *given capital,* employed in the *purchase* and *improvement* of a piece of land, is greater or less, than that of a like capital employed in the prosecution of a manufactory: or whether the *whole value produced* from a *given capital* and a *given quantity of labour,* employed in one way, be greater or less, than the *whole value produced* from an *equal capital* and an *equal quantity of labour* employed in the other way: or rather, perhaps whether the business of Agriculture or that of Manufactures will yield the greatest product, according to a *compound ratio* of the quantity of the Capital and the quantity of labour, which are employed in the one or in the other.

The solution of either of these questions is not easy. It involves numerous and complicated details, depending on an accurate knowledge of the objects to be compared. It is not known that the comparison has ever yet been made upon sufficient data properly ascertained and analysed. To be able to make it on the present occasion with satisfactory precision would demand more previous inquiry and investigation, than there has been hitherto either leisure or opportunity to accomplish.

Some essays however have been made towards acquiring the requisite information; which have rather served to throw doubt upon, than to confirm the Hypothesis, under examination. But it ought to be acknowledged, that they have been too little diversified, and are too imperfect, to authorize a definite conclusion either way; leading rather to probable conjecture than to certain deduction. They render it probable, that there are various branches of manufactures, in which a given Capital will yield a greater *total* product, and a considerably greater *nett* product, than an equal capital invested in the purchase and improvement of lands; and that there are also *some* branches, in which both the *gross* and the nett produce will exceed that of the Agricultural industry; according to a compound ratio of capital and labour. But it is on this last point, that there appears to be the greatest room for doubt. It is far less difficult to infer generally, that the *nett produce* of Capital engaged in manufacturing enterprises is greater than that of Capital engaged in Agriculture.

In stating these results, the purchase and improvement of lands, under previous cultivation are alone contemplated. The comparison is more in favour of Agriculture, when it is made with reference to the settlement of new and waste lands; but an argument drawn from so temporary a circumstance could have no weight in determining the general question concerning the permanent relative productiveness of the two species of industry. How far it ought to influence the policy of the United States, on the score of particular situation, will be adverted to in another place.

The foregoing suggestions are *not designed to inculcate an opinion that manufacturing industry is more productive than that of Agriculture.* They are intended rather to show that the reverse of this proposition is not ascertained; that the general arguments which are brought to establish it are not satisfactory; and, consequently that a supposition of the superior productiveness of Tillage ought to be no obstacle to listening to any substantial inducements to the encouragement of manufactures, which may be otherwise perceived to exist, through an apprehension; that they may have a tendency to divert labour from a more to a less profitable employment.

It is extremely probable, that on a full and accurate development of the matter, on the ground of fact and calculation, it would be discovered that there is no material difference between the aggregate productiveness of the one, and of the other kind of industry; and that the propriety of the encouragements, which may in any case be proposed to be given to either ought to be determined upon considerations irrelative to any comparison of that nature.

II. But without contending for the superior productiveness of Manufacturing Industry, it may conduce to a better judgment of the policy, which ought to be pursued respecting its encouragement, to contemplate the subject, under some additional aspects, tending not only to confirm the idea, that this kind of industry has been improperly represented as unproductive in itself; but to evince in addition that the establishment and diffusion of manufactures have the effect of rendering the total mass of useful and productive labor, in a community, *greater than it would otherwise be*. In prosecuting this discussion, it may be necessary briefly to resume and review some of the topics, which have been already touched.

To affirm, that the labour of the Manufacturer is unproductive, because he consumes as much of the produce of land, as he adds value to the raw materials which he manufactures, is not better founded, than it would be to affirm, that the labour of the farmer, which furnishes materials to the manufacturer is unproductive, *because he consumes an equal value of manufactured articles*. Each furnishes a certain portion of the produce of his labor to the other, and each destroys a correspondent portion of the produce of the labour of the other. In the mean time the maintenance of two Citizens, instead of one, is going on; the State has two members instead of one; and they together consume twice the value of what is produced from the land.

If instead of a farmer and artificer, there were a farmer only, he would be under the necessity of devoting a part of his labour to the fabrication of clothing and other articles, which he would procure of the artificer, in the case of there being such a person; and of course he would be able to devote less labor to the cultivation of his farm; and would draw from it a proportionable less product. The whole quantity of production, in this state of things, in provisions, raw materials and manufactures, would certainly not exceed in value the amount of what would be produced in provisions and raw materials only, if there were an artificer as well as a farmer.

Again—if there were both an artificer and a farmer, the latter would be left at liberty to pursue exclusively the cultivation of his farm. A greater quantity of provisions and raw materials would of course be produced—equal at least—as has been already observed, to the whole amount of the provisions, raw materials and manufactures, which would exist on a contrary supposition. The artificer, at the same time would be going on in the production of manufactured commodities; to an amount sufficient not only to repay the farmer, in those commodities, for the provisions and materials which were procured from him, but to furnish the artificer himself with a supply of similar commodities for his own use. Thus then, there would be two quantities or values in existence, instead of one; and the revenue and consumption would be double in one case, what it would be in the other.

If in place of both of these suppositions, there were supposed to be two farmers, and no artificer, each of whom applied a part of his labour to the culture of land, and another part to the fabrication of Manufactures—in this case, the portion of the labour of both bestowed upon land would produce the same quantity of provisions and raw materials only, as would be produced by the entire sum of the labour of one applied in the same manner—and the portion of the labour of both bestowed upon manufactures, would produce the same quantity of manufactures only, as would be produced by the entire sum of the labour of one, applied in the same manner. Hence the produce of the labour of the two farmers would not be greater than the produce of the labour of the farmer and artificer; and hence, it results, that the labour of the artificer is as positively productive as that of the farmer, and, as positively, augments the revenue of the Society.

The labour of the Artificer replaces to the farmer that portion of his labour, with which he provides the materials of exchange with the Artificer, and which he would otherwise have been compelled to apply to manufactures: and while the Artificer thus enables the farmer to enlarge his stock of Agricultural industry, a portion of which he purchases for his own use, *he also supplies himself with the manufactured articles of which he stands in need.* He does still more—Besides this equivalent which he gives for the portion of Agricultural labour consumed by him, and this supply of manufactured commodities for his own consumption—he furnishes still a surplus, which compensates for the use of the Capital advanced either by himself or some other person, for carrying on the business. This is the ordinary profit of the Stock employed in the manufactory, and is, in every sense, as effective an addition to the income of the Society, as the rent of the land.

The produce of the labour of the Artificer consequently, may be regarded as composed of three parts: one by which the provisions for his subsistence and the materials for his work are purchased of the farmer, one by which he supplies himself with manufactured necessities, and a third which constitutes the profit on the Stock employed. The two last portions seem to have been overlooked in the system, which represents manufacturing industry as barren and unproductive.

In the course of the preceding illustrations, the products of equal quantities of the labour of the farmer and artificer have been treated as if equal to each other. But this is not to be understood as intending to assert any such precise equality. It is merely a manner of expression adopted for the sake of simplicity and perspicuity. Whether the value of the produce of the labour of the farmer be somewhat more or less, than that of the artificer, is not material to the main scope of the argument, which hitherto has only aimed at showing, that the one, as well as the other, occasions a positive augmentation of the total produce and revenue of the Society.

It is now proper to proceed a step further, and to enumerate the principal circumstances, from which it may be inferred—that manufacturing establishments not only occasion a positive augmentation of the Produce and Revenue of the Society, but that they contribute essentially to rendering them greater than they could possibly be, without such establishments. These circumstances are—

1. The division of labour.
2. An extension of the use of Machinery.
3. Additional employment to classes of the community not ordinarily engaged in the business.
4. The promoting of emigration from foreign Countries.
5. The furnishing greater scope for the diversity of talents and dispositions which discriminate men from each other.
6. The affording a more ample and various field for enterprize.
7. The creating in some instances a new, and securing in all, a more certain and steady demand for the surplus produce of the soil.

Each of these circumstances has a considerable influence upon the total mass of industrious effort in a community: Together, they add to it a degree of energy and effect, which are not easily conceived. Some comments upon each of them, in the order in which they have been stated, may serve to explain their importance.

I. As to The Division of Labour

It has justly been observed, that there is scarcely any thing of greater moment in the œconomy of a nation than the proper division of labour. The separation of occupations causes each to be carried to a much greater perfection, than it could possibly acquire, if they were blended. This arises principally from three circumstances—

1st. The greater skill and dexterity naturally resulting from a constant and undivided application to a single object. It is evident, that these properties must increase, in proportion to the separation and simplification of objects and the steadiness of the attention devoted to each; and must be less in proportion to the complication of objects, and the number among which the attention is distracted.

2nd. The œconomy of time, by avoiding the loss of it, incident to a frequent transition from one operation to another of a different nature. This depends on various circumstances—the transition itself—the orderly disposition of the implements, machines and materials employed in the operation to be relinquished—the preparatory steps to the commencement of a new one—the interruption of the impulse, which the mind of the workman acquires, from being engaged in a particular operation—the distractions, hesitations and reluctances, which attend the passage from one kind of business to another.

3rd. An extension of the use of Machinery. A man occupied on a single object will have it more in his power, and will be more naturally led to exert his imagination in devising methods to facilitate and abrige labour, than if he were perplexed by a variety of independent and dissimilar operations. Besides this the fabrication of Machines, in numerous instances, becoming itself a distinct trade, the Artist who follows it, has all the advantages which have been enumerated, for improvement in his particular art; and in both ways the invention and application of machinery are extended.

And from these causes united, the mere separation of the occupation of the cultivator, from that of the Artificer, has the effect of augmenting the *productive powers* of labour, and with them, the total mass of the produce or revenue of a Country. In this single view of the subject, therefore, the utility of Artificers of Manufacturers, towards promoting an increase of productive industry, is apparent.

II. As to an extension of the use of Machinery, a point which, though partly anticipated requires to be placed in one or two additional lights

The employment of Machinery forms an item of great importance in the general mass of national industry. 'Tis an artificial force brought in aid of the natural force of man; and, to all the purposes of labour, is an increase of hands; an accession of strength, *unencumbered too by the expense of maintaining the laborer*. May it not therefore be fairly inferred, that those occupations, which give greatest scope to the use of this auxiliary, contribute most to the general Stock of industrious effort, and, in consequence, to the general product of industry?

It shall be taken for granted, and the truth of the position referred to observation, that manufacturing pursuits are susceptible in a greater degree of the application of machinery, than those of Agriculture. If so all the difference is lost to a community, which, instead of manufacturing for itself, procures the fabrics requisite to its supply from other Countries. The substitution of foreign for domestic manufactures is a transfer to foreign nations of the advantages accruing from the employment of Machinery, in the modes in which it is capable of being employed, with most utility and to the greatest extent.

The Cotton Mill, invented in England, within the last twenty years, is a signal illustration of the general proposition, which has been just advanced. In consequence of it, all the different processes for spinning Cotton are performed by means of Machines, which are put in motion by water, and attended chiefly by women and Children; and by a smaller number of persons, in the whole, than are requisite in the ordinary mode of spinning. And it is an advantage of great moment, that the operations of this mill continue with convenience during the night as well as through the day. The prodigious effect of such a Machine is easily conceived. To this invention is to be attributed essentially the immense progress, which has been so suddenly made in Great Britain, in the various fabrics of cotton.

III. As to the additional employment of classes of the community, not originally engaged in the particular business

This is not among the least valuable of the means, by which manufacturing institutions contribute to augment the general stock of industry and production. In places where those institutions prevail, besides the persons regularly engaged in them, they afford occasional and extra employment to industrious individuals and families, who are willing to devote the leisure resulting from the intermissions of their ordinary pursuits to collateral labours, as a resource for multiplying their acquisitions or their enjoyments. The husbandman himself experiences a new source of profit and support from the increased industry of his wife and daughters; invited and stimulated by the demands of the neighboring manufactories.

Besides this advantage of occasional employment to classes having different occupations, there is another, of a nature allied to it, and of a similar tendency. This is—the employment of persons who would otherwise be idle (and in many cases a burthen on the community) either from the bias of temper, habit, infirmity of body, or some other cause, indisposing or disqualifying them for the toils of the

Country. It is worthy of particular remark, that, in general, women and Children are rendered more useful, and the latter more early useful by manufacturing establishments, than they would otherwise be. Of the number of persons employed in the Cotton Manufactories of Great Britain, it is computed that four sevenths nearly are women and children; of whom the greatest proportion are children, and many of them of a very tender age.

And thus it appears to be one of the attributes of manufactures, and one of no small consequence, to give occasion to the exertion of a greater quantity of Industry, even by the *same number* of persons, where they happen to prevail, than would exist, if there were no such establishments.

IV. AS TO THE PROMOTING OF EMIGRATION FROM FOREIGN COUNTRIES.

Men reluctantly quit one course of occupation and livelihood for another, unless invited to it by very apparent and proximate advantages. Many who would go from one country to another, if they had a prospect of continuing with more benefit the callings, to which they have been educated, will often not be tempted to change their situation, by the hope of doing better, in some other way. Manufacturers, who, listening to the powerful invitations of a better price for their fabrics, or their labour, of greater cheapness of provisions and raw materials, of an exemption from the chief part of the taxes, burthens and restraints, which they endure in the old world, of greater personal independence and consequence, under the operation of a more equal government, and of what is far more precious than mere religious toleration—a perfect equality of religious privileges; would probably flock from Europe to the United States to pursue their own trades or professions, if they were once made sensible of the advantages they would enjoy, and were inspired with an assurance of encouragement and employment, will, with difficulty, be induced to transplant themselves, with a view to becoming Cultivators of Land.

If it be true then, that it is the interest of the United States to open every possible avenue to emigration from abroad, it affords a weighty argument for the encouragement of manufactures; which, for the reasons just assigned, will have the strongest tendency to multiply the inducements to it.

Here is perceived an important resource, not only for extending the population, and with it the useful and productive labour of the country, but likewise for the prosecution of manufactures, without deducting from the number of hands, which might otherwise be drawn to Tillage and even for the indemnification of Agriculture for such as might happen to be diverted from it. Many, whom Manufacturing views would induce to emigrate, would afterwards yield to the temptations, which the particular situation of this Country holds out to Agricultural pursuits. And while Agriculture would in other respects derive many signal and unmingled advantages, from the growth of manufactures, it is a problem whether it would gain or lose, as to the article of the number of persons employed in carrying it on.

V. As to the furnishing greater scope for the diversity of talents and dispositions, which discriminate men from each other.

This is a much more powerful means of augmenting the fund of national Industry than may at first sight appear. It is a just observation, that minds of the strongest and most active powers for their proper objects fall below mediocrity and labour without effect, if confined to uncongenial pursuits. And it is thence to be inferred, that the results of human exertion may be immensely increased by diversifying its objects. When all the different kinds of industry obtain in a community, each individual can find his proper element, and can call into activity the whole vigour of his nature. And the community is benefitted by the services of its respective members, in the manner, in which each can serve it with most effect.

If there be any thing in a remark often to be met with—namely that there is, in the genius of the people of this country, a peculiar aptitude for mechanic improvements, it would operate as a forcible reason for giving opportunities to the exercise of that species of talent, by the propagation of manufactures.

VI. As to the affording a more ample and various field for enterprise.

This also is of greater consequence in the general scale of national exertion, than might perhaps on a superficial view be supposed, and has effects not altogether dissimilar from those of the circumstance last noticed. To cherish and stimulate the activity of the human mind, by multiplying the objects of enterprise, is not among the least considerable of the expedients, by which the wealth of a nation may be promoted. Even things in themselves not positively advantageous, sometimes become so, by their tendency to provoke exertion. Every new scene which is opened to the busy nature of man to rouse and exert itself, is the addition of a new energy to the general stock of effort.

The spirit of enterprise, useful and prolific as it is, must necessarily be contracted or expanded in proportion to the simplicity or variety of the occupations and productions, which are to be found in a Society. It must be less in a nation of mere cultivators, than in a nation of cultivators and merchants; less in a nation of cultivators and merchants, than in a nation of cultivators, artificers and merchants.

VII. As to the creating, in some instances, a new, and securing in all a more certain and steady demand, for surplus produce of the soil.

This is among the most important of the circumstances which have been indicated. It is a principal mean, by which the establishment of manufactures contributes to an augmentation of the produce or revenue of a country, and has an immediate and direct relation to the prosperity of Agriculture.

It is evident, that the exertions of the husbandman will be steady or fluctuating, vigorous or feeble, in proportion to the steadiness or fluctuation, adequateness or inadequateness, of the markets on which he must depend, for the vent of the surplus, which may be produced by his labor; and that such surplus in the ordinary course of things will be greater or less in the same proportion.

For the purpose of this vent, a domestic market is greatly to be preferred to a foreign one; because it is in the nature of things, far more to be relied upon.

It is a primary object of the policy of nations, to be able to supply themselves with subsistence from their own soils; and manufacturing nations, as far as circumstances permit, endeavor to procure from the same source, the raw materials necessary for their own fabrics. This disposition, urged by the spirit of monopoly, is sometimes even carried to an injudicious extreme. It seems not always to be recollected, that nations who have neither mines nor manufactures, can only obtain the manufactured articles, of which they stand in need, by an exchange of the products of their soils; and that, if those who can best furnish them with such articles are unwilling to give a due course to this exchange, they must of necessity, make every possible effort to manufacture for themselves; the effect of which is that the manufacturing nations abridge the natural advantages of their situation, through an unwillingness to permit the Agricultural countries to enjoy the advantages of theirs, and sacrifice the interests of a mutually beneficial intercourse to the vain project of *selling every thing* and *buying nothing*.

But it is also a consequence of the policy, which has been noted, that the foreign demand for the products of Agricultural Countries is, in a great degree, rather casual and occasional, than certain or constant. To what extent injurious interruptions of the demand for some of the staple commodities of the United States, may have been experienced from that cause, must be referred to the judgment of those who are engaged in carrying on the commerce of the country; but it may be safely affirmed, that such interruptions are at times very inconveniently felt, and that cases not unfrequently occur, in which markets are so confined and restricted as to render the demand very unequal to the supply.

Independently likewise of the artificial impediments, which are created by the policy in question, there are natural causes tending to render the external demand for the surplus of Agricultural nations a precarious reliance. The differences of seasons, in the countries, which are the consumers, make immense differences in the produce of their own soils, in different years; and consequently in the degrees of their necessity for foreign supply. Plentiful harvests with them, especially if similar ones occur at the same time in the countries, which are the furnishers, occasion of course a glut in the markets of the latter.

Considering how fast and how much the progress of new settlements in the United States must increase the surplus produce of the soil, and weighing seriously the tendency of the system, which prevails among most of the commercial nations of Europe, whatever dependence may be placed on the force of natural circumstances to counteract the effects of an artificial policy, there appear strong reasons to regard the foreign demand for that surplus as too uncertain a reliance, and to desire a substitute for it, in an extensive domestic market.

To secure such a market, there is no other expedient, than to promote manufacturing establishments. Manufacturers who constitute the most numerous class, after the Cultivators of land, are for that reason the principal consumers of the surplus of their labour.

This idea of an extensive domestic market for the surplus produce of the soil is of the first consequence. It is, of all things, that which most effectually conduces to a flourishing state of Agriculture. If the effect of manufactories should be to detach a portion of the hands, which would otherwise be engaged in Tillage, it might possibly cause a smaller quantity of lands to be under cultivation; but, by their tendency to procure a more certain demand for the surplus produce of the soil, they would, at the same time, cause the lands which were in cultivation to be better improved and more productive. And while, by their influence, the condition of each individual farmer would be meliorated, the total mass of Agricultural production would probably be increased. For this must evidently depend as much, if not more, upon the degree of improvement than upon the number of acres under culture.

It merits particular observation, that the multiplication of manufactories not only furnishes a Market for those articles which have been accustomed to be produced in abundance in a country, but it likewise creates a demand for such as were either unknown or produced in inconsiderable quantities. The bowels as well as the surface of the earth are ransacked for articles which were before neglected. Animals, Plants and Minerals acquire a utility and a value which were before unexplored.

The foregoing considerations seem sufficient to establish, as general propositions, that it is the interest of nations to diversify the industrious pursuits of the individuals who compose them—that the establishment of manufactures is calculated not only to increase the general stock of useful and productive labour; but even to improve the state of Agriculture in particular, certainly to advance the interests of those who are engaged in it. There are other views, that will be hereafter taken of the subject, which, it is conceived, will serve to confirm these inferences.

10

Letter to George Washington, Accompanying Hamilton's Final Draft of Washington's Farewell Address, July 30, 1796

In the summer of 1796, with his second term as president coming to an end, George Washington decided to offer a Farewell Address to the nation. He sought to make clear that he had no interest in remaining in office for a third term, and he wanted to leave the country with some words of wisdom. The ensuing 6,000-word document was never delivered as a speech. On September 19, 1796, it was published in the *American Daily Advertiser*, a newspaper in Philadelphia, which was the nation's capital.

Washington's address was quickly picked up by other newspapers and reprinted across the republic. Within a week or two, it reached most parts of the nation. It was probably not accidental that Washington's late summer timing limited how long the nation could spend wrangling over his successor before the presidential election in November.

James Madison had drafted a parting speech for Washington as his first term was coming to an end four years earlier, and it was put aside when Washington agreed to run for a second term. In 1796, it was dusted off and revised, first by Washington and then extensively by Hamilton, who also prepared a new draft for Washington's consideration. It was the new draft, with some final revisions by Washington, that was released to newspapers and the public. The main points reflect Washington's thoughts as well as Hamilton's core philosophy, their joint paramount belief in the importance of the Union and the strength of the national government, and their pride in the creation of the great American experiment in democracy. It also discusses three dangers: political partisanship, sectional conflict, and foreign entanglements, especially permanent alliances with foreign powers.

The country more or less ignored the prescient warnings on the first two items. Vitriolic partisanship was as endemic in the first decades after the Constitution was ratified as at any other time in America's history, and nineteenth-century America was the story of sectional conflict and open warfare. Wariness concerning foreign entanglements certainly informed American foreign policy in very powerful ways until the attack on Pearl Harbor 145 years later. Although a large part of the writing was Hamilton's, the ideas represented Washington and Hamilton's deep agreement on these issues throughout their twenty-year relationship.

Reprinted here are Hamilton's last draft of the Farewell Address and the letter that he sent to Washington along with the draft on July 30, 1796. Readers interested in the Farewell Address as Washington released it to newspapers may find the complete text online at the National Archives website Founders Online.

New York July 30. 1796

Sir

I have the pleasure to send you herewith a certain draft which I have endeavoured to make as perfect as my time and engagements would permit. It has been my object to render this act *importantly* and *lastingly* useful, and avoiding all just cause of present exception, to embrace such reflections and sentiments as will wear well, progress in approbation with time, & redound to future reputation. How far I have succeeded you will judge.

I have begun the second part of the task—the digesting the supplementary remarks to the first address which in a fortnight I hope also to send you—yet I confess the more I have considered the matter the less eligible this plan has appeared to me. There seems to me to be a certain awkwardness in the thing—and it seems to imply that there is a doubt whether the assurance without the evidence would be believed. Besides that I think that there are some ideas which will not wear well in the former address, & I do not see how any part can be omitted, if it is to be given as the thing formerly prepared. Nevertheless when you have both before you you can better judge.

If you should incline to take the draft now sent—and after perusing and noting any thing that you wish changed & will send it to me I will with pleasure shape it as you desire. This may also put it in my power to improve the expression & perhaps in some instances condense.

I rejoice that certain clouds have not lately thickened & that there is a prospect of a brighter horison.

With affectionate & respectful attachment I have the honor to be Sir   Yr. Very Obed Serv[*]

A Hamilton

The President of the UStates

---

[*]Your Very Obedient Servant

To George Washington

The period for a new election of a Citizen to administer the Executive Gov of the U states being not very distant and the time actually arrived when your thoughts must be employed in designating the person who is to be cloathed with that important trust for another term, it appears to me proper, and especially as it may conduce to a more distinct expression of the public voice, that I should now apprize you of the resolution I have formed to decline being considered among the number of those out of whom a choice is to be made.

I beg you nevertheless to be assured that the resolution, which I announce, has not been taken without a strict regard to all the considerations attached to the relation which as a dutiful Citizen I bear to my Country; and that in withdrawing the tender of my service, which silence in my situation might imply, I am influenced by no diminution of zeal for its future interest nor by any deficiency of grateful respect for its past kindness, but by a full conviction that such a step is compatible with both.

The acceptance of and continuance hitherto in the office to which your suffrages have twice called me has been a uniform sacrifice of private inclination to the opinion of public duty coinciding with what appeared to be your wishes. I had constantly hoped that it would have been much earlier in my power consistently with motives which I was not at liberty to disregard to return to that retirement from which those motives had reluctantly drawn me.

The strength of my desire to withdraw previous to the last election had even led to the preparation of an address to declare it to you—but deliberate reflection on the very critical and perplexed posture of our affairs with foreign nations and the unanimous advice of men of every way intitled to my confidence obliged me to abandon the idea.

I rejoice that the state of your national Concerns external as well as internal no longer renders the pursuit of my inclination incompatible with the sentiment of duty or propriety, and that whatever partiality any portion of You may still retain for my services, they, under the existing circumstances of our Country, will not disapprove the resolution I have formed.

The impressions under which I first accepted the arduous trust of chief Magistrate of the U States were explained on the proper occasion. In the discharge of this trust I can only say that I have with pure intentions contributed towards the organisation and administration of the Government the best exertions of which a very fallible judgment was capable. Not unconscious at the outset of the inferiority of my qualifications for the station, experience in my own eyes and perhaps still more in those of others has not diminished in me the diffidence of myself—and every day the increasing weight of years admonishes me more and more that the shade of retirement is as necessary to me as it will be welcome to me. Satisfied that if any circumstances have given a peculiar value to my services they were temporary, I have the consolation to believe that while inclination and prudence urge me to recede from the political scene patriotism does not forbid it— May I also have that of perceiving in my retreat that the involuntary errors which I have probably committed have been the causes of no serious or lasting mischief to my Country and thus be spared the anguish of regrets which would disturb the repose of my retreat and embitter the remnant of my life! I may then expect to realize without alloy the purest enjoyment of partaking, in the midst of my fellow citizens of the benign influence of good laws under a free Government; the ultimate object of all my wishes and to which I look as the happy reward I hope of our mutual cares labours and dangers.

In looking forward to the moment which is to terminate the carreer of my public life, my sensations do not permit me to suspend the deep acknowlegements required by that debt of gratitude which I owe to my beloved country for the many honors it has conferred upon me still more for the distinguished and steadfast confidence it has reposed in me and for the opportunities it has thus afforded me of manifesting my inviolable attachment by services faithful and persevering— however the inadequateness of my faculties may have ill seconded my zeal. If benefits have resulted to you my fellow Citizens from these services, let it always be remembered to your praise and as an instructive example in our annals that the constancy of your support amidst appearances sometimes dubious vicissitudes of fortune often discouraging and in situations in which not infrequently want of success has seconded the criticisms of malevolence was the essential prop of the efforts and the guarantee of the measures by which they were atchieved. Profoundly penetrated with this idea, I shall carry it with me to my retirement and to my grave as a lively incitement to unceasing vows (the only returns I can henceforth make) that Heaven may continue to You the choicest tokens of the beneficence merited by national piety and morality—that your union and brotherly affection may be perpetual—that the free constitution, which is the work of your own hands may be sacredly maintained—that its administration in every department may be stamped with wisdom and virtue—that in fine the happiness of the People of these States under the auspices of liberty may be made complete by so careful a preservation & so prudent a use of this blessing as will acquire them the glorious satisfaction of recommending it to the affection the praise—and the adoption of every nation which is yet a stranger to it.

Here perhaps I ought to stop. But a solicitude for your welfare, which cannot end but with my life, and the fear that there may exist projects unfriendly to it against which it may be necessary you should be guarded, urge me in taking leave of you to offer to your solemn consideration and frequent review some sentiments the result of mature reflection confirmed by observation & experience which appear to me essential to the permanency of your felicity as a people. These will be offered with the more freedom as you can only see in them the disinterested advice of a parting friend who can have no personal motive to tincture or byass his counsel.

Interwoven as is the love of Liberty with every fibre of your hearts no recommendation is necessary to fortify your attachment to it. Next to this that unity of Government which constitutes you one people claims your vigilant care & guardianship—as a main pillar of your real independence of your peace safety freedom and happiness.

This being the point in your political fortress against which the batteries of internal and external enemies will be most constantly and actively however covertly and insidiously levelled, it is of the utmost importance that you should appreciate in its full force the immense value of your political Union to your national and individual happiness—that you should cherish towards it an affectionate and immoveable attachment and that you should watch for its preservation with jealous solicitude.

For this you have every motive of sympathy and interest. Children for the most part of a common country, that country claims and ought to concentrate your affections. The name of American must always gratify and exalt the just pride of patriotism more than any denomination which can be derived from local discrimination. You have with slight shades of difference the same religion manners habits & political institutions & principles. You have in a common cause fought and triumphed to gether. The independence and liberty you enjoy are the work of joint councils efforts—dangers sufferings & successes. By your Union you atchieved them, by your union you will most effectually maintain them.

The considerations which address themselves to your sensibility are greatly strengthened by those which apply to your interest. Here every portion of our Country will find the most urgent and commanding motives for guarding and preserving the Union of the Whole.

The North in free & unfettered intercourse with the South under the equal laws of one Government will in the production of the latter many of them peculiar find vast additional resources of maritime and commercial enterprise and precious materials of their manufacturing industry. The South in the same intercourse will share in the benefits of the Agency of the North will find its agriculture promoted and its commerce extended by means of Navigation which the North more abundantly affords and while it contributes to extend the national navigation will participate in the protection of a maritime strength to which itself is unequally adapted. The East in a like intercourse with the West finds and in the progressive improvement of internal navigation will more & more find, a valuable vent for the commodities which it brings from abroad or manufactures at home. The West derives through this Channel an essential supply of its wants—and what is far more important to it, it must owe the secure and permanent enjoyment of the indispensable outlets for its own productions to the weight influence & maritime resources of the Atlantic States directed by an indissoluble community of interest. The tenure by which it could hold this advantage either from its own separate strength or by an apostate and unnatural connection with any foreign Nation must be intrinsically & necessarily precarious at every moment liable to be disturbed by the fluctuating combinations of those primary European interests which constantly regulate the conduct of every portion of Europe—And where every part finds a particular interest in the Union All the parts of our Country will find in their Union greater independence from the superior abundance & variety of production incident to the diversity of soil & climate, all the parts of it must find in the aggregate assemblage & reaction of their mutual population production greater strength, proportional security from external danger, less frequent interruption of their peace with foreign nations and what is far more valuable an exemption from those broils & wars between the parts if disunited which their own rivalships fomented by foreign intrigue, or the opposite alliances with foreign nations engendered by their mutual jealousies would inevitably produce—a consequent exemption from the necessity of those military establishments upon a large scale which bear in every country so menacing an aspect toward Liberty.

These considerations speak a conclusive language to every virtuous and considerate mind. They place the continuance of our Union among the first objects of patriotic desire. Is there a doubt whether a common government can long embrace so extensive a sphere? Let Time & Experience decide the question. Speculation in such a case ought not to be listened to—And tis rational to hope that the auxiliary agency of the governments of the subdivisions, with a proper organisation of the whole will secure a favourable issue to the Experiment. Tis allowable to believe that the spirit of party the intrigues of foreign nations, the corruption & the ambition of Individuals are likely to prove more formidable adversaries to the unity of our Empire than any inherent difficulties in the scheme. Tis against these that the guards of national opinion national sympathy national prudence & virtue are to be erected. With such obvious motives to Union there will be always cause from the fact itself to distrust the patriotism of those who in any quarter may endeavour to weaken us bands. And by all the love I bear you My fellow Citizens I conjure you as often as it appears to frown upon the attempt.

Besides the more serious causes which have been hinted at, as endangering our Union there is another less dangerous but against which it is necessary to be on our guard. I mean the petulance collisions & disgusts of party differences of Opinion. It is not uncommon to hear the irritations which these excite vent themselves in declarations that the different parts of the Union are ill assorted and cannot remain together—in menaces from the inhabitants of one part to those of another that it will be dissolved by this or that measure. Intimations of the kind are as indiscreet as they are intemperate. Though frequently made with levity and without being in earnest they have a tendency to produce the consequence which they indicate. They teach the minds of men to consider the Union as precarious as an object to which they arc not to attach their hopes and fortunes and thus weaken the sentiment in its favour. By rousing the resentment and alarming the pride of those to whom they are addressed they set ingenuity to work to depreciate the value of the object and to discover motives of Indifference to it. This is not wise. Prudence demands that we should habituate ourselves in all our words and actions to reverence the Union as a sacred and inviolable palladium of our happiness—and should discountenance whatever can lead to a suspicion that it can in any event be abandonned.

Tis matter of serious concern that parties in this Country for some time past have been too much characterised by geographical discriminations—Northern and Southern States Atlantic and Western Country. These discriminations of party which are the mere artifice of the spirit of party (always dexterous to avail itself of every source of sympathy of every handle by which the passions can be taken hold of and which has been careful to turn to account the circumstance of territorial vicinity) have furnished an argument against the Union as evidence of a real difference of local interests and views and serve to hazard it by organising large districts of country under the direction of the leaders of different factions whose passions & prejudices rather than the true interests of the Country, will be too apt to regulate the use of their influence. If it be possible to correct this poison in the affairs of our Country it is worthy the best endeavours of moderate & virtuous men to effect it.

One of the expedients which the partisans of Faction employ towards strengthening their influence by local discriminations is to misrepresent the opinions and views of rival districts—The People at large cannot be too much on their guard against the jealousies which grow out of these misrepresentations. They tend to render aliens to each other those who ought to be tied together by fraternal affection. The Western Country have lately had a useful lesson on this subject. They have seen in the negotiation by the Executive & in the unanimous ratification of the Treaty with Spain by the Senate & in the universal satisfaction at that event in all parts of the Country a decisive proof how unfounded have been the suspicions that have been instilled in them of a policy in the Atlantic States & in the different departments of the General Government hostile to their interests in relation to the Mississipian. They have seen two treaties formed which secure to them every thing that they could desire to confirm their prosperity. Will they not henceforth rely for the preservation of these advantages on that union by which they were procured? Will they not reject those counsellors who would render them alien to their brethren & connect them with Aliens?

To the duration and efficacy of your Union a Government extending over the whole is indispensable. No alliances however strict between the parts could be an adequate substitute. These could not fail to be liable to the infractions and interruptions which all alliances in all times have suffered. Sensible of this important truth you have lately established a Constitution of General Government, better calculated than the former for an intimate union and more adequate to the direction of your common concerns. This Government the offspring of your own choice uninfluenced and unawed, completely free in its principles, in the distribution of its powers uniting energy with safety and containing in itself a provision for its own amendment is well entitled to your confidence and support—Respect for its authority, compliance with its laws, acquiescence in its measures, are duties dictated by the fundamental maxims of true Liberty. The basis of our political systems is the right of the people to make and to alter their constitutions of Government. But the constitution for the time, and until changed by an explicit and authentic act of the whole people, is sacredly binding upon all. The very idea of the right and power of the people to establish Government presupposes the duty of every individual to obey the established Government.

All obstructions to the execution of the laws—all <u>combinations</u> and <u>associations</u> under whatever plausible character with the real design to direct counteract countroul influence or awe the regular deliberation or action of the constituted authorities are contrary to this fundamental principle & of the most fatal tendency. They serve to organise Faction to give it an artificial force; and to put in the stead of the delegated will of the whole nation the will of a party, often a small but artful & enterprising minority of the community—and according to the alternate triumphs of different parties to make the public administration reflect the ill concerted schemes and projects of faction rather than the wholesome plans of common councils and deliberations. However combinations or associations of this description may occasionally promote popular ends and purposes they are likely to produce in the course of time and things the most effectual engines by which artful ambitious and unprincipled men will be enabled to subvert the power of the people and usurp the reins of Government.

Towards the preservation of your government and the permanency of your present happy state, it is not only requisite that you steadily discountenance irregular oppositions to its authority but that you should be upon your guard against the spirit of innovation upon its principles however specious the pretexts. One method of assault may be to effect alterations in the forms of the constitution tending to impair the energy of the system and so to undermine what cannot be directly overthrown. In all the changes to which you may be invited remember that time and habit are as necessary to fix the true character of governments as of any other human institutions, that experience is the surest standard by which the real tendency of existing constitutions of government can be tried—that changes upon the credit of mere hypothesis and opinions exposes you to perpetual change from the successive and endless variety of hypothesis and opinion—and remember also that for the efficacious management of your common interests in a country so extensive as ours a Government of as much force and strength as is consistent with the perfect security of liberty is indispensable. Liberty itself will find in such a Government, with powers properly distributed and arranged, its surest guardian—and protector. In my opinion the real danger in our system is that the General Government organised as at present will prove too weak rather than too powerful.

I have already observed the danger to be apprehended from founding our parties on Geographical discriminations. Let me now enlarge the view of this point and caution you in the most solemn manner against the baneful effects of party spirit in general. This spirit unfortunately is inseperable from human nature and has its root in the strongest passions of the human heart.—It exists under different shapes in all governments but in different degrees stifled controuled or repressed in those of the popular form it is always seen in its utmost vigour & rankness and it is their worst enemy. In republics of narrow extent, it is not difficult for those who at any time possess the reins of administration, or even for partial combinations of men, who from birth riches and other sources of distinction have an extraordinary influence by possessing or acquiring the direction of the military force or by sudden efforts of partisans & followers to overturn the established order of things and effect a usurpation. But in republics of large extent the one or the other is scarcely possible. The powers and opportunities of resistance of a numerous and wide extended nation defy the successful efforts of the ordinary military force or of any collections which wealth and patronage may call to their aid—especially if there be no city of overbearing force resources and influence. In such Republics it is perhaps safe to assert that the conflict of popular faction offer the only avenues to tyranny & usurpation. The domination of one faction over another stimulated by that spirit of Revenge which is apt to be gradually engendered and which in different ages and countries have produced the greatest enormities is itself a frightful despotism. But this leads at length to a more formal and permanent despotism. The disorders and miseries which result predispose the minds of men to seek repose & security in the absolute power of a single man. And some leader of a prevailing faction more able or more fortunate than his competitors turns this disposition to the purpose of an ambitious and criminal self aggrandisement.

Without looking forward to such an extremity (which however ought not to be out of sight) the ordinary and continual mischief of the spirit of party make it the interest and the duty of a wise people to discountenance and repress it.

It serves always to distract the Councils & enfeeble the administration of the Government. It agitates the community with ill founded jealousies and false alarms embittering one part of the community against another, & producing occasionaly riot & insurrection. It opens inlets for foreign corruption and influence—which find an easy access through the channels of party passions—and cause the true policy & interest of our own country to be made subservient to the policy and interest of one and another foreign Nation; sometimes enslaving our own Government to the will of a foreign Government.

There is an opinion that parties in free countries are salutary checks upon the administration of the Government & serve to invigorate the spirit of Liberty. This within certain limits is true and in governments of a monarchical character or byass patriotism may look with some favour on the spirit of party. But in those of the popular kind in those purely elective, it is a spirit not to be fostered or encouraged. From the natural tendency of such governments, it is certain there will always be enough of it for every salutary purpose and there being constant danger of excess the effort ought to be by force of public opinion to mitigate & correct it. Tis a fire which cannot be quenched but demands a uniform vigilance to prevent its bursting into a flame—lest it should not only warm but consume.

It is important likewise that the habits of thinking of the people should tend to produce caution in their agents in the several departments of Government, to retain each within its proper sphere and not to permit one to encroach upon another—that every attempt of the kind from whatever quarter should meet with the discountenance of the community, and that in every case in which a precedent of encroachment shall have been given, a corrective be sought in (revocation be effected by) a careful attention to the next choice of public Agents. The spirit of encroachment tends to absorb & consolidate the powers of the several branches and departments into one, and thus to establish under whatever forms a despotism. A just knowlege of the human heart, of that love of power which predominates in it, is alone sufficient to establish this truth. Experiments ancient and modern—some in our own country and under our own eyes serve to confirm it. If in the public opinion the distribution of the constitutional powers be in any instance wrong or inexpedient—let it be corrected by the authority of the people in a legitimate constitutional course—Let there be no change by usurpation, for though this may be the instrument of good in one instance, it is the ordinary and natural instrument of the destruction of free Government—and the influence of the precedent is always infinitely more pernicious than any thing which it may atchieve can be beneficial.

To all those dispositions which promote political happiness, Religion and Morality are essential props. In vain does that man claim the praise of patriotism who labours to subvert or undermine these great pillars of human happiness these firmest foundations of the duties of men and citizens. The mere politician equally with the pious man ought to respect and cherish them. A volume could not trace all their connections with private and public happiness. Let it simply be asked where is the security for property for reputation for life if the sense of moral and religious obligation deserts the oaths which are administered in Courts of Justice? Nor ought we to flatter ourselves that morality can be separated from religion. Concede as much as may be asked to the effect of refined education in minds of a peculiar structure—can we believe—can we in prudence suppose that national morality can be maintained in exclusion of religious principles? Does it not require the aid of a generally received and divinely authoritative Religion?

Tis essentially true that virtue or morality is a main & necessary spring of popular or republican Governments. The rule indeed extends with more or less force to all free Governments. Who that is a prudent & sincere friend to them can look with indifference on the ravages which are making in the foundation of the Fabric? Religion? The uncommon means which of late have been directed to this fatal end seem to make it in a particular of manner the duty of the Retiring Chief of a nation to warn his country against tasting of the poisonous draught.

Cultivate also industry and frugality. They are auxiliaries of good morals and great sources of private and national prosperity. Is there not room for regret that our propensity to expence exceeds the maturity of our Country for expense? Is there not more luxury among us, in various classes, than suits the actual period of our national progress? Whatever may be the apology for luxury in a Country mature in all the arts which are its ministers and the means of national opulence—can it promote the advantage of a young agricultural Country little advanced in manufactures and not much advanced in wealth?

Cherish public Credit as a mean of strength and security. As one method of preserving it, use it as little as possible. Avoid occasions of expence by cultivating peace—remembering always that the preparation against danger by timely and provident disbursements is often a mean of avoiding greater disbursements to repel it. Avoid the accumulation of debt by avoiding occasions of expence and by vigorous exertions in time of peace to discharge the debts which unavoidable wars may have occasionned—not transferring to posterity the burthen which we ought to bear ourselves. Recollect that towards the payment of debts there must be Revenue, that to have revenue there must be taxes, that it is impossible to devise taxes which are not more or less inconvenient and unpleasant—that they are always a choice of difficulties—that the intrinsic embarrassment which never fails to attend a selection of objects ought to be a motive for a candid construction of the conduct of the Government in making it—and that a spirit of acquiescence in those measures for obtaining revenue which the public exigencies dictate is in an especial manner the duty and interest of the citizens of every State.

Cherish good faith and Justice towards, and peace and harmony with all nations. Religion and morality enjoins this conduct. And It cannot be, but that true policy equally demands it. It will be worthy of a free enlightened and at no distant period a great nation to give to mankind the magnanimous and too novel example of a people invariably governed by those exalted views. Who can doubt that in a long course of time and events the fruits of such a conduct would richly repay any temporary advantages which might be lost by a steady adherence to the plan? Can it be that Providence has not connected the permanent felicity of a nation with its virtue? The experiment is recommended by every sentiment which ennobles human nature. Alas! is it rendered impossible by its vices?

Toward the execution of such a plan nothing is more essential than that antipathies against particular nations and passionate attachments for others should be avoided—and that instead of them we should cultivate just and amicable feelings towards all. That nation, which indulges towards another a habitual hatred or a habitual fondness is in some degree a slave. It is a slave to its animosity or to its affection—either of which is sufficient to lead it astray from its duty and interest. Antipathy against one nation which never fails to beget a similar sentiment in the other disposes each more readily to offer injury and insult to the other—to lay hold of slight causes of umbrage and to be haughty and intractable when accidental or trifling differences arise. Hence frequent quarrels and bitter and obstinate contests. The nation urged by resentment and rage sometimes impels the Government to War contrary to its own calculations of policy. The Government sometimes participates in this propensity & does through passion what reason would forbid—at other times it makes the animosity of the nations subservient to hostile projects which originate in ambition & other sinister motives. The peace often and sometimes the liberty of Nations has been the victim of this cause.

In like manner a passionate attachment of one nation to another produces multiplied ills. Sympathy for the favourite nations, promoting the illusion of a supposed common interest in cases where it does not exist and communicating to one the enmities of the one betrays into a participation in its quarrels & wars without adequate inducements or justifications. It leads to the concession of privileges to one nation and to the denial of them to others—which is apt doubly to injure the nation making the concession by an unnecessary yielding of what ought to have been retained and by exciting jealousy ill will and retaliation in the party from whom an equal privilege is witheld. And it gives to ambitious corrupted or deluded citizens, who devote themselves to the views of the favourite foreign power, facility in betraying or sacrificing the interests of their own country without odium & even with popularity gilding with the appearance of a virtuous impulse the base yieldings of ambition or corruption.

As avenues to foreign influence in innumerable Ways such attachments are peculiarly alarming to the enlightened independent Patriot. How many opportunities do they afford to intrigue with domestic factions to practice with success the arts of seduction—to mislead public opinion—to influence or awe the public Councils! Such an attachment of a small or weak towards a great & powerful Nation destines the former to revolve round the latter as its satellite.

Against the Mischiefs of Foreign Influence all the Jealousy of a free people ought to be constantly continually exerted. All History & Experience prove that foreign influence is one of the most baneful foes of republican Governt—but that jealousy of it to be useful must be impartial else it becomes an instrument—of the very influence to be avoided instead of a defence against it.

Excessive partiality for one foreign nation & excessive dislike of another, leads to see danger only on one side and serves to viel & second the arts of influence on the other. Real Patriots who resist the intrigues of the favorite become suspected & odious. Its tools & dupes usurp the applause & confidence of the people to betray their interests.

The great rule of conduct for us in regard to foreign Nations ought to be to have as little <u>political</u> connection with them as possible—so far as we have already formed engagements let them be fulfilled—with circumspection indeed but with perfect good faith. Here let us stop.

Europe has a set of primary interests which have none or a very remote relation to us. Hence she must be involved in frequent contests the causes of which will be essentially foreign to us. Hence therefore it must necessarily be unwise on our part to implicate ourselves by an artificial connection in the ordinary vicissitudes of European politics—in the combination, & collisions of her friendships or enmities.

Our detached and distant situation invites us to a different course & enables us to pursue it. If we remain a united people under an efficient Government the period is not distant when we may defy material injury from external annoyance—when we may take such an attitude as will cause the neutrality we shall at any time resolve to observe to be violated with caution—when it will be the interest of belligerent nations under the impossibility of making acquisitions upon us to be very careful how either forced us to throw our weight into the opposite scale—when we may choose peace or war as our interest guided by justice shall dictate.

Why should we forego the advantages of so felicitous a situation? Why quit our own ground to stand upon Foreign ground? Why by interweaving our destiny with any part of Europe should we intangle our prosperity and peace in the nets of European Ambition rivalship interest or Caprice?

Permanent alliance, intimate connection with any part of the foreign world is to be avoided, so far (I mean) as we are now at liberty to do it: for let me never be understood as patronising infidelity to preexisting engagements. These must be observed in their true and genuine sense. But tis not necessary nor will it be prudent to extend them. Tis our true policy as a general principle to avoid permanent or close alliance—Taking care always to keep ourselves by suitable establishments in a respectably defensive posture we may safely trust to occasional alliances for extraordinary emergencies.

Harmony liberal intercourse and commerce with all nations are recommended by justice humanity & interest. But even our commercial policy should hold an equal hand—neither seeking nor granting exclusive favours or preferences—consulting the natural course of things—<u>diffusing</u> and <u>diversifying</u> by gentle means the streams of Commerce but forcing nothing—establishing with powers so disposed in order to give to Trade a stable course, to define the rights of our Merchants and enable the Government to support them—conventional rules of intercourse the best that present circumstances and mutual opinion of interest will permit but temporary—and liable to be abandonned or varied as time experience & future circumstances may dictate—remembering alway that tis folly in one nation to expect disinterested favour in another—that to accept any thing under that character is to part with a portion of its independence—and that it may find itself in the condition of having given equivalents for nominal favours and of being reproached with ingratitude in the bargain. There can be no greater error in national policy than to desire expect or calculate upon real favours. Tis an illusion that experience must cure, that a just pride ought to discard.

In offering to you My Countrymen! these counsels of an old and affectionate friend—counsels suggested by labourious reflection and matured by a various experience—I dare not hope that they will make the strong and lasting impressions I wish—that they will controul the current of the passions or prevent our nation from running the course which has hitherto marked the destiny of all nations. But if they even produce some partial benefits, some occasional good—that they sometimes recur to moderate the violence of party spirit—to warn against the evils of foreign intrigue—to guard against the impositions of pretended patriotism—the having offered them must always afford me a precious consolation.

How far in the execution of my present Office I have been guided by the principles which have been inculcated the public records & the external evidences of my conduct must witness. My conscious assures me that I have at least believed myself to be guided by them.

In reference to the present War of Europe my Proclamation of the 22d of April 1793 is the key to my plan. Sanctioned by your approving voice and that of your representatives in Congress the spirit of that measure has continually governed me uninfluenced and unawed by the attempts of any of the warring powers their agents or partizans to deter or divert from it. After deliberate consideration and the best lights I could obtain (and from men who did not agree in their views of the origin progress & nature of that war) I was satisfied that our Country, under all the circumstances of the case, had a right and was bound in propriety and interest to take a neutral position—And having taken it, I determined as far as should depend on me to maintain it steadily and firmly.

Though in reviewing the incidents of my administration I am unconscious of intentional error—I am yet too sensible of my own deficiencies not to think it probable that I have committed many errors. I deprecate the evils to which they may tend—and fervently implore the Almighty to avert or mitigate them. I shall carry with me nevertheless the hope that my motives will continue to be viewed by my Country with indulgence & that after forty five years of my life devoted with an upright zeal to the public service the faults of inadequate abilities will be consigned to oblivion as myself must soon be to the mansions of rest.

Neither Ambition nor interest has been the impelling cause of my actions. I never designedly misused any power confided to me. The fortune with which I came into office is not bettered otherwise than by that improvement in the value of property which the natural progress and peculiar prosperity of our country have produced. I retire without cause for a blush—with a pure heart with no alien sentiment to the ardor of those vows for the happiness of his Country which is so natural to a Citizen who sees in it the native soil of himself and his progenitors for four generations.